Indo-Pacific Region: Political and Strategic Prospects

Indo-Pacific Region: Political and Strategic Prospects

Editors

Rajiv K. Bhatia

Vijay Sakhuja

Vij Books India Pvt Ltd
New Delhi (India)

Indian Council of World Affairs
Sapru House, New Delhi

Published by

Vij Books India Pvt Ltd
(Publishers, Distributors & Importers)
2/19, Ansari Road
Delhi – 110 002
Phones: 91-11-43596460, 91-11-47340674
Fax: 91-11-47340674
e-mail: vijbooks@rediffmail.com
web : www.vijbooks.com

First Published in 2014

Paperbak Edition 2015

The views expressed in this book are of the contributors in their personal capacity and do not represent the views of editors or the ICWA.

Contents

Foreword   vii

Keynote Address   ix

     Mr Salman Khurshid, External Affairs Minister

Contributors   xiii

Abbreviations   xv

1   Indo-Pacific Region as a Spatial Concept   1
     K. V. Bhagirath

2   The Emergent Vistas of the Indo-Pacific   5
     Lawrence W. Prabhakar

3   China and the Indo-Pacific Area as a Region   17
     Michimi Muranushi

4   Australia Re-Discovering the Indo-Pacific   37
     Melissa Conley Tyler and Samantha Shearman

5   Indo-Pacific Region: Perspectives from Southeast and East Asia   51
     Sumathy Permal

6   ASEAN and the Indo-Pacific Region   70
     Chan Git Yin

7   The Indo-Pacific Region or India's Rise in Asia-Pacific?: A View from Russia   83
     Evgeny Kanaev

8   Indo-Pacific Region: Perspectives from Russia   97
     Ekaterina Koldunova

9   Indo-Pacific Region: Perspectives from the US   107
     Daniel P. Leaf

10   India and the Indo-Pacific Region   110
     Hemant Krishan Singh

11   Prospects for Economic Integration   115
     Zhu Cuiping

12   Indo-Pacific Region: Perspectives from Indian Ocean   118
      Noellie Alexander

13   Indo-Pacific Region: Perspectives from Indian Ocean   121
      M. R. Khan

14   The Indo-Pacific Region: A European Perspective   126
      Joachim Krause

15   Indo-Pacific Region: Perspectives from Indian Ocean   135
      Hoseana B. Lunogelo

16   India in the Indo-Pacific: Maritime Stakes and Challenges 138
      Raghavendra Mishra

17   Prospects for Economic Integration in Indo-Pacific Region:
      A Perspective from Sri Lanka   164
      Asanga Abeyagoonasekera and Amali Wedagedara

Index   181

Foreword

The 'Indo-Pacific' as a spatial concept has been in use for long in reference to a precise bio-geographic region in marine science and first appeared in 1948 when the Food and Agriculture Organisation (FAO) set up the 'Indo-Pacific Fisheries Council' in Baguio in the Philippines. In the changes geo-political scenario today, several experts believe that 'Indo-Pacific' is 'a more credible and contemporary' phrase now name than the older term 'Asia-Pacific.'

Moving beyond the debate about names, the more fundamental question is: what does the concept mean? The multi-faceted globalization has now ensured, more than ever before, that security and development, defined in the widest sense, in the region stretching from the Suez Canal to the Sea of Japan or from African shores of the Indian Ocean to the western Pacific, are strongly inter-related and mutually dependent. Hence using this relatively new spatial concept, a tool in understanding the geopolitics of the 21st century, would be instructive. This is especially so because stakes are high. Approximately 77 per cent of the world population resides in the 'Indo-Pacific' region.

This volume underlines the intrinsic significance of the Indo-Pacific region, at least from three different angles. Firstly, it highlights the maritime dimension in inter-state relations. Secondly, it provides a platform to examine competing political priorities, converging and diverging economic interests, and changing security perspectives. In this context, a variety of issues such as identification of 21st century as 'the Asian Century', the shift of power from the west to the east, the rise of China, the US 'pivot', re-balancing or even a newer edition of the policy approach, and strategic responses from ASEAN, Japan, Australia and others are addressed. Thirdly, this volume helps us to move away from the previously nurtured and narrow views of the cartographic imaginations of Indian and Pacific Oceans. It also endeavours to enhance our understanding of the two oceans and encourage the idea of 'confluence of the seas.'

Viewing these questions from the perspective of India, it is fair to assert that oceanic linkages moulded India through the millennia. Its commercial, cultural and civilizational exchanges with the regions east, south and west of India, flourished through the sea routes. This experience and tradition became prominent in India's strategy, particularly during the past two decades.

This volume emerges from a conference hosted by the Indian Council of World Affairs (ICWA) in March 2013 as part of our annual Asian Relations Conference (ARC) series. We hope that it will provide valuable insights into the contemporary discourse on 'Indo-Pacific' and will inform the readers of various regional perspectives.

Rajiv K. Bhatia

Director General
Indian Council of World Affairs

Keynote Address

Salman Khurshid, External Affairs Minister, India

Resurgence of Asia

The Asian Relations Conference, a milestone event in 1947, was the fruit of labour of Pandit Jawaharlal Nehru, a great visionary, a great statesman who realised that it was time for "Asian resurgence" which would be marked by the beginning of the end of the colonial era in Asia and the beginning of intellectual, political, social, economic and cultural resurgence of the continent. Over six decades later, as the centre of gravity of global economy and politics inexorably shifts to Asia, it is but natural to revisit the vision and see its applicability in this modern age.

The gap of sixty years poses an important question. How has the concept of "Asian resurgence" flowered, or has it floundered? The Conference then was an assertion of Asia's identity, an expression of freedom, of Asian people breaking their shackles of colonial rule which pushed back their lives by centuries, and finally of Asian people seeking a new destiny. This trend of Asian resurgence continued into the 1950s and even early 1960s. An important contribution of Asia to international political discourse at that time was the "Non-Aligned Movement" and the policy of "Panchsheel", putting India in a high moral pedestal and at complete variance with the regressive power politics practised by the West. Though geopolitics has changed over the past two decades, these principles seem eternal and relevant even in this day and age.

Post 1950s, the fact that the economy and social fabric of many Asian countries was in tatters due to colonial mismanagement meant that many countries had to channelise their energies for decades on internal reconstruction. The East Asian economies (Japan & Korea) and the Asian tigers (Singapore, Taiwan, Malaysia and Thailand) were first on their feet, China followed suit and India also was not far behind. Today, Asia is the engine of growth; it is driving the global economic agenda with China and India being at the forefront. Since the Asian Relations Conference sixty years ago, the world has transformed into a much smaller, intertwined entity, Asia is once again asserting itself to take its rightful position in global political and economic order. Economic growth has been backed by impressive levels of innovation and enterprise marking the beginning of an "Asian Century".

The global economic crisis of 2008 has brought into focus the shift of the economic epicentre towards Asia. What is in witness is that the geo-strategic focus is moving towards the Pacific and further into Asia. It was therefore apt and commendable that the first Conference of this series was in 2009, focussing on China. The second Conference in 2010 was on a region critical to India's economic and energy security. The third Conference in 2012 was on our immediate neighbourhood, the indispensability of which needs no elaboration. Looking it in concentric circles, the next obvious stop is the ocean which is our lifeline connecting us to the rest of the world. I would assume that the theme of this year's conference, "Geopolitics of the Indo-Pacific Region" is, therefore, equally relevant and topical.

"Indo-Pacific" as a Concept

Some scholars and analysts tend to look upon Indo-Pacific as an integrated geo-political and geo-economic theatre, but there are others who do not favour this approach. They argue that while Indo-Pacific can be regarded as a single entity from the economic perspective, when it comes to the security and strategic dimension, they make a distinction. It is important to pay attention to this subtle but significant differentiation also.

The term Indo-Pacific has been in use in scientific and marine circles for quite some time, though its use in geo-political circles has gained currency only in recent years. It is pertinent that the term has started finding articulation in official statements also. Former US Secretary of State Ms Hillary Clinton used it in her Honululu Speech of October 2010 as did Australia's Defence Minister in 2012. The term has gained acceptance particularly in the US, Australia and some countries in the region.

There are some countries, however, who have misgivings about the concept, viewing it as directed towards "balancing" or "diluting" the influence of certain powers in the region, referring to the so-called 'encirclement' theory or to the 'pivot' to Asia policy.

The "India-Pacific region" could also be viewed as a spatial concept wherein the strengths and complementarities of the Indian Ocean and the Pacific Ocean are in full play. Oceans neither begin nor end at any particular point; they connect and interact with each other creating numerous possibilities and opening new horizons. We are in an exciting era in this region where the Indian and Pacific Oceans meet and the countries and people on its rim are embarked in the pursuit of a new paradigm of peace, prosperity and stability.

India and Indian-Pacific Region

Maritime supremacy is the hallmark of a great power. There can be no two views about the fact that India's future lies in its ability to harness the power of the Ocean- the Indian Ocean and the extended "Indian-Pacific" Ocean region. The remnants of our cultural interactions found today in Southeast Asia are living testimonies to the maritime invincibility that we enjoyed more than a millennium ago. Even today, this geo-political advantage has put us in a pre-eminent position in the region and this advantage needs to be calibrated carefully to serve our national interests.

Confabulating on the theme looks more relevant when one considers the fact that India is the current chair of the IOR-ARC, a grouping of twenty countries from the Indian Ocean's rim looking to discuss the future cooperative architecture in areas as significant and diverse such as maritime security, disaster management, trade and investments, scientific research, fisheries and tourism.

Conceptually, from India's perspective, the concept of 'Indo-Pacific' could be looked upon as a natural corollary of the country's modern version of Look East policy, the most important dimension of India's foreign policy apparatus over the past decade or two. The Look East policy, in its modern version, has contributed to expanding and deepening of India's traditional relations with Southeast and East Asia and beyond, and increasing the country's interests and presence beyond the Malacca Strait. Last December India celebrated the 20th anniversary of India's dialogue partnership with the ASEAN and the 10th anniversary of Summit level interaction with the regional body. India-ASEAN trade is now over US$ 80 billion and the Free Trade Agreement (FTA) in goods, negotiations on FTA in Services and Investments have also been concluded.

Similarly, India's relations with China have expanded multi-fold, making the country India's largest trade partner in merchandise goods. Relations with Japan and Republic of Korea have also expanded and deepened with Comprehensive Economic Partnership Agreements being established with both countries. India is the largest recipient of Japanese ODA and Japan is making significant investments in India. These economic relationships have acquired a deeper significance with the establishment of strategic partnerships.

Protecting the sea lines of communication traversing the Indian Ocean into the Pacific and vice-versa has become our common interest and responsibility. There has been good international cooperation to secure these from pirates and other disruptive factors. IOR-ARC is finding its relevance particularly in this domain. Thus, one could summarise, that while the logic of our Look East policy has increased our links East of Malacca, the export driven growth models of East and South Asia and China's rise has not only increased trade and commerce in the Pacific but also contributed to greater inter-link across the Indian and Pacific Oceans.

The Road Ahead

The challenge Asia faces is to evolve a transparent, open and balanced regional architecture for itself, both in the economic and security arenas. The region also has challenges pertaining to equity, competition for resources and even sovereignty issues. A new regional architecture comprising of major powers in the region is emerging. The interplay of this path breaking economic and strategic developments has propelled India's Look East policy into a wider context.

The significance of deliberating this theme lies in bringing on a common platform views and perspectives from different parts of Asia and the world, and generate a discussion and an exchange of views which would contribute to greater understanding and harmonisation of perspectives and enhance confidence in the region.

Contributors

Ambassador (Retd) Rajiv K Bhatia, Director General, Indian Council of World Affairs (ICWA), New Delhi.

Dr Vijay Sakhuja, Director (Research) Indian Council of World Affairs (ICWA), New Delhi.

Ambassador K. V. Bhagirath, Secretary-General, Indian Ocean Rim Association for Regional Cooperation (IOR-ARC), Mauritius.

Dr. Lawrence W Prabhakar, Associate Professor, Madras Christian College (MCC), Chennai, India.

Professor Michimi Muranushi, University of Gakushuin, Tokyo, Japan.

Ms Melissa H. Conley Tyler, National Executive Director, Australian Institute of International Affairs (AIIA), Deakin, Australia.

Ms Samantha Shearman, Research intern, Australian Institute of International Affairs (AIIA), Deakin, Australia.

Ms Sumathy Permal, Senior Researcher, Maritime Institute of Malaysia (MIMA), Kuala Lumpur, Malaysia.

Ms Chan Git Yin, Rajaratnam School of International Studies (RSIS), Nanyang Technological University, Singapore.

Dr. Evgeny Kanaev, leading Researcher at the Centre for Asia-Pacific Studies, Institute of World Economy and International Relations, Moscow, Russia.

Ekaterina Koldunova, Associate Professor, Asian and African Studies Department, Moscow State Institute of International Relations University, the MFA of Russia.

Lt. Gen. (Retd) Daniel P. Leaf, Asia Pacific Centre for Security Studies (APCSS), Hawaii, USA.

Ambassador (Retd) Hemant Krishan Singh, Chair Professor, ICRIER-Wadhwani Programme.

Dr Zhu Cuiping, Deputy Director, Regional Institute for Indian Ocean Economies (RIIOE), Yunnan University, Kunming, China.

Ambassador (Retd) Noellie Alexander, Seychelles.

Commodore (Retd) M R Khan, Centre for Air Power Studies (CAPS), New Delhi.

Professor Joachim Krause, Aspen Institute, University of Kiel, Berlin, Germany.

Dr. Hoseana B. Lunogelo, Executive Director, Economic and Social Research Foundation (ESRF), Dar-es-Salaam, Tanzania.

Commander Raghavendra Mishra, National Maritime Foundation (NMF), New Delhi.

Mr Asanga Abeyagoonasekara, Executive Director, Lakshman Kadirgamar Institute of International Relations and Strategic Studies (LKIIRS), Colombo, Sri Lanka.

Ms Amali Wedagedara, Research Associate, Lakshman Kadirgamar Institute of International Relations and Strategic Studies (LKIIRS), Colombo, Sri Lanka.

Abbreviations

ADMM plus	ASEAN Defence Ministers Meeting Plus
AIIA	Australian Institute of International Affairs
AIP	ASEAN Information-Sharing Portal
AMF	ASEAN Maritime Forum
ANU	Australian National University
ARF	ASEAN Regional Forum
ASEAN	Association of South-East Asian Nations
AU	African Union
CSGs	Carrier Strike Groups
EAMF	Expanded ASEAN Maritime Forum
EAS	East Asia Summit
EEZ	Exclusive Economic Zone
EWG	Experts' Working Groups
FDI	Foreign Direct Investment
FTA	Free Trade Agreement
HOA	Horn of Africa
ICJ	International Court of Justice
IFC	Information Fusion Centre
ILO	International Liaison Officers

IMB	International Maritime Bureau
IOR-ARC	Indian Ocean Rim Association for Regional Cooperation
IOTC	Indian Ocean Tuna Commission
LCS	Littoral Combat Ships
MED	Mutual Economic Dependence
NDP	National Defence Policy
NTIS	National Technical Information Service
OEF	Operation Enduring Freedom
ONGC	Oil and Natural Gas Corporation
QDR	Quadrennial Defense Review
RCEP	Regional Comprehensive Economic Partnership
SAARC	South Asian Association for Regional Cooperation
SAF	Singapore Armed Forces
SFA	Strategic Framework Agreement
SLOC	Sea Lines of Communication
SOMs	Straits of Malacca
SPRI	Stockholm Peace Research Institute
TAC	Treaty of Amity and Cooperation
TPP	Trans-Pacific Partnership
VLCC	Very Large Crude Carrier
WNC	World News Connections

1

Indo-Pacific Region as a Spatial Concept

K. V. Bhagirath

The 'Indo-Pacific Region' as a spatial concept highlights the immediacy of the narrative that focuses on the Indian and Pacific Ocean rims and the strategic importance of this vast area. The opportunities are as promising, as are the challenges daunting. How the enduring and emerging economic strengths of this region will impact existing and evolving regional configurations, and secure peace and stability in the Indo-Pacific is the inescapable question.

We are witnessing an immense increase in the flow of cyber-information, the opaque movement of investment capital, the introduction of innovative technologies, the mobility of human resources across borders and the massive acquisition of state-of-the-art weaponry in the Indo-Pacific region. Regional partnerships, which were few till recently, have multiplied in number and expanded in their mandates. The patterns of cooperation in the Indian Ocean region are being inevitably redefined and will be influenced by developments in the new geo-strategic realities in the Pacific. Paradoxically, while economic partnerships have grown in strength, the geo-political framework remains fluid. In essence, the Indo-Pacific is a unique challenge with promise and problems.

The situation in the Indian Ocean has been fairly stable, as opposed to the rather complex situation in the Pacific region. With the widely held view that the centre of world economic gravity is shifting towards the Asian continent, washed by both the Indian and the Pacific Oceans, it would not be out of place to suggest that regionalism, as we understand it, may be a thing of the past and new patterns of regional cooperation in the Indo-Pacific are under formulation and would require considered examination.

Much has been said about the critical geo-strategic importance of the Indian Ocean. This region, interfacing three politically, economically, socially and culturally diverse and hugely populated continents, carrying half of the world's container ships, transporting one-third of global bulk cargo and shipping two-thirds of the world's oil, has witnessed high rates of growth, helping it to realize its considerable potential for development.

The Indian Ocean Rim Association for Regional Cooperation (IOR-ARC) is a unique regional forum founded in 1997 and is based in Mauritius. Its membership, comprising countries from Southern and Eastern Africa, the Middle East, South Asia, Southeast Asia and Australia, totalling 20 countries, lie along the Indian Ocean rim, forming a veritable arc, from South Africa in the west to Australia in the east. Importantly, it also has six Dialogue Partner states, namely, China, Egypt, France, Japan, the United Kingdom (UK) and the United States of America (USA). The IOR-ARC, in principle, already straddles across the western Indian Ocean touching the western Pacific Rim in its engagement.

The IOR-ARC does not have a political mandate. When the then South African President Nelson Mandela first voiced during his visit to India in 1995, the importance of a regional community in the Indian Ocean, clearly envisioned an organization which would be an instrument for multilateral economic cooperation in the region. Consequently, the charter of IOR-ARC confines to the interaction of IOR-ARC member states and dialogue partners or trade, commerce, investment and academic pursuits. The charter meticulously enunciates that the IOR-ARC will "promote sustained growth and balanced development and create a common ground for regional economic cooperation". The attraction that this narrative of regional partnership may hold within the Indo-Pacific construct, at this point of time is, perhaps, debatable.

With India taking over as Chair in November 2011, the IOR-ARC Council of Ministers Meeting in Bengaluru, re-defined its priorities into six areas of co-operation, namely, maritime safety and security, marine resources and fisheries management, trade and investment facilitation, disaster risk management, science and technology, and tourism. With Australia taking over as Vice Chair at the same juncture, the two countries injected a new dynamism into the organization, the momentum of which will continue to accelerate.

Australia will take over as Chair in November 2013 during the next IOR-ARC Council of Ministers Meeting in Perth. It may be noted that Indonesia has already been elected as the next Vice Chair, and will assume that responsibility at the same time. Consequently, the fulcrum of the IOR-ARC will inevitably move towards the Pacific region.

With India, Australia and Indonesia providing leadership to IOR-ARC organization, the Indo-Pacific concept is an inevitable element in regional engagement. Strengthening the economic framework of cooperation among the nations of the Indo-Pacific will be one of the primary principles of the IOR-ARC. The priority in this vast region will be for sustained economic development.

The IOR-ARC sees itself as a useful player in the Indo-Pacific, with the formulation of a new road map for economic cooperation, which is in consonance with the new and emerging geo-strategic regional architecture in the Indo-Pacific region. The ultimate objective is to make the IOR-ARC a dynamic ocean community enjoying a durable regional partnership.

Initiatives related to trade and investment promotion have always been a high priority and the IOR-ARC is organizing the first-ever Ministerial Economic and Business Conference of Member States and Dialogue Partners in Mauritius on 4-5 July, 2013. There will be a special focus on the ocean economy.

Further, bringing both government and businesses from the Indian and Pacific Rim states together is an important economic and commercial exercise. A platform needs to be created for cooperation from which the prosperity that the Indian Ocean rim has seen in the last decade can be extended and shared through partnership with the Pacific Rim. Within the unquestionable centrality of the Indian Ocean to the global economy, the possibility of a greater economic and strategic regional system stretching across the Indian and Pacific Oceans is being envisioned. Cumulatively, the Indo-Pacific region accounts for over two-third of global economic activity.

The Indo-Pacific concept, which has evidently gained a swift and increasingly shrill strategic narrative, merits rigorous study. Its global transformational dimensions could well change the history of the world. There is tremendous potential for an Indo-Pacific regional economic architecture, which could be the foundation for multi-faceted Indo-Pacific partnership, presenting the opportunity for creating an institutional framework that underlines the principle of cooperation instead of confrontation, and inclusion, rather than exclusion.

2

The Emergent Vistas of the Indo-Pacific

Lawrence W. Prabhakar

The Indo-Pacific has emerged from the different debates of the new discourse on maritime power that seeks to define the seamless linkages between the Indian and Pacific Oceans and the linkages of the rim states of the two oceans linked by economic interdependence, growing maritime commerce and the security ties that have emerged from the growth of these powers. It also represents the rise of the Asian maritime power evident in China and India as well the continuity of the world's dominant resident maritime power—the United States. The three maritime powers do determine the pivot of the Indo-Pacific in their respective contexts even as they vie with each other for dominance and influence. Since World War II, the Indo-Pacific has been in constant focus and attention vying with the Euro-Atlantic as the expansive maritime theatre of economic growth and security competition. Spatially, the region needs to be defined and characterised in the context of the contemporary geo-politics and geo-economics. This chapter seeks to elucidate the contexts of the Indo-Pacific, the vistas of the region and its varied definitions, the emergent power game and the strategies in pursuit.

The Indo-Pacific is the new spatial definition and framework of the maritime convergence of India, China and the United States as the pivotal powers in the world's largest maritime expanse. The region is representative of the competing and converging dyads of the three premier powers, i.e. India-US, US-China and India-China strategic relationships that are being churned in the maritime domain on the basis of competitive, cooperative and convergent relationships. Even as economic interdependence, maritime trade and commerce are intense among the three powers, the security competition for a dominant influence in the region has become inevitable. The Indo-Pacific has also emerged as a highly volatile region with nuclear and missile developments with several states in their proliferation drive. Escalation and brinkmanship in the Korean peninsula and its attendant impact on Japan and the United States is very intense. To define the Indo-Pacific a multiple sources of meanings and implications can be derived. In Constructivist terms, the Indo-Pacific presents the idea and imagery of the two oceanic regions of the Indian and Pacific Oceans that comprise of the 'institutional frameworks and inter-state operations that mesh the two oceans together.'[1] In terms of Regionalism, the 'regions of the Indian and Pacific Oceans portray the dynamic evolution of interests and operations of the powers are shaped up.[2] In its geo-political essence the origins of the concept was elucidated by Karl Haushofer who coined the term 'Indopazifischen Raum'. Haushofer elucidated that 'dense Indo-Pacific concentration of humanity and cultural empire of India and China, which . . . are geographically sheltered behind the protective veil of the offshore island arcs.'[3]

In his classic treatise on sea power, Alfred T. Mahan emphasized the primacy of sea power in the Indian and Pacific Oceans. He viewed the two oceans hedging the continental world island and decisive of the impact that it created in terms of security and strategy. Nicholas Spykman termed the Indo-Pacific as the 'circumferential maritime highway which links the whole area together in terms of sea power.'[4] In the 1980s and 1990s, the Asia-Pacific was the construct that was deployed that envisaged 'the discourse of 'Pacific Rim,' evident in the regional economic arrangements of the Asia Pacific Economic Cooperation and the East Asia Summit, etc. The year 2010 witnessed the construct of the 'Indo-Pacific' created to evoke

---

1 Peter Katzenstein elucidates that regions are the social constructions of politics and are cognitive constructs rooted in political perception and practice. See Peter Katzenstein, "Regionalism and Asia," in Shaun Breslin (ed.), *New Regionalism in the Global Political Economy* (London: Routledge, 2002), p.105.

2 Bruce Cumings, "Rimspeak; or the Discourse of the 'Pacific Rim,'" in Arif Dirlik (ed.), *What is in a Rim?: Critical Perspectives on the Pacific Region Idea* (Oxford: Rowman & Littlefield, 1998), 2nd ed., pp.53-72.

3 Ernst Haushofer, An English Translation and Analysis of Major Karl Ernst Haushofer's Geopolitics of the Pacific Ocean, trans. Lewis Tambs and Ernst Brehm (Lampeter: Edwin Mellor, 2002), p.141.

4 Nicholas Spykman, *The Geography of the Peace* (New York: Harcourt, Brace, 1944), p.38.

the India-US perspectives of the maritime and strategic convergence of the Indian and Pacific oceans.[5]

Frameworks about the Indo-Pacific

The Indo-Pacific region in its evolutionary design could be debated from several perspectives. There could be seven approaches that characterize the design of the Indo-Pacific. These are: (a) 'Constructivism of the Indo-Pacific'; (b) 'Balance of Power in the Indo-Pacific'; (c) 'Power Shift in the Indo-Pacific'; (d) 'Strategic Autonomy Choices in the region'; (e) 'Concert of Democracies in the Indo-Pacific'; (f) 'Indo-Pacific Regionalism' and (g) 'Indo-Pacific Commons.'

Constructivism of the Indo-Pacific' envisages that the ideas and images of the Indo-Pacific have been the construction of regionalism and geopolitics. The construction reveals the confluence of the two oceanic theatres of their profiles and competing interests. Constructivism posits the view that the Indian and Pacific Oceans present the respective institutional and operational entities that are unique to the region but the dynamic evolution of interests of the states in the two regions present a seamless maritime region.[6] Viewed from classical geopolitics, the Indo-Pacific region represents the physical-spatial definition. The critical geopolitics dimension introduces the significance of the perceptions and ambitions of the states in the region. Constructivism also envisages in the conceptualization of the political and diplomatic dimensions of strategy and operations of the major powers in the region and the extra-regional powers. Yet another dimension of Constructivism is the ability to view scope of the economic dimensions of engagement of the major powers of the region.

'Balance of Power in the Indo-Pacific' elucidates the changing power dynamics in the region. The regional balance witnesses the emergent complexities of a multi-polar balance emerging (US, China, India, Japan, Australia and the secondary powers of East and Southeast Asia). While the United States is the dominant and resident power of the region, and China

---

5 John Bradford, "The Maritime Strategy of the United States: Implications for Indo-Pacific Sealanes," *Contemporary Southeast Asia*, vol. 33, no. 2 (2011), pp.183-208.

6 David Scott, The "Indo-Pacific"—New Regional Formulations and New Maritime Frameworks for US-India Strategic Convergence, *Asia-Pacific Review*, vol. 19, no.2 (2012), p. 86.

is the emerging economic and strategic power, the power changes between the two and the other major powers in the region are seen as responses to China's power rise. The US rebalancing in the region and the creation of the Asian 'Pivot' is seen as a strategic response to China's military assertiveness and the spiraling of crisis and conflicts in the East and South China Seas.[7] A variant of the Balance of Power dynamics is Power Transition. Power transitions between the US and China is hastening the military competition between China and the US and it has increased the regional concerns of the states responding to the power rise of China. Power Transition is the process that commences with the dissatisfaction of the rising powers towards the dominant overlay of the regional and global hegemon, who's economic and security guarantees to the region could be challenged by the rising power dissatisfied with the system. The Balance of Power in the Indo-Pacific has been evident in the naval and air forces modernization and the revamping of their capabilities of the regional states and the extra-regional powers.

'Power Shift in the Indo-Pacific' is exemplified in the US rebalancing efforts that is conceptually and operationally a counter-response to the power rise of China and the arguments about the US decline. Power Shift is also discussed in the context of China's assertive rise and the strides in economic and strategic areas in the face of regional apprehensions in Southeast and East Asia. The US rebalance vis-à-vis China is bringing into focus the rejuvenation of economic and commercial interdependence of the US with the region as well as the alliances that are reinforced with its traditional allies and the new partners.[8] Power Shift in effect pushes the Southeast Asian states to focus on the Indo-Pacific as a means to counter-balance China with the US, Japan, India, Australia and South Korea joining the dynamics. The US sponsored Trans-Pacific Partnership (TPP) is the economic dimension of the US reengagement in the region and also serves to provide the ballast to the 'pivot' that it has been proposing and developing in the region.

'Strategic Autonomy Choices in the region' feature the regional perspective of how rising powers could envision their role and scope of engagement in the region. The Indian perspective on the Indo-Pacific is yet

---

7 John Bradford, The Maritime Strategy of the United States: Implications for Indo-Pacific Sealanes, *Contemporary Southeast Asia*, vol. 33, no. 2 (August 2011), p.186-208.

8 Michael Auslin, Getting it Right, Japan and Trans-Pacific Partnership, *Asia-Pacific Review*, vol. 19, no. 1, 2012, pp. 23-24.

unclear even as India has a divided opinion of an expansive engagement in the Indo-Pacific even as it is incrementally engaging the neighbourhood in Southeast Asia. While the broad consensus links the Indian and the US interests in convergence for the Indo-Pacific, certain sections of the Indian strategic community view the necessity of an Indian approach to the Indo-Pacific as independent of other approaches.[9] Strategic Autonomy choices entails that India could be driven by its strategic core interests of the scope and momentum of its Indo-Pacific engagement. India's expanding engagement with Japan, Australia and South Korea presents the prospect of an emergent Indo-Pacific perspective that is determined by its own interests and space of operations. On the other hand, the constricted view of India's strategic autonomy lies in the perspective that its interests would be better served through regional constructs like the ASEAN and EAS that would provide a substantial engagement. India's pivot in the Indo-Pacific emerges from the Strategic Partnerships that it has developed with the US, Japan, South Korea and the emerging partnership with Australia. Meanwhile, Strategic Partnerships involving the US-Japan-South Korea-Australia and the India-Japan-South Korea; India-Japan-Australia dimensions are still evolving.

'Concert of Democracies in the Indo-Pacific' has been a well-elucidated concept that has been employed in the contexts of unity and convergence of democracies in the region with the United States. The theme of Concert of Democracies had been used in the World War II contexts of fighting against authoritarian governments. The Concert of Democracies has been employed as a norm of the US-led alliance partners and friends in the region to portray and project allied interests in economic and political fronts. In the contemporary context it has its purported employment vis-à-vis China and North Korea as an enabling tool for Japan, South Korea and Australia. Concert of Democracies is employed in the context of the neo-liberal economic interdependence and the free transit and passage on the seas of the region.[10] The post-Tsunami relief operations in 2005 under the Operation Unified Assistance drew the democratic powers of the US, Japan, Australia and India into concerted maritime based humanitarian relief rehabilitation operations in the Southeast Asian region and the

---

9 Priya Chacko, India and the Indo-Pacific An Emerging Regional Vision, *Policy Brief,* Issue 5, November 2012, Indo-Pacific Governance Research Centre, Adelaide.

10 C. Raja Mohan, Great Powers and Asia's Destiny: A View from Delhi, *Political Science,* December 2012 vol. 64, no. 2, December 2012.

expanse of the Indian Ocean. The Malabar 07-02 naval exercises in 2007 involving the US, India, Japan, Singapore and Australia exemplified the ethos of the confluence of democratic states in the region. It had also evoked predictable and strong reactions from Beijing. Democracy and its diffusion in Asia has been a primary goal of the US and also it had engaged in its pursuit with India, Japan, Australia, South Korea and the countries of the ASEAN.

'Indo-Pacific Regionalism' provides the maritime basis of the region that is based on the primacy of maritime power and trade linking the countries throughout the region.[11] It is thus the emergent framework of the region that has the accents of strong economic growth, growing interdependence and also features high levels of military expenditure leading to arms race. The regional frameworks of Indo-Pacific regionalism are built on the basis of the existing economic regional arrangements of the ASEAN, ARF, EAS, APEC and the new TPP is also gaining accent to undergird the economic foundations of the Indo-Pacific. Indo-Pacific regionalism also envisages the scope of the US alliances in the region and its impact on India and the other countries.

'Indo-Pacific Commons' is yet another framework that defines the maritime commons that is formed on the linkages of the countries. The Indo-Pacific commons comprise of the sub-regions of Northeast, Southeast, and Southern Asia and the waterways of the Indian Ocean, Bay of Bengal, Straits of Malacca, South China Sea, Taiwan Straits and the Pacific expanse. The commons include thousands of miles of coastline in the Indo-Pacific region, key aerial transit routes, and undersea passages and the outer space. The framework has two triangles of countries that are concentric that have critical interests in the security and stability of the region, and the tranquil transit and trade amongst them. An inner triangle of countries of Southeast Asia (Malaysia, Singapore, Indonesia, Vietnam, Philippines) that enclose the South China Sea and an outer triangle of India, South Korea, Japan and Australia that have critical interests in the stability of the region.[12]

---

11 Dennis Rumley, Timothy Doyle & Sanjay Chaturvedi, 'Securing' the Indian Ocean? Competing Regional Security Constructions, *Policy Brief*, Issue 3, April 2012. Indo-Pacific Governance Research Centre, Adelaide.

12 Michael Auslin, Security in the Indo-Pacific Commons Toward a Regional Strategy (Washington DC: American Enterprise Institute, December 2010). Accessed http://www.aei.org/papers/foreign-and-defense-policy/regional/asia/security-in-the-indo-pacific-

Strategies of Great Powers in the Indo-Pacific

Great Power engagement in the Indo-Pacific has resulted in several competing strategies. The economic future of the region is increasingly tied towards China even as all regional powers have strong economic partnerships with China creating net dependence on China for their economic growth, while their security relationships are tied with the United States and seek greater US involvement in the region in the face of increasing China's military assertiveness.

The 'Hub and Spokes' has been the traditional US bilateral mutual security agreements with Japan, South Korea and Australia (1951), Philippines (1952), South Korea (1953), Thailand (1954) and Japan (1960). It has resulted in the forward basing of forces in Japan and South Korea. The US has increased its intelligence cooperation with Australia and its access to bases in Singapore and Thailand; it has enhanced the conventional forces pre-positioning as well as deployment of tactical nuclear weapons in South Korea and theatre missile defences in the region. The US reconfiguration of its power matrices in the Southeast Asian and East Asian theatres was made through its global forward basing power realignments in 2004. It signified that the US, while continuing to access the world's oceans and seas reduced its priority attention in the region and in its quest to build a cooperative and engaged relations with China preferred to 'stay neutral' in the South China Sea issues. It however did not preclude the rise of China with its hard power and the emergence of its dominating economic overlay throughout the Asian region. Alliance dynamics is being reinvigorated in the Indo-Pacific even as traditional 'Hub and Spoke' arrangements of the US with Japan, South Korea and Australia are buttressed by partnerships with Philippines, Thailand and Singapore.

The 'Regional Pivot' has emerged as the principal US response to the Chinese military power rise since 2012. Rebalancing of naval and air forces in the region and robust interoperability have become the standard operational initiatives of the US in the region. The pivot is based on strengthening alliances; deepening partnerships with emerging powers; building a stable, productive and constructive relationship with China; empowering regional institutions; and helping to build a regional economic architecture that can sustain shared prosperity.[13]

---

commons/.

13 Trefor Moss, America's Pivot to Asia: A Report Card, *The Diplomat*, May 5 2013. Accessed http://thediplomat.com/2013/05/05/americas-pivot-to-asia-a-report-card/.

The Chinese counter-responses could be envisaged through the following:

(a) **Soft balancing**: China has preferred this optimal external strategy as it does not attract immediate international or contending hegemonic responses of hard balancing. It has been engaged in a limited arms buildup, initiated *ad hoc* cooperative exercises, and has engaged in several collaborative initiatives with regional or international institutions. However, China has the option to convert these into open, hard-balancing strategies if and when security competition becomes intense. China contends the United States, Japan and India among the powers from where it expects concerted aggressive opposition to its rising power.

(b) **Internal balancing**: A variant of soft balancing, China has diligently sought to soften and to blunt the aggressiveness of the US, and Japanese economic and strategic power through a complex process of "engagement with the adversary's economic power base". This engagement is known as internal balancing. China has been increasing its potential power by focusing on economic development with synergies to convert its wealth into military might at a more propitious time. China's strategy of internal balancing is less likely to arouse immediate security concerns among other states by its constant manipulation of its relative economic and military capabilities. Internal balancing for China would be an optimal strategy to manoeuvre into a delicate balance between the poles of economic and military power.

China's combination of soft balancing in the external realm and internal balancing of economic development, which it calls as "peaceful rise" and "peaceful development" would be the blunting instruments of hegemonic power of its adversaries.

(c) **Asymmetric military strategy: China's most favoured strategy against its foes.** China's Taiwan strategy is based on a strategy of denial of American intervention power in its hubs of operation. Asymmetry is defined as the prevalent lopsided balance in power and capabilities in a contention between two sides. Asymmetry however weighs in great advantage for the weaker power to resort to a variety of hostile deceptive and denial actions against the stronger adversary. China's asymmetric strategy is pivoted on the "Assassin's mace" that consists of short and medium range ballistic missiles and long range land attack cruise missiles armed with electro-magnetic pulse, anti-radar, thermobaric and conventional warheads. China's asymmetric weapons are designed to neutralize and defeat a formidable superpower like the United States in a conventional conflict including the DF21-D to defeat the US carrier power in the Pacific.

(d) Encouraging the Brinkmanship states is one of the strategies of China to encourage them to pursue revisionist policies challenging the prevalent international status quo. Encouraging Brinkmanship states provides China strategic gain to create the leverage to secure China's position vis-à-vis the United States and its Asian allies. Brinkmanship states like North Korea, Iran and Pakistan provide important leverages for China even as the US re-balances and its alliances in the region are being reinvigorated.

The Emerging Great Game in the Indo-Pacific

A Great Game is being played in the Indo-Pacific with the US, China and India in the competitive deployments of naval forces and air forces joined by Japan, South Korea and Australia evident by the trends. Military transformation developments have been steadily progressing with the United States leading the initiatives and the allied countries have been following the various initiatives.[14]

'Reinforcing naval access and basing strategies' has been a prominent military transformation development that has resulted in robust forward basing of naval and air assets including Unmanned Aerial Vehicles and other surveillance equipment. The US rebalancing has resulted in new deployments of naval and air assets in Singapore, South Korea and Japan that has enhanced the efficacy of air and naval expeditionary capabilities. Joint exercises have increased the interoperability of the forward based forces with the regional powers.

'Ramping of naval and air expeditionary capabilities' has resulted

---

14 Richard A. Bitzinger, Military Modernization in the Asia-Pacific: Assessing New Capabilities, in Ashley Tellis, Andrew Marble and Travis Tanner (eds), *Strategic Asia 2010-11, Asia's Rising Power and America's Continued Purpose* (Seattle, WA: National Bureau of Asian Research).

in the investments made in the order of battle of the Southeast Asian states, South Korea, Japan and Australia. The emphasis on naval and air expeditionary capabilities reflect the nature of future wars in the air-sea domains even as the maritime disputes in the region seem to move into high contestation. The US has been transferring military hardware to Southeast Asia as well and has transferred relevant technology to its allied partners that has created and enhanced new capabilities.

Development of anti-access and area denial capabilities (A2AD) and countermeasures has resulted in the response and counter-responses in the technologies that has resulted in the development of anti-access and area denial capabilities. The US-China arms competition has seen the slew of new missile technologies that are being unleashed by both sides even as they battle in area dominance and denial operations. The development of anti-access and area denial capabilities are in tune with the regional and theatre military strategies of the US and China.

Air-Sea and Space-Cyber architectures would form the operational framework and constitute the main operational framework of the emerging capabilities, even as the US and China build the capabilities to contend and neutralize the other. The US led initiatives have now been built into allied capabilities of Japan, Australia and South Korea that presents a strategic interdependence of the US and its allies in the region. Chinese responses to the new architectures have been robust and have continued with the increasing investments into the frontier area of technologies.

Forward Basing and strengthening of regional alliances have been achieved by the United States that brings in renewed US troop presence in Darwin, Australia as well as the stationing of unmanned aerial assets in the region to maintain surveillance over the South China Sea. The US rebalancing efforts have increased the efficacy of its forward deployed forces throughout the region and have been able to surge its naval and air assets during the recent Korean flashpoint crisis by North Korea.

New Thresholds of sea-based nuclear forces—nuclear ballistic and cruise missile deployments have been the accents by which the US, China and India are now investing and building sea-based assets in the form of nuclear propelled platforms as well as nuclear tipped ballistic and cruise missiles.[15] Deployments of the nuclear ballistic and cruise missiles and

---

15 C. Raja Mohan, *Samudra Manthan: Sino-Indian Rivalry in the Indo-Pacific* (Washington

their platforms raise the threshold of the strategic competition. The United States however has the predominance in terms of the two classes of nuclear tipped missiles and in the number of platforms that operate in the Pacific Command. Sea-based nuclear forces have their scope and purpose in coercion and compellance missions and also aid in the extended nuclear deterrence of the allied partners.

Sea-based missile defences have proven their increasing relevance in the age of ballistic and cruise missile proliferation. The United States, Japan and South Korea have increased the numbers of the cruisers and destroyers that deploy sea-based ballistic missiles that have been deployed to counter the North Korean ballistic missile threat.

Thus, a variety of military transformations are in effect in the region even as the region posits the prospect of economic growth as well as strategic competition. The Indo-Pacific's seamless maritime space thus presents the scope for the re-energised alliance dynamics based on maritime partnerships of trade and security.

Concluding Remarks

It could be surmised that the Indo-Pacific as a regional commons presents the world's largest spatial area that encompasses several regional and subregional systems that feature economic interdependence and security arrangements. The region's economic interdependence and the net worth of economic transactions would be grossly higher than any region. Thus, the spatial contexts of the Indo-Pacific envisage new frameworks that feature competitive and convergent security evident in the light of power shifts in the region. While the prospect of exploiting the peaceful dimensions of this vast maritime commons is often promised and debated; the prospect of a spiralling competition between the region's powers and China on one hand and the US intervening in this crisis is as alarming as ever. Similarly the prospect of brinkmanship actors like North Korea or even terrorist groups disturbing the region is also prominent.

The triangular strategic contexts of the US, China and India engagement reveals that China and India reserve more of strategic autonomy to determine their respective pivots. The strategic reality of the US decline stares clearly in the transformation and evolution of the

DC: Carnegie Endowment for International Peace, 2012).

alliance dynamics in the region which is now being buttressed by renewed energy in alliance realignments and economic engagement of the US in the region. The maritime basis of the Indo-Pacific provides the new emphasis in the development of expeditionary capabilities of naval and air forces that have gained optimal synergy in the face of the technology revolutions. It is, however, China's power rise and sustained strategic modernization that attracts the compulsive attention of the US and its allies to sustained engagement. Indo-Pacific alliance dynamics would be influenced more in terms of how partners like India interpret their respective strategic autonomy and China's response by its own 'pivot'.

3

China and the Indo-Pacific Area as a Region

Michimi Muranushi

Regions are usually regarded in world politics as a matter of geographical division of the earth. However, East Asia, Southeast Asia, South Asia, the Middle East reflect the way Europeans looked at the map of the world.

This simple division dependent on the linear distance from Europe is convenient, but sometimes misleading. The first problem comes from the difficulty in determining the borders of the region thus divided. Whether Burma is seen as a state in Southeast Asia or South Asia; it has close relations with India and Bangladesh as well as Thailand. Usually countries relate more naturally with their neighbours in a different region than a distant country of the same region.

The second problem comes from states spreading across regions. Some big states are too big to be confined into a single region. Russia is partly Asia, and partly Europe. China is partly Central Asia and partly East Asia; Sudan is partly sub-Saharan Africa and partly North Africa.

The third problem comes from the fact that the ocean connects many parts of the world and sharing the ocean can mean a community. Just as the Polynesian islands are connected by sea, Japan, North Korea, China, Southeast Asia, South Asia are also connected by the sea. The concept of the Indo-Pacific area is based on this notion. Not only the sea but also the great rivers like the Mekong and the Nile can create a region.

The fourth problem is that geographical proximity is only one of the factors connecting one country to another. A country has strong relations with far away countries because of the country's need. The Middle East exports oil and natural gas to Europe and Japan. Growing China looks for natural resources all over the world, and in this sense, the strength of the connections among states can change over time.

Probably the field of world politics should try to find alternatives to geographical division. One such alternative which this chapter tries to propose is regions as 'being mentioned together'. For example, salt and pepper are in the same region, but salt and gasoline are not in the same, while gasoline and natural gas are in the same groups. There is probably much stronger connection between salt and sugar than between salt and honey, because the former pair is mentioned much more frequently than the latter pair. This does not mean, however, that salt is similar to sugar. In fact, sugar is more similar to honey than to salt.

This chapter proposes that it is possible to construct regions on the basis of what countries and people put together in their mind. When country A is mentioned together with country B, A and B are in the same group. When A, B and C are mentioned together, then A, B and C are in the same group. This does not necessarily mean that these countries are friends. In fact, the opposite may be true, just as salt and sugar. When the US and the USSR are mentioned together, they were in the same group of superpowers but they were adversaries to each other. Nevertheless, the fact they are mentioned together means that there is at least one issue concerning the two; the two states are in this sense connected.

One can move a step forward and define that two states, A and B, are connected to the extent that A is mentioned together with B frequently. If A and B are mentioned in many speeches, newspaper articles, or TV programs, there are probably many issues involving both A and B. The more articles mention A and B together, the more strongly A and B are connected. This does not necessarily mean, however, that other states are not related to the issue. In fact other states, C, may also be involved. If A, B and C are mentioned together, this means A and B are connected, that B and C are connected, and that C and A are connected. If A and B are mentioned together by 100 articles and B and C are mentioned together by 200 articles, B and C are twice as strongly connected as A and B.

A difficult part of continuing this research is what data to use to count such numbers. There are so many instances in which A and B are mentioned all over the world. Then what is the best source of information

CHINA AND THE INDO-PACIFIC AREA AS A REGION

on which one can decide the degree that A and B are mentioned together frequently? This chapter depends on the online database of world newspaper and other articles named 'World News Connections[1] (WNC)' produced by the National Technical Information Service (NTIS), the US Government. WNC translates into English thousands of articles published daily in newspapers or aired in various languages.

This chapter selected 20 countries or political entities. Many of them share the Indo-Pacific Ocean. Japan, North Korea, South Korea, Taiwan, China, the Philippines, Indonesia, Vietnam, Cambodia, Thailand, Indonesia, Myanmar, Bangladesh, Nepal, India, Pakistan, Russia, the US, Sudan (and Southern Sudan) and Brazil. The purpose of including Sudan and Brazil is to compare the relations among the rest of the group with the relations with far away countries.

The matrix of the relations in 2012 means how many articles of WNC in 2012, mentioned A and B together. If, for example, an article says that North Korea launched a missile and the US and Japan protested, the article is counted as one instance of North Korea–Japan relations, one instance of North Korea–US relations, and one instance of Japan–US relations. It does not matter how often two countries are mentioned in the same article. A matrix of the relations among the 20 countries this chapter selected in 1997 are given below:

---

1   http://wnc.fedworld.gov/

Table 1: Connection of Countries in 1997 (The number of WNC articles mentioning both countries/areas).

	Japan	North Korea	South Korea	Taiwan	China	Viet-nam	Philip-pine	Cam-bodia	Thai-land	Myan-mar	Indo-nesia	Paki-stan	Bang-ladesh	India	Nepal	Sri Lanka	Russia	USA	Sudan
Japan																			
N. Korea	420																		
S. Korea	1,355	2,034																	
Taiwan	782	245	499																
China	2,593	729	1,447	5,464															
Vietnam	187	38	151	120	568														
Philippines	268	50	197	184	519	283													
Cambodia	603	24	66	107	385	281	191												
Thailand	448	36	259	191	735	388	475	572											
Myanmar	28	2	2	11	169	87	58	59	109										
Indonesia	303	21	21	130	456	261	427	188	531	68									
Pakistan	151	24	24	42	534	41	44	19	61	20	70								
Bangladesh	36	3	3	16	137	39	26	14	55	43	51	159							
India	301	26	26	109	799	100	62	39	110	44	128	1,158	190						
Nepal	22	2	10	24	334	12	12	1	15	15	15	44	73	153					
Sri Lanka	18	2	9	9	100	10	13	10	26	9	21	85	65	95	53				
Russia	1,417	243	571	200	2,317	212	90	70	131	25	174	362	30	692	19	26			
USA	1,814	768	1,698	1,303	4,058	216	297	178	478	52	302	478	56	559	34	33	2,224		
Sudan	9	6	3	4	48	5	2	1	9	3	9	15	7	9	2	2	30	105	
Brazil	77	4	56	38	164	10	20	3	19	1	37	20	5	62	6	3	124	158	1

Source: Based on WNC 1997.

Let us look at how each of the following countries is connected with other countries according to the WNC articles in 1997.

Japan

Japan is most strongly connected to China (2,593 articles) and then to the US (1,814 articles), Russia (1,417 articles) and South Korea (1,355 articles). It is a little counter intuitive that Japan's connection to the US is weaker than Japan's connection to China. Japan's connection to India (301) is much smaller than Japan's connection to Cambodia (603), Thailand (448), Taiwan (782) and Indonesia (303). Likewise, Japan is very weakly connected to Myanmar (28), Sri Lanka (18) and Nepal (22). Japan is very weakly connected to Brazil (77) and Sudan (9). Japan's connection seems to be related to geographical distance.

North Korea

North Korea is most strongly connected to South Korea (2,034 articles) and strongly connected to China (729) and the US (768). North Korea is modestly connected to Japan (420), Russia (243) and Taiwan (245). North Korea is weakly related to many other states such as Pakistan (24) and India (26).

South Korea

South Korea is most strongly connected to North Korea (2,034 articles) but it is almost equally strongly connected to the US (1,698) and it is strongly connected to China (1,447). South Korea is weakly connected to states such as Pakistan (24), Bangladesh (3), and India (26); South Korea is weakly connected to Sudan (3) and Brazil (56). Like the case of Japan, South Korea's pattern seems to be related to geographical distance.

Taiwan

Taiwan is most strongly connected to China (5,464 articles). It is a little strongly connected to the US (1,303) and Japan (782). It is weakly connected to the rest of Southeast Asia and South Asia. It is also weakly connected to Sudan (4) and Brazil (38).

China

China is most strongly connected to Taiwan (5,464 articles). It is very

21

strongly connected to the US (4,058), Japan (2,593) and Russia (2,317). It is modestly connected to North Korea (729), but its connection to South Korea (1,447) is much stronger. China is modestly connected to Pakistan (534) but China's connection with India (799) is stronger. This result seems counter intuitive, given the already long history of Chinese friendship with Pakistan. China is far more strongly connected to the US (4,058) than Japan is connected to the US (1,814).

China is more strongly connected to Southeast Asia and South Asia than other states in these regions, including India. For example, China is about equally connected to Sri Lanka (100) as India is connected to Sri Lanka (95). China is more strongly connected to Nepal (334) than India is connected to Nepal (153). China is weakly connected to the Sudan (48) and Brazil (164), but China's connections to these countries is stronger than the US connection to the Sudan (105) and Brazil (158).

Vietnam

Vietnam is most strongly connected to China (568 articles). Its connection to Japan is not strong (187). This was counter intuitive, given the amount of Japanese ODA to Vietnam, and the history of territorial dispute between China and Vietnam. Vietnam has some connections with nearby countries such as Thailand (388), but its connections seem weak. It is also only weakly connected to the Sudan (5) and Brazil (10).

The Philippines

The Philippines are most strongly connected to China (519 articles), but it is about equally connected to Indonesia (427) and Thailand (475). Its connection to the US is modest (297). Its connections to the Sudan (2) and Brazil (20) are weak.

Cambodia

Cambodia is most strongly connected to Japan (603 articles) and it is strongly connected to Thailand (572). It is relatively strongly connected to China (385) and the US (178) and Indonesia (188). It is weakly related to the rest of Southeast Asia and South Asia. It is very weakly related to the Sudan (1) and Brazil (3).

Thailand

Thailand is most strongly related to China (735 articles) and strongly related to Cambodia (572), Japan (448) Indonesia (531) and the US (472). Thailand is relatively weakly connected to the rest of Southeast Asia and South Asia. It is weakly connected to the Sudan and Brazil.

Myanmar

Myanmar's connection to the rest of the world is weak, but its strong connection is with China (169 articles). It has relatively strong connection to Thailand (109) and the US (52). In 1997, this was a rather isolated country and its degree of isolation seems stronger than that of North Korea.

Indonesia

Indonesia is most strongly connected to Thailand (531 articles) and it is relatively strongly connected to China (456). It is interesting to find that Indonesia may be the only country whose connection to China is not particularly strong. Compared with Vietnam, for example, Indonesia has conditions to keep distance from China. Indonesia's connection to Japan (301) is about as strong as its connection to the US (302). Indonesia has weak connection to the Sudan and Brazil.

Pakistan

Pakistan is most strongly connected to India (1,158 articles). It is strongly connected to China (534) and the US (478). It is not strongly connected to the rest of Southeast Asia or South Asia. One could say that Pakistan has a little bit strong connection to Sudan (15) and Brazil (20).

Bangladesh

Bangladesh is most strongly connected to India (190 articles) but also strongly connected to China (137) and Pakistan (159). It is weakly connected to the rest of the world.

India

India is most strongly connected to Pakistan (1,158 articles) and China (799). This is interesting in the sense that India is a country tied to relatively hostile environment. Another characteristic of India is its connection to

Russia (692) is stronger than its connection to the US (559). Compared with Pakistan, India's connection to the Sudan is weaker (9 articles) but India's connection to Brazil is stronger (62).

Nepal

Nepal is most strongly connected to China (334 articles) and strongly connected to India (153). It is weakly connected to the rest of the world.

Sri Lanka

Sri Lanka is most strongly connected to China (100 articles), and it is strongly connected to India (95). Perhaps the position of Sri Lanka can be comparable to that of North Korea. Whereas China has dominant position in its relations with North Korea, India cannot do the same in its relations with Sri Lanka.

Russia

Russia is most strongly connected to China (2,317 articles), and it is almost equally strongly connected to the US (2,224). This suggests a possibility that China is not only the centre of Asia but also the centre of the world already in 1997, according to the data this chapter uses. It is also strongly connected to Japan (1,417).

The USA

The US is most strongly connected to China (4,058 articles), than to Russia (2,224). It is obvious that the US is already more strongly connected to China than to Russia, or to Japan (1,814) or to South Korea (1,698). American connection to Sudan and Brazil is not particularly stronger than Chinese connection to these two.

Sudan

The Sudan has relatively strong connection to China (48 articles), Pakistan (15), Russia (30) and the US (105).

Brazil

Brazil has relatively strong connection to China (164 articles), Russia (164) and the US (158).

The above observation can be roughly summarized in the following.

Figure 1: Connection of Different Countries in 1997 based on Very Strong Connections.

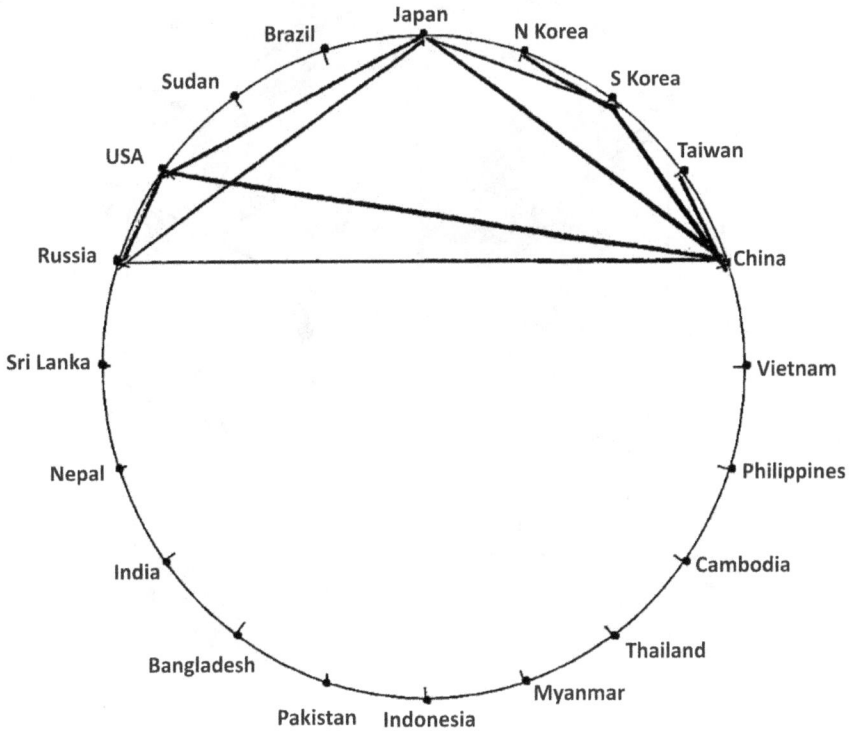

Figure 2: Connection of Different Countries in 1997 based on Relatively Strong Connections.

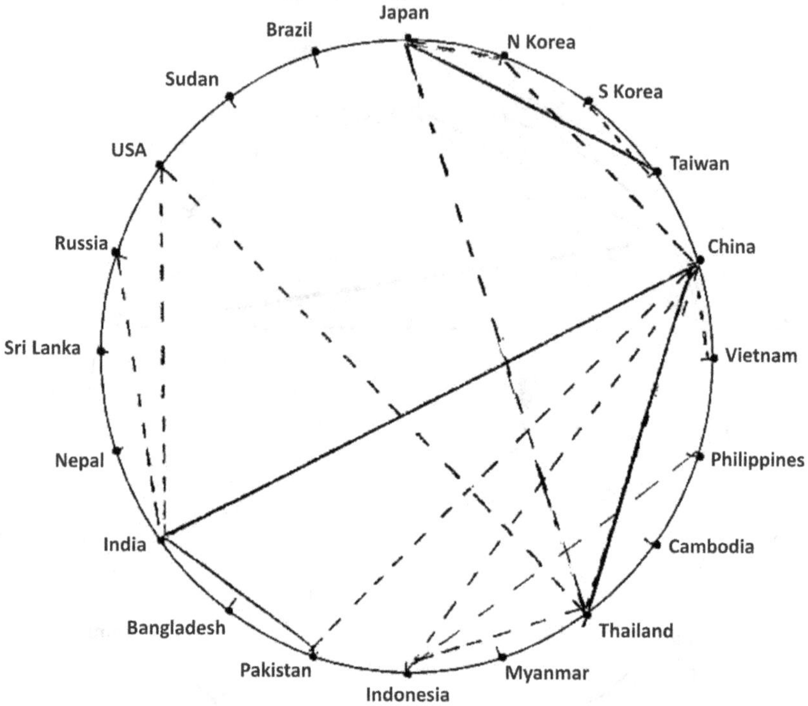

The number of articles in WNC in 2012 is much bigger than in 1997. It is not meaningful to compare absolute numbers between 1997 and 2012, but it will be meaningful to compare the structure of connection in 1997 and that in 2012.

Table 2: Connection of Countries in 2012 (The Number of WNC articles mentioning both countries/areas).

	Japan	N Korea	S Korea	Taiwan	China	Vietnam	Philippine	Cambodia	Thailand	Myanmar	Indonesia	Pakistan	Bangladesh	India	Nepal	Sri Lanka	Russia	USA	Sudan	Brazil
Japan																				
N Korea	5506																			
S Korea	9393	15774																		
Taiwan	4404	420	2289																	
China	12617	7039	11205	14509																
Vietnam	1395	608	1158	1201	4480															
Philippines	1471	464	1026	1251	3825	1699														
Cambodia	695	419	572	328	2855	1083	768													
Thailand	1420	442	1131	771	9815	1394	1092	1293												
Myanmar	561	424	526	199	2332	653	389	586	1378											
Indonesia	1402	612	1286	814	3697	1261	1364	843	1486	669										
Pakistan	1234	581	726	269	6172	519	425	166	467	484	1096									
Bangladesh	485	347	295	105	1748	328	209	171	377	805	578	1893								
India	2908	907	213	1027	12455	1192	889	516	1365	1048	1652	16978	3888							
Nepal	128	287	134	58	914	100	82	73	110	147	134	453	477	804						
Sri Lanka	313	101	235	142	1142	167	138	77	211	421	278	972	503	1509	235					
Russia	4772	3603	3698	819	17014	1334	683	430	421	421	1417	3343	567	6014	176	375				
USA	8164	5762	8216	4289	22778	2039	3097	3097	1088	1088	2380	11433	1710	10594	249	745	22193			
Sudan	252	168	171	56	1584	67	82	50	141	141	278	589	216	630	60	136	810	1536		
Brazil	871	343	788	284	2943	248	153	88	78	78	479	163	159	1880	79	95	2015	2396	163	

Source: Based on WNC 2012.

Japan

Japan is most strongly connected to China (12,617 articles). This is the same as 1997, whereas the US-Japan tie came second in 1997, and third in 2012 (8,164). Japan's connection to South Korea (9,393) seems stronger. Japan's connection to North Korea (5,506) and to Taiwan (4,404) and to Russia (4,772) follow the Japan-US connection. And it is only after these ties that Japan's connection to India (2,908) comes.

Japan was already surpassed by China in 1997 in the sense that Japan's connection to the countries selected are weaker than those of China, with the exception of connection to Cambodia. But in 2012, the gap between Japan and China further widened. China's connections to Southeast Asia and South Asia are three to five times as strong as Japan's connections to the regions.

North Korea

North Korea is most strongly connected to South Korea (15,774 articles). It is also strongly connected to China (7,039), the US (5,762), Japan (5,506), and Russia (3,603).

South Korea

South Korea is most strongly connected to North Korea (15,774 articles). It is also strongly connected to China (11,205), Japan (9,393), the US (8,216) and Russia (3,698).

Taiwan

Taiwan is most strongly connected to China (14,509 articles). It is also strongly connected to the US (4,289).

China

China is most strongly connected to the US (22,778 articles). This may be the strongest bilateral relations of the world. China has strong connection to Russia (17,014), Taiwan (14,509), Japan (12,817) and to India (12,455). China has stronger connections to the countries this chapter selected than the US, with the exception of Pakistan and Russia. Namely, China-Pakistan

(6,172) versus the US-Pakistan (11,433), China-Russia (17,014) versus the US-Russia (22,193). The tie between Pakistan and China seems more modest than its history suggests. China has strong connection to the Sudan (1,584) and Brazil (2,943). These connections are as strong as American connections to these countries.

Vietnam

Vietnam is most strongly connected to China (4,480 articles). Vietnam is also relatively strongly connected to the US (2,039).

The Philippines

The Philippines is most strongly connected to China (3,825 articles). It also has strong connection to the US (3,097). Comparison of Vietnam and the Philippines suggests that the Philippines has more freedom to keep distance from China and come near to the US.

Cambodia

Cambodia is most strongly connected to the US (3,097 articles). It is also strongly connected to China (2,855). Cambodia's connection to Japan (695) seems relatively much weaker.

Myanmar

The political changes in Myanmar made it much less isolated. But Myanmar is still most strongly connected to China (2,332 articles). It is also strongly connected to Thailand (1,378). Myanmar's connection to India (1,048) is strengthened. Myanmar's connection to the US (1,098) is also strengthened.

Indonesia

Indonesia was more strongly connected to Thailand than to China in 1997. This was exceptional in Southeast Asia in 1997. But Indonesia came nearer to China in 2012. Indonesia is most strongly connected in 2012 to China (3,697 articles). It is strongly connected to the US (2,380). Indonesia is relatively strongly connected to Japan (1,402), South Korea (1,286), Vietnam (1,281), the Philippine (1,364), Thailand (1,486), India (1,652), Russia (1,417). Indonesia may have given China a leading position while keeping equidistance from other states.

Pakistan

Pakistan is most strongly connected to India (16,978 articles). It is also strongly connected to the US (11,433) and to China (6,172).

Bangladesh

Bangladesh is most strongly connected to India (3,889 articles). It is strongly connected to China (1,748). Compared with 1997, India has become more connected to Bangladesh.

India

India is most strongly connected to Pakistan (17,978 articles). But it is also strongly connected to China (12,455). This should be compared with India's connection to Japan (2,908). India has reasonably strong connection to Sudan (630) and Brazil (1,880). This may mean that India has begun to widen its relations with the world outside Southeast Asia and South Asia.

Nepal

Nepal is most strongly connected to China (914 articles). It is also strongly connected to India (804).

Sri Lanka

Sri Lanka is most strongly connected to India (1,509 articles). While it is strongly connected to China (1,142), the situation may be improving for India.

Russia

Russia is most strongly related to the US (22,193 articles). It is also strongly related to China (17,014). Compared with 1997, Russia may have come slightly nearer to the US and slightly far from China.

The USA

With the exception of Russia, the countries in this chapter are more strongly connected to China than to the US. But compared with Japan, which seems totally surpassed by China in this game of connection building, the US is still racing with China.

Sudan

The Sudan is strongly connected to China (1,584 articles), to India (630), to Pakistan (589), Russia (810) and the US (1,536).

Brazil

Brazil is strongly connected to China (2,943 articles), India (1,980), Russia (2,015) and the US (2,396).

Comparison

Figure 3 shows the result of the numbers of 2012 divided by the number of 1997.

The above observations can be roughly summarized this way.

Figure 3: Comparison between the results of 2012/1997 on 'Very Strong Connections' countries.

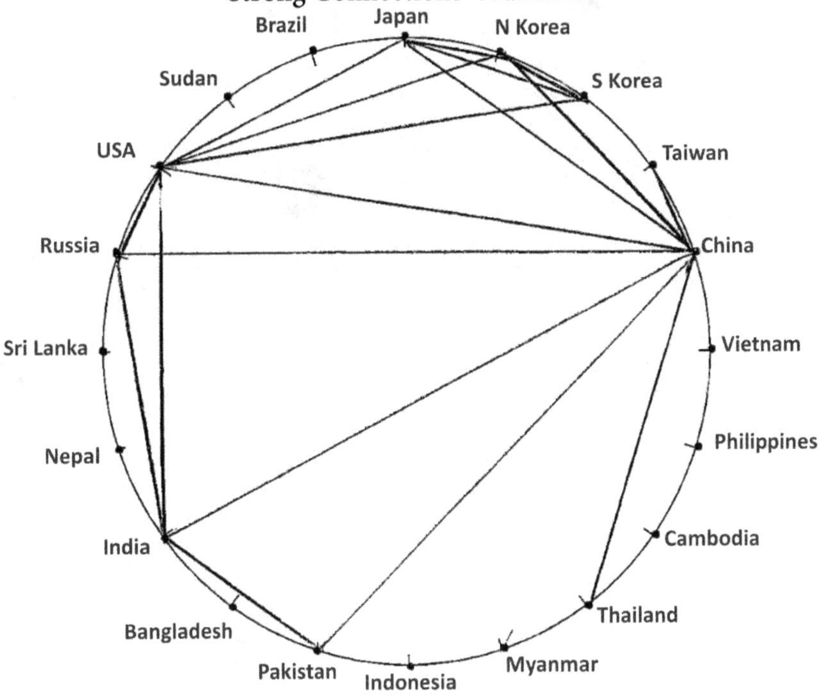

Figure 4: Comparison between the results of 2012/1997 on 'Relativelv

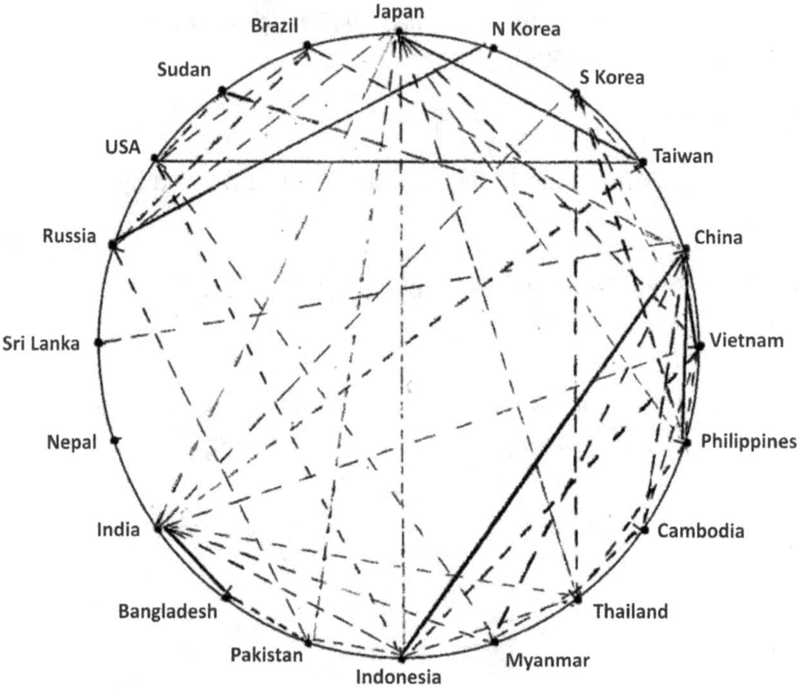

	Japan	N Korea	S Korea	Taiwan	China	Vietnam	Philippine	Cambodia	Thailand	Myanmar	Indonesia	Pakistan	Bangladesh	India	Nepal	Sri Lanka	Russia	USA	Sudan	Brazil
Japan	13																			
N Korea	7	7.8																		
S Korea	6	1.7	4.6																	
Taiwan	5	9.7	7.8	2.6																
China	7	16	7.7	10	7.9															
Vietnam	5.5	9.5	5.2	6.8	7.4	6														
Philippines	6.7	17	8.7	3	7.4	3.9	4.5													
Cambodia	3.2	12	0.5	4	13.4	3.6	2.3	2.3												
Thailand	20	212	22.9	18	13.4	7.5	6.7	10	12.7											
Myanmar	4.6	29	5.8	6.3	8.1	4.8	3.2	4.5	2.8	9.8										
Indonesia	8.2	24	11	6.4	11.2	12.7	9.7	8.8	7.7	24.2	15.7									
Pakistan	13.5	11.6	6.7	6.6	12.8	8.4	8	12	6.9	18.8	11.3	12								
Bangladesh	9.7	35	15	9.4	15.6	12	14.3	13.2	12.4	19	12.9	14.7	20							
India	5.8	13	13.4	2.4	2.7	8.3	6.8	73	7.3	9.8	8.9	4	6.5	5.3						
Nepal	17.3	51	26	15.8	11.4	16.7	10	7.7	8.1	23.4	13.2	11.1	7.7	15.9	4.4					
Sri Lanka	3.4	15	6.4	4	7.3	6.3	7.6	6.1	6.2	17	8.1	9.2	18.9	8.7	9.3	14.4				
Russia	4.5	6.9	4.8	3.3	5.6	9.4	10.4	5.5	4.8	21	7.9	5	30.5	19	7.3	22.5	9.7			
USA	28	57	57	14	33	13.4	4	50	9.8	47	3.1	40	30.9	70	30	68	27	14.6		
Sudan																				
Brazil	11.3	14	7.4	7.4	18	24.8	7.7	29	10	78	12.9	8.1	31.8	30.3	13.1	32	16.3	15.1		163

Source: Based on WNC.

Analysis

(a) Two states divided by birth are strongly connected to each other. Taiwan–China, North Korea–South Korea, India–Pakistan are examples.

(b) Landlocked state, Nepal, is relatively isolated.

(c) Island states such as the Philippines and Indonesia may have better conditions than continental states to be free from China.

(d) Some countries are known to be in conflict with China, but they are in fact more strongly connected with China than with other countries. Such examples are Vietnam and the Philippines.

(e) The centrality of China in this selected group of 20 countries is already clear in 1997. The two states most strongly connected are China and the US. China is in the very centre of South Asia and Southeast Asia. Also, China is in the centre of the 20 states or areas this chapter selected. It is neither the US, Russia nor Japan. China is most strongly connected with the rest of the group than any other states. US-China relations are stronger than US-Japan and US-Russia relations. For many countries, relations with China are stronger than the relations with their neighbours.

(f) Russia may have begun to regain its previous connection to the US.

(g) Japan has considerably lost its connection to Southeast Asia and South Asia. It is not succeeding in translating its economic assistance to building connection. US-Japan tie is often said to be the most important bilateral tie of the world. This statement is not supported by the data used here. Rather, the most important set of bilateral relations in the sense that the two states are mentioned together, is US-China relations.

(h) North Korea is not so isolated; it is connected to a set of countries.

(i) The US is still in Southeast Asia and South Asia, but it cannot make stronger connection, with the exception of Pakistan.

(j) China is well connected not only with nearby states but also with

34

far away states. India follows China.

(k) Myanmar, which has been relatively isolated in 1997, began to be connected with many countries very fast in 2012. But its connection to China remains strong.

(l) Relations with China are not only important among the group of big states such as Russia, the US, Japan, but also among the group of China's neighbours. China has strong relations with the rest of Asian states than the US, Japan or Russia.

(m) Besides having strong connections with the rest of Asia, China has strong connections with distant countries such as Sudan and Brazil. The degree that China is connected to these countries can exceed that of the US and Russia, despite geographical distance.

(n) The neighbours of India and Vietnam, namely, Bangladesh, Pakistan, Cambodia and Laos, are strongly connected with China. This may be a kind of combination of direct and indirect encirclement of the countries around China. The same observation can be made in Northeast Asia. While the power of Japan is declining, China has increasingly strong connections with South Korea and North Korea, as if these countries are encircling Japan.

(o) China is more strongly connected to such states as Brazil and Sudan than the US and Russia. China's connection is not only strong within the group of the Indo-Pacific region but also with the countries outside the group.

Region plus one?

For China, the best way to deal with other countries is to use one-to-one relations. China uses this in its dispute with Vietnam, the Philippines, Taiwan and other countries over the Spratly islands and the Paracel islands. When states try to cope with China as the ASEAN, China wedges the group by using continental states of Cambodia. In the dispute with Japan over the Senkaku islands, it will never agree to take the issue to the International Court of Justice (ICJ). China can think, with good reason, that by letting the others group may deprive China of power.

China is not going to be a global superpower. This is not contradictory to the fact that China began to take more aggressive measures in East Asia or Southeast Asia. Its renunciation of a global status is for preventing others from creating a bigger group including the US. It pledges not to be a hegemon because there is a trade-off between global status and regional interests. China's goal will be to obtain a position like what the Monroe doctrine used to mean for the US, and extend its relations to the outside world.

European concept of geographical division helps China. For Europe, the world is square, with Europe in its west. For China, the world is round, with China in the centre. China can divide the rest of the world to stand in a better position in negotiation. In this sense, regions should be rethought and created in a different way. What China does not tell is that, if China is the centre, the circles around the centre can be a region.

The rise of China means that China has increased power over the bilateral relations or traditional regional relations. The regions or countries in dispute with China should rather fight along with countries with different regions. The region, when discussed as area of dialogue, should be expanded. ASEAN is already a little old-fashioned concept. Japan should be willing to be involved in South Asian or Southeast Asian affairs, in which Japan was less interested before. However, India pays more attention to the Northeast Asian affairs. The new concept of region should not be based on a flat map. It should be based on flexible connection with special attention to China.

4

Australia Re-Discovering the Indo-Pacific

Melissa Conley Tyler and Samantha Shearman

In May 2012 incoming Secretary of the Department of Foreign Affairs and Trade Peter Varghese, returning from his posting as High Commissioner to India, was asked to speak on the topic of Australia and India in the Asian century. He suggested that the crucial concept would be the Indo-Pacific: 'Today, it makes more sense to think of the Indo-Pacific, rather than the Asia Pacific, as the crucible of Australian security.'[1] This reflects the extent to which the Indo-Pacific concept has emerged as a topic of current debate in Australia.

The Indo-Pacific concept shifts Australia's focus from the Asia-Pacific to a broader region comprising both the Indian and Pacific Oceans. Both domestic and external factors have been central causes for the re-emergence of the concept. Domestic factors include the Western Australian mining boom and increased focus on Australia's northern and western oceans. External factors include the increased economic and strategic links between the Indian and Pacific Oceans and the increasing use of the Indo-Pacific concept by US policy-makers.

While the term 'Indo-Pacific' is not new in Australian discourse, it more recently re-emerged in 2005. Since then, the term has been used by government officials and commentators. A two-sided debate has emerged: proponents promote the concept as a valid description of the regional reality while opponents view the concept with concern, arguing that it is designed

---

1 Peter Varghese, 'Australia and India in the Asian Century: An address by H.E. Peter Varghese AO', Institute of Peace and Conflict Studies, May 2012. http://www.ipcs.org/pdf_file/issue/SR127-AustraliaandIndiaintheAsianCentury.pdf (accessed 5 May 2013), p. 2.

to serve the US' strategic interests and may be perceived to exclude China. The issue seems to have been settled with the wholesale adoption in the *Defence White Paper 2013* of the Indo-Pacific as a description of Australia's wider region and one of Australia's four key strategic interests.[2]

The implications of using the Indo-Pacific as a key concept in Australian foreign policy have yet to be played out. Australia is in a delicate strategic position as it attempts to balance its alliance with the US and its economic relationship with China; it does not want to upset this balance. Australia is likely to increase its engagement with Indo-Pacific powers and invest in regional institutions as a way of engaging the region and nurturing cooperation. While the future remains unclear, many other states face a similar position; they are strategically linked to the US but increasingly linked to China economically. Therefore, Australia is in a position where its choices are being watched by others as something of a regional 'bellwether'. How Australia manages these choices provides a window into a rapidly changing Asia.

Defining the Indo-Pacific Concept

Various definitions of the Indo-Pacific region have been proposed in Australia. According to the Government, Australia in the Asian Century White Paper: 'Under such a conception, the western Pacific Ocean and the Indian Ocean would come to be considered as one strategic arc.'[3] Similarly, the Indo-Pacific Governance Research Centre defines the Indo-Pacific as the region 'spanning the western Pacific Ocean to the western Indian Ocean along the eastern coast of Africa.'[4] Lowy Institute analyst Rory Medcalf defines the region as an 'emerging Asian strategic system that encompasses both the Pacific and Indian Oceans, defined in part by the geographically expanding interests and reach of China and India, and the continued strategic role and presence of the United States in both.'[5]

---

2 Commonwealth of Australia, Defence White Paper 2013 (Canberra: Department of Defence, 2013). http://www.defence.gov.au/whitepaper2013/docs/WP_2013_web.pdf (accessed 5 May 2013), p. 7.

3 Commonwealth of Australia, *Australia in the Asian Century White Paper* (Canberra: Department of the Prime Minister and Cabinet, 2012). http://asiancentury.dpmc.gov.au/white-paper (accessed 5 May 2013), p. 74.

4 Indo-Pacific Governance Research Centre, University of Adelaide, 'Indo-Pacific'. http://www.adelaide.edu.au/indo-pacific-governance/ (accessed 2 April 2013).

5 Rory Medcalf, 'Pivoting the Map: Australia's Indo-Pacific System', Paper No. 1, *Centre of*

While the broad geographic shape of the region is clear, defining exact boundaries would be arbitrary to some extent. The definition given by the Indo-Pacific Governance Research Centre offers the greatest level of specificity when defining the borders of the Indo-Pacific. Based on this, the geographic limitations of the region can be defined as the western Pacific Ocean to the western Indian Ocean, including the eastern coast of Africa. However, as Medcalf highlights, the Indo-Pacific region is defined by more than its geographic constraints.

Causes for the Emergence of the Indo-Pacific Concept in Australia

Domestic Factors

The economic growth of Western Australia has influenced the emergence of the Indo-Pacific concept in Australia. While just 10 per cent of the Australian population lives in Western Australia, over 30 per cent of exports leave from its shores.[6] The state alone was responsible for more than 50 per cent of Australia's economic growth from 2011 to 2012.

The importance of Western Australia has three impacts on Australia's foreign outlook. First, Australia's traditionally eastern focus has shifted to the north and west. Exports have made the Indian Ocean and the security of its sea-lanes fundamental to Australia's interests.[7] Second, resource exports have entrenched a connection between Australia and Indo-Pacific powers such as China and India, which rely on foreign imports. Third, Western Australia has become strategically important. This shift is already visible: the 2012 Australia-United States Ministerial Consultations (AUSMIN) held in Perth symbolise the importance of the West to the alliance. HMAS Stirling provides the US with invaluable port access to the Indian Ocean.[8] Strategists are also discussing the possibility of using the Cocos (Keeling)

Gravity Series, Strategic and Defence Studies Centre, The Australian National University, November 2012. http://ips.cap.anu.edu.au/sdsc/cog/COG1_Medcalf_Indo-Pacific.pdf (accessed 5 May 2013), p. 2.

6   Julie Bishop, 'Charting the future of Australia-India relations', *Australian Polity*, vol. 2, no. 3 (March 2012). http://australianpolity.com/australian-polity/charting-the-future-of-australia-india-relations (accessed 19 March 2013).

7   Julie Bishop, 'Charting the future of Australia-India relations', *Australian Polity*, vol. 2, no. 3 (March 2012). http://australianpolity.com/australian-polity/charting-the-future-of-australia-india-relations (accessed 19 March 2013).

8   Rory Medcalf, 'The West is Poised for Strategic Role as Hub of the Indo-Pacific Age', *The Australian*, 12 November 2012.

Islands, an Australian territory located in the Indian Ocean approximately 2,800 km Northwest of Perth, as a potential location for maritime air patrol and surveillance activities.[9]

This has led to a change of perspective among policy-makers, as has the prominence of Western Australians in foreign affairs and defence issues, including Minister for Defence Stephen Smith and Shadow Minister for Foreign Affairs Julie Bishop. Ms. Bishop speaks for other Western Australians when she says 'I'm very conscious that Australia is bound by the Indian Ocean, the Pacific Ocean and we are unmistakably located in Asia.'[10] The growth of Western Australia has increased Australia's focus on the Indian Ocean region, contributing to the emergence of the Indo-Pacific concept.

External Factors

In addition to these changes within Australia, external factors are crucial in explaining the emergence of the Indo-Pacific concept. Asia is increasingly economically and strategically linked, drawing together the Indian and Pacific Oceans. At the heart of this is the rise of China and India. Their rapidly increasing reliance on imports has forged a myriad of trade connections. India's oil needs grew by over two-and-a-quarter times from 1990 to 2007 while China's tripled; over 80 per cent of oil required by Asia's major powers is sourced from the Gulf.[11] Many resources are also imported from Africa. Approximately two-thirds of the world's oil shipments and one-third of bulk cargo pass through the Indian Ocean.[12] This creates a trade highway that connects the Indian and Pacific Ocean. According to Australian National University Professor Michael Wesley:

---

9   Thomas Mahnken, 'Strengthening the Australia-US alliance in a period of constraint', *The Strategist,* Australian Strategic Policy Institute, 18 March 2013. http://www.aspistrategist.org.au/strengthening-the-australia-us-alliance-in-a-period-of-constraint/ (accessed 2 May 2013).

10 Julie Bishop, 'Address to Australia-Indonesia Dialogue', Australian Institute of International Affairs, Sydney, 4 March 2013. http://www.juliebishop.com.au/speeches/1223-address-to-australia-indonesia-dialogue.html (accessed 2 May 2013).

11 Michael Wesley, *There Goes the Neighbourhood: Australia and the Rise of Asia* (Sydney: UNSW Press, 2011), p. 87.

12 Commonwealth of Australia, *Australia in the Asian Century White Paper* (Canberra: Department of the Prime Minister and Cabinet, 2012). http://asiancentury.dpmc.gov.au/white-paper (accessed 5 May 2013), p. 74.

"By the end of the first decade of the supposedly Asia Pacific century, Asia's internal trade was more than two-and-a-quarter times the size of cross-Pacific trade."[13]

The reliance on imports from across the Indian Ocean has stretched the geographic reach of the major Asian powers' interests and created a focus on maritime and naval security.[14] China, for example, is developing port access from Hong Kong to Iraq. India has implemented a Look East policy as strategic and economic integration with Asia that is fundamental to its growth.[15]

These connections also create strategic links that traverse the two oceans. For many states it is vital that the sea-lanes across the Indo-Pacific are secure. This reliance creates a sense of vulnerability. As each state attempts to protect its interests through increased military presence those surrounding it feel less secure.[16] Those states therefore develop strategic alignments, creating a complex web of strategic links across both the Indian and Pacific Oceans that further draws the two oceans together.

Beyond an economically and strategically linked Asia, the Indo-Pacific term is emerging in Australia as a result of the US pivot to Asia. The US engagement with Asia demonstrably extends beyond the Asia-Pacific.[17] In the words of the US Secretary of State Hilary Clinton: 'We are also expanding our alliance with Australia from a Pacific partnership to an Indo-Pacific one, and indeed a global partnership.'[18] Given Australia's

---

13 Michael Wesley, *There Goes the Neighbourhood: Australia and the Rise of Asia* (Sydney: UNSW Press, 2011), p. 86-87.

14 Rory Medcalf, 'Pivoting the Map: Australia's Indo-Pacific System', Paper No. 1, *Centre of Gravity Series*, Strategic and Defence Studies Centre, The Australian National University, November 2012. http://ips.cap.anu.edu.au/sdsc/cog/COG1_Medcalf_Indo-Pacific.pdf (accessed 5 May 2013), p. 3.

15 Amar Nath Ram (ed.), *Two Decades of India's Look East Policy: Partnership for Peace, Progress and Prosperity* (New Delhi: Manohar Publishers and Indian Council of World Affairs, 2012).

16 Michael Wesley, *There Goes the Neighbourhood: Australia and the Rise of Asia* (Sydney: UNSW Press, 2011), pp. 87-88.

17 Rory Medcalf, 'Pivoting the Map: Australia's Indo-Pacific System', Paper No. 1, *Centre of Gravity Series*, Strategic and Defence Studies Centre, The Australian National University, November 2012. http://ips.cap.anu.edu.au/sdsc/cog/COG1_Medcalf_Indo-Pacific.pdf (accessed 5 May 2013), p. 3.

18 Hillary Clinton, 'America's Pacific Century', *Foreign Policy*, vol. 189 (November 2011), p. 59.

geographic position and the long-standing alliance, Australia will be a useful location from which the US can engage with the extended Asian region.[19] The Indo-Pacific was a theme at both the 2011 and 2012 AUSMIN consultations. The simple fact that 'Indo-Pacific' appears in the US policy discourse has assisted its emergence in Australia.

'Indo-Pacific' in Australian Discourse

The Re-Emergence of an Old Debate

The 'Indo-Pacific' is not a new term in Australian debates. In the 1950s 'Indo-Pacific' was used to discuss the decolonisation of dominions surrounding Australia.[20] It was used again in 1965 and 1966 at two seminars held by the Australian Institute of International Affairs (AIIA) and the Australian National University (ANU) discussing nuclear proliferation and Commonwealth responsibilities within the region.[21] During the 1970s the term was used to describe an 'Indo-Pacific balance' which would ensure Australia's security.[22] For around 30 years the term was not prominent until its re-emergence in 2005. For Michael Richardson, the inclusion of India, Australia and New Zealand in the East Asia Summit (EAS) symbolised a more unified 'Indo-Pacific' region. Richardson hypothesised about how the region would evolve:

> Slowly and probably fitfully, reflecting the geographic, political, economic and cultural diversity of such a vast region, the deep mistrust and rivalry among some of its countries, …

---

19 Rory Medcalf, 'Pivoting the Map: Australia's Indo-Pacific System', Paper No. 1, *Centre of Gravity Series*, Strategic and Defence Studies Centre, The Australian National University, November 2012. http://ips.cap.anu.edu.au/sdsc/cog/COG1_Medcalf_Indo-Pacific.pdf (accessed 5 May 2013), p. 3.

20 I.M. Cumpton, 'Consolidation by conference?' *Australian Outlook*, vol. 10, no. 2 (1956), pp. 61-64.

21 Australian Institute of International Affairs and The Australian National University, Defence Studies Project, *Proceedings of the seminar on nuclear dispersal in Asia and the Indo-Pacific region* (Canberra: Australian Institute of International Affairs and The Australian National University, 1965);

Australian Institute of International Affairs and The Australian National University, Defence Studies Project, *Proceedings of the seminar on Commonwealth responsibilities for security in the Indo-Pacific region* (Canberra: Australian Institute of International Affairs and The Australian National University, 1966).

22 H.G. Gelber, 'Nuclear arms and the Pacific', *Australian Outlook*, vol. 25, no. 3 (1971), pp. 295-308.

and the reluctance to surrender decision-making powers of the state to supra-national agencies.[23]

He proposed that a cohesive Indo-Pacific region would increase stability and growth.

The term 'Indo-Pacific' subsequently started to appear in Australian foreign policy discourse. For example, Minister for Defence Stephen Smith noted: In this century, the Asia-Pacific and the Indian Ocean Rim, what some now refer to as the Indo-Pacific, will become the world's strategic centre of gravity.[24]

Two Oceans of Thought: Proponents of the 'Indo-Pacific'

The term has been embraced by some as realistically describing the region in which Australia is situated. Australian National University Professor Michael Wesley explores the fundamental reasons for the concept's emergence, highlighting the economic and strategic links through Asia:

> The Indo-Pacific power highway takes the pivot of world power away from the northern Pacific and northern Atlantic and shifts it to the southern and eastern coasts of the Asian landmass. It is here that the dynamism of the world economy will course, and where rivalries and alignments that shape the way the world works will be played out.[25]

He therefore urges Australia to react to the changing region, to alter its traditional foreign policy approaches (focussed on the US alliance and multilateral organisations) and to acknowledge that the centre of world affairs is moving closer to its shores.[26] Lowy Institute analyst Rory Medcalf also embraces the concept for its descriptive power:

---

23 Michael Richardson, 'Australia-Southeast Asia Relations in the East Asia Summit', *Australian Journal of International Affairs*, vol. 59, no. 3 (September 2005), p. 363.

24 Stephen Smith, 'Paper presented by Stephen Smith MP, Minister for Defence, to the Lowy Institute on the 2013 Defence White Paper', Sydney, 9 August 2012. http://www.lowyinstitute.org/publications/paper-presented-stephen-smith-mp-minister-defence-lowy-institute-2013-defence-white (accessed 7 March 2013).

25 Michael Wesley, *There Goes the Neighbourhood: Australia and the Rise of Asia* (Sydney: UNSW Press, 2011), pp. 89-90.

26 Michael Wesley, *There Goes the Neighbourhood: Australia and the Rise of Asia* (Sydney: UNSW Press, 2011), pp. 172-173.

In both an economic and a strategic sense, the Indo-Pacific is a valid and objective description of the greater regional system in which Australia now finds itself.[27]

Both Medcalf and Wesley argue that China is an essential player in the description and must therefore be included in the Indo-Pacific region.

Two Oceans of Thought: Opponents and Sceptics

At the same time, there has been criticism of adopting the Indo-Pacific concept too readily. La Trobe University Professor Nick Bisley and University of Queensland Lecturer Andrew Phillips argue:

> there has been virtually no debate about what precisely the term means, whose interests it serves and the significant risks as well as opportunities involved in uncritically absorbing the concept into Australia's strategic lexicon.[28]

It is highlighted that adopting the concept would serve political aims such as emphasizing Australia's strategic strengths to the US and binding the US to the region. Bisley and Phillips argue that the concept is interpreted by Beijing to exclude China and increase the US', India and Australia's role in the region. The creation of a perceived US Indo-Pacific coalition may alienate Australia's largest trading partner and reduce rather than enhance stability.

University of Western Australia Professor Dennis Rumley, University of Adelaide Professor Timothy Doyle and Punjab University Professor Sanjay Chaturvedi propose a similar argument. They argue that the term is:

> propagated by conservative practitioners and commentators concerned principally with the use of collective traditional security and hard power.[29]

---

27 Rory Medcalf, 'Pivoting the Map: Australia's Indo-Pacific System', Paper No. 1, *Centre of Gravity Series*, Strategic and Defence Studies Centre, The Australian National University, November 2012. http://ips.cap.anu.edu.au/sdsc/cog/COG1_Medcalf_Indo-Pacific.pdf (accessed 5 May 2013), p. 3.

28 Nick Bisley and Andrew Phillips, 'The Indo-Pacific: What does it actually mean?', *East Asia Forum*, 6 October 2012. http://www.eastasiaforum.org/2012/10/06/the-indo-pacific-what-does-it-actually-mean/ (accessed 5 May 2013).

29 Dennis Rumley, Timothy Doyle and Sanjay Chaturvedi, '"Securing" the Indian Ocean? Competing Regional Security Constructions', *Journal of the Indian Ocean Region*, vol. 8,

They are concerned that the Indo-Pacific concept of the region may be depicted as 'exclusive' and designed to alienate China.[30] Furthermore, it is argued that the concept inhibits other regional constructs from being seriously considered and allows the US to share the burden of maritime security with India and Australia.

Director of the Strategic Advice and Geopolitical Estimates International John Bruni argues that Australia is 'too small in size, mind and political culture' to engage diplomatically with the Indian Ocean littoral and therefore the Indo-Pacific is only of benefit to Australia should it engage the region under the US strategy.[31]

Adopting the Indo-Pacific

This debate between these two camps was fairly even until May 2013 with the Indo-Pacific not yet concretely embedded into Australian foreign policy. The 2012 Government White Paper on Australia in the Asian Century included a mention that the Indo-Pacific may have a greater place in foreign policy in the future – but this was in a side box rather than in the main text.[32] This was still a long way from giving the concept official endorsement for the long history of linking Australian foreign policy to an "Asia-Pacific" view of Australia's region.

This changed with the release of the Defence White Paper 2013 on May 3. In outlining the strategic outlook for Australia, the White Paper identified "a new Indo-Pacific strategic arc... connecting the Indian and Pacific Oceans through Southeast Asia".[33]

The White Paper noted that the "new strategic construct" of the Indo-Pacific is being forged by a range of factors, including India "emerging as

---

no. 1 (February 2012), p. 2.

30 Ibid.

31 John Bruni, 'Australia's proposed 'Indo-Pacific' Strategy: A case of biting off more than it can chew?', SAGE International, 2012. http://sageinternational.com.au/details.php?prod Id=114&category=1&secondary=&keywords= (accessed 5 May 2012), p. 4.

32 Commonwealth of Australia, *Australia in the Asian Century White Paper* (Canberra: Department of the Prime Minister and Cabinet, 2012). http://asiancentury.dpmc.gov.au/ white-paper (accessed 5 May 2013), p. 74.

33 Commonwealth of Australia, Defence White Paper 2013 (Canberra: Department of Defence, 2013). http://www.defence.gov.au/whitepaper2013/docs/WP_2013_web.pdf (accessed 5 May 2013), p. 7.

an important strategic, diplomatic and economic actor, 'looking East', and becoming more engaged in regional frameworks" as well as growing trade, investment and energy flows that are strengthening economic and security interdependencies in the broader region.[34]

Presenting the Indo-Pacific as a "logical extension" of what the 2009 Defence White Paper called the "wider Asia-Pacific region", the White Paper adopts the concept which "adjusts Australia's priority strategic focus to the arc extending from India though Southeast Asia to Northeast Asia, including the sea lines of communication on which the region depends".[35]

The White Paper then sets "a Stable Indo-Pacific" as one of Australia's four key strategic interests: (1) a secure Australia; (2) a secure South Pacific and Timor-Leste; (3) a stable wider region, which we now conceptualise as the emerging Indo-Pacific; and (4) a stable, rules-based global order.[36]

This makes the capacity to "contribute to military contingencies in the Indo-Pacific" one of the Australian Defence Force's four principal tasks.[37] It is hard to imagine a fuller incorporation of the Indo-Pacific concept into a government policy document.

Implications of an Indo-Pacific Worldview

There are a number of implications of adopting an Indo-Pacific worldview. First, Australia will need to assess the implications of the Indo-Pacific concept for its key relationships with the US and China. The US is Australia's primary Strategic Partner, with a strong alliance lasting more than 60 years and a tradition of cooperation across many fields. However, Australia also has a key economic relationship with China that is underpinned by mutually beneficial trade ties; in 2009 China became Australia's top trading partner.[38] Australia aims to maintain positive relations with both China and the US. In the words of Prime Minister Julia Gillard:

---

34 Ibid

35 Ibid

36 Ibid, p. 24.

37 Ibid, p. 28.

38 Department of Foreign Affairs and Trade, 'Australia's trade in goods and services by top 10 partners, 2009'. http://www.dfat.gov.au/publications/tgs/2009_top10_exports_GandS.pdf (accessed 2 April 2013).

For Australia this is not an either-or question... We can have our strong, long-standing friendship and alliance with the United States, based as it is on shared values, as well as have a positive and constructive engagement with China.[39]

However, should the relationship between the two superpowers degrade Australia would be placed in a difficult position. The Australian Government thus advocates finding ways to accommodate China's greater weight and the development of mechanisms to deal with instability between the US and China which may be created by miscommunication or miscalculation. According to Secretary of the Department of Foreign Affairs and Trade Peter Varghese:

China has every right to seek greater strategic influence to match its economic weight. The extent to which this can be peacefully accommodated will turn ultimately on both the pattern of China's international behaviour and the extent to which the existing international order intelligently finds more space for China.[40]

While Australia will attempt to continue to balance the delicate relationship it remains an ongoing challenge. This position magnifies the sensitivity around adopting the Indo-Pacific concept as it may be perceived to tie Australia closer to the US and alienate China. As Medcalf highlights, it is Australia's responsibility to ensure its diplomatic signals do not portray the concept as a balancing tactic.[41] Bisley and Phillips argue that to create a stable region the concept must not be the US centred and exclude China; the Indo-Pacific should not be code for 'dialling up Australia's alliance commitments to 11'.[42] Early indications of China's response to the Defence White Paper 2013 were positive. China correspondent John Garnaut

---

39 Quoted in Matthew Franklin and Michael Sainsbury, 'Julia Gillard's China-US balancing act', *The Australian*, 26 April 2011.

40 Quoted in 'DFAT Secretary Peter Varghese - Asialink Chairman's Welcome Address', *Asialink*, 20 February 2013. http://www.asialink.unimelb.edu.au/__data/assets/pdf_file/0008/716885/Peter_Varghese_release.pdf (Accessed 19 March 2013).

41 Rory Medcalf, 'The West is Poised for Strategic Role as Hub of the Indo-Pacific Age', *The Australian*, 12 November 2012.

42 Nick Bisley and Andrew Phillips, 'The Indo-Pacific: What does it actually mean?', *East Asia Forum*, 6 October 2012. http://www.eastasiaforum.org/2012/10/06/the-indo-pacific-what-does-it-actually-mean/ (accessed 5 May 2013).

judged that compared with the 2009 White Paper which had "Chinese generals, military strategists and security experts lined up to show they were apoplectic at Australia", the 2013 White Paper would "barely raise a yawn".[43] This suggests that the use of the term "Indo-Pacific" is less of a concern to China than the characterisation of China as a potential threat.

Second, as Australia must consider how to build relationships with Indo-Pacific powers as it adopts the Indo-Pacific concept into its foreign policy. It is useful to be aware of how each Indo-Pacific power approaches the concept. For example, the Indian view of the concept focuses on enhancing cooperation, forwarding India's domestic economic goals, achieving the Look East policy and maintaining strategic autonomy. However, the US view of the concept is underpinned by a desire to maintain a strong role in the region and its global position.[44] If Australia was to become a true Indo-Pacific power it will need to engage strongly with many other regional players, for example, with India, Indonesia, Japan, Vietnam, South Korea, Thailand and key African countries, as well as with China and the US. Regional issues would need to be addressed through engagements that include security dialogue and operational cooperation.[45] As Wesley highlights, in an Indo-Pacific region Australia cannot rely on its traditional foreign policy focus, but it must begin to 'rebalance its centres of attention and effort' to promote Australia's interests widely.[46]

Third, Australia will need to invest time and effort in building Indo-Pacific institutions. Multilateral institutions play a central role in facilitating regional cooperation. These institutions include the Indian Ocean Rim

---

43 John Garnaut, 'New white paper waves white flag', *The Age*, 4 May 2013. http://www.theage.com.au/national/new-white-paper-waves-white-flag-20130503-2iylc.html (accessed 5 May 2013); see also Daniel Flitton, 'A bland defence posture that may be just right for our times', *The Age*, 4 May 2013. http://www.theage.com.au/opinion/politics/a-bland-defence-posture-that-may-be-just-right-for-our-times-20130503-2iyj4.html (accessed 5 May 2013).

44 Priya Chacko, 'India and the Indo-Pacific: An Emerging Regional Vision', Indo-Pacific Governance Research Centre Policy Brief, Issue 5, November 2012. http://www.adelaide.edu.au/indo-pacific-governance/policy/Chacko_PB.pdf (accessed 5 May 2013), p. 2.

45 Rory Medcalf, 'Pivoting the Map: Australia's Indo-Pacific System', Paper No. 1, *Centre of Gravity Series*, Strategic and Defence Studies Centre, The Australian National University, November 2012. http://ips.cap.anu.edu.au/sdsc/cog/COG1_Medcalf_Indo-Pacific.pdf (accessed 5 May 2013), p. 5.

46 Michael Wesley, *There Goes the Neighbourhood: Australia and the Rise of Asia* (Sydney: UNSW Press, 2011), pp. 172-173.

Association for Regional Cooperation (IOR-ARC) and the East Asia Summit (EAS). Given Australia is set to take over the chair of IOR-ARC in late 2013 it is well-positioned to lead the association to greater facilitation of regional cooperation. According to Shadow Minister for Foreign Affairs Julie Bishop:

> Injecting greater purpose and momentum into the Indian Ocean Rim Association for Regional Cooperation will also help coordinate our efforts to combat issues such as fisheries management, terrorism and extremism, ... piracy and illegal migration in the region.[47]

The EAS also includes the major Indo-Pacific powers, providing a space for cooperation and regional development and putting it in a position to deal with many issues the region may face. This was foreseen as early as 2010 by Michael Wesley.[48] According to Secretary of the Department of Foreign Affairs and Trade Peter Varghese:

> This new construct of the Indo-Pacific neatly matches the recently expanded East Asian Summit (EAS). And it sets the scene to make the EAS the premier regional institution potentially capable of addressing both the strategic and economic challenges facing the Indo-Pacific region.[49]

The EAS has been reported to be a key part of Australia's foreign policy. Senior correspondent to *The Age*, Daniel Flitton reports the view that the Department of Foreign Affairs and Trade is currently prioritising Australian foreign policy according to the following formula: 'six + two + n'. The 'six' refers to Australia's key relationships with China, India, Indonesia, Japan, South Korea and the United States while 'n' refers to Australia's South Pacific neighbourhood. According to Flitton: 'The "two" refers to the multilateral meetings that Australia is putting most energy

---

47 Julie Bishop, 'Charting the future of Australia-India relations', *Australian Polity*, vol. 2, no. 3 (March 2012). http://australianpolity.com/australian-polity/charting-the-future-of-australia-india-relations (accessed 19 March 2013).

48 Michael Wesley, 'Australia Faces a Changing Asia', *Current History*, September 2010, pp. 227-231.

49 Peter Varghese, 'Australia and India in the Asian Century: An address by H.E. Peter Varghese AO', Institute of Peace and Conflict Studies, May 2012. http://www.ipcs.org/pdf_file/issue/SR127-AustraliaandIndiaintheAsianCentury.pdf (accessed 5 May 2013), p. 2.

into – the East Asia Summit and the Group of 20'.[50] Perhaps surprisingly, given Australia's current membership of the UN Security Council, this does not make the "two". This suggests that Australia's multilateral focus is increasingly turning towards Indo-Pacific institutions.

Conclusion

While the term Indo-Pacific has resurfaced in Australian discussions, until recently it remained a contested concept that had not yet been fully adopted given Australia's delicate position balancing its alliance with the US and economic relationship with China. This changed with the adoption of the concept in the Defence White Paper 2013. The implications of the adoption of the concept are still unknown, but are likely to include a continuing focus on key relationships, increasing focus on other Indo-Pacific powers and investment in Indo-Pacific institutions.

Many other Indo-Pacific powers are in a similar position to Australia; they are strategically aligned with the US but economically aligned with China. This means that Australian debates and Australian choices are receiving more attention than they would previously have received as other states watch for indications of how others will respond to similar forces. This makes Australia somewhat of a bellwether state within the region and makes Australia's future choices regarding the Indo-Pacific concept of even greater significance. Given this, it is likely that debates around the concept will continue.

---

50 Daniel Flitton, 'Chief diplomat spells out Australia's rules of engagement', *The Age,* January 29, 2013. http://www.theage.com.au/opinion/politics/chief-diplomat-spells-out-australias-rules-of-engagement-20130128-2dgse.html (accessed 2 May 2013).

5

Indo-Pacific Region: Perspectives from Southeast and East Asia

Sumathy Permal

Introduction

One of the earliest literatures in contemporary strategic studies describes the Indo-Pacific as a "shorthand for the wider region of the Asia-Pacific area plus South Asia and the Indian Ocean region: hence Indo and Pacific."[1] The term is increasingly used in the global strategic and geo-political discourse as a concept in international relations in referring to the maritime space comprising the Indian Ocean and the Western Pacific. Scholars suggest that the Indo-Pacific is an emerging Asian strategic system defined in part by the geographically expanding interests and reach of China and India, and the continued strategic role and presence of the United States in both areas.[2] Major actors in the region include India, China, US, Australia, Japan, South Korea and Indonesia. The global economic power shift from West to East (with the rise of newly industrialized countries in the 1980s and 1990s) coupled with increasing trade, investment and production in the area spanning the Indian and Pacific Ocean regions has increasingly defined the Indo-Pacific region. Australia's 2012 White Paper notes that China and India have tripled their share of the global economy and increased their absolute economic size almost six fold over in the past 20 years. By 2025, the region will account for almost half the world's output.[3]

---

1 James Ferguson (2000). The Indo-Pacific Region, The Department of International Relations, SHSS, Bond University, Queensland, Australia.

2 C. Raja Mohan, 2012. Samudra Manthan: Sino-Indian Rivalry in the Indo-Pacific, Carnegie Endowment for International Peace.

3 Australia in the Asia Century, (2012) White Paper, Australian Government. http://asiancentury.dpmc.gov.au/white-paper.

China alone is expected to reach 19.8 per cent of global GDP by 2030[4] and the combined economic, social and political clout of the countries in Asia has prompted the western powers' pivot to Asia. Asia is the second fastest growing region in the world[5] and the emergence of India as a new military power in South Asia are factors contributing to the new concept of the Indo-Pacific.

Recent discourses and scholarly studies in international relations have given birth to the views of many leaders through their comments and speeches. The tone of international relations around the world has shifted from being Asia-Pacific to Indo-Pacific centric. Among the major nations that have recognised the importance of the Indo-Pacific region are the United States, Australia, Japan and India.

As a superpower that has a large deployment of forces worldwide, the United States' strong presence in the Indian Ocean as well as in the Pacific subscribes to the Indo-Pacific concept. In a speech at Honolulu in October 2010, Secretary of State Hillary Clinton mentioned "Indo-Pacific" to describe a newly emerged and integrated theatre and that the US was "expanding our work with the Indian Navy in the Pacific because we understand how important the Indo-Pacific basin is to global trade and commerce."[6] This is an explicit and significant reflection of the growing strategic convergence between the two countries with respect to the region.

Further, former US Secretary of Defence Leon Panetta had mentioned "…as American forces withdraw from Iraq by the end of 2011, and continue to draw down in Afghanistan, US policy makers in Washington, DC are turning their full attention to the challenges of maintaining American influence in the Indo-Pacific region.."[7]

The Japanese view on the Indo-Pacific was provided by Prime

---

4 Barry Desker, 2013. Why the world must listen more carefully to Asia's rising powers, Europe World. http://www.europesworld.org/NewEnglish/Home_old/ Article/tabid/191/ArticleType/ArticleView/ArticleID/22077/language/en-US/ WhytheworldmustlistenmorecarefullytoAsiasrisingpowers.aspx.

5 Regional Programming For Asia, Strategy Document, 2007-2013, European Commission. http://ec.europa.eu/europeaid/where/asia/regional-cooperation/index_en.htm.

6 Hillary Rodham Clinton, (2010), America's Engagement in the Asia-Pacific, Honolulu. http://www.state.gov/secretary/rm/2010/10/150141.htm.

7 2012 U.S. Force Posture Strategy in the Asia Pacific Region: An Independent Assessment, Center for Strategic and International Studies, Washington DC.

Minister Shinzo Abe in his speech in India in August 2007. He coined the phrase 'Confluence of the Two Seas', advocating an idea that Japan and India, as like-minded maritime democracies, should promote freedom and prosperity in the 'broader Asia' under a 'strategic global partnership' between the two states. A scholar from Japan has argued that the "Asia-Pacific may be insufficient for describing the dynamism in this region... the Indo-Pacific Rim has the potential to reach an unprecedented level of prosperity, freedom, and stability in this century".[8]

The Australian Government's 2012 White Paper described Australia in the Asian Century and recognises the Indian Ocean in surpassing the Atlantic and the Pacific as "the world's busiest and most strategically significant trade corridor". India and Australia acknowledged the greater potential for further growth in the relationship. This was based on the idea that the "India-Australia relationship is anchored in shared values as liberal democracies, converging interests and shared opportunities in the Asian Century." The bilateral Strategic Partnership is given effect through rapidly expanding trade and investment ties, common interest in a stable and outward looking Indo-Pacific region.

India's Prime Minister, Manmohan Singh, was quoted as "introducing a new term 'Indo-Pacific' in the political practices and used this term in his speech at the India–ASEAN (Association of South-East Asian Nations) Delhi summit in 2012. The term widens the scope of the Asia-Pacific region and underlines India's growing interests in the region.

For the European Union, a rising Indo-Pacific Region is significant as it facilitates trade movements between East Asia via the Indian Ocean to Europe. The EU's interest in the region is primarily to secure and protect critical maritime trade routes; however, political and geo-strategic considerations are prevalent as to its normative power position. To this end the EU wants to "...re-enter the Indo-Pacific space as a full-fledged geostrategic actor that helps to balance power and ensure that no particular power's rise disturbs the smaller countries".[9]

---

8   Tetsuo Kotani, Geopolitical Change in Asia and Legal Warfare at Sea, Maritime Asia.

9   Piotr Maciej Kaczynski and James Rogers (2012) Putting back European in the Indo Pacific Zone.

Indo-Pacific Region: What it means to ASEAN

Southeast Asia is located strategically at the crossroads of the Indian Ocean and the Pacific Ocean, and its history has been shaped as much by the influence of great civilizations as the impact of great powers. Historically, trade, politics and culture of Southeast Asia were defined or driven by maritime connections across the Indian Ocean arena, rather than the Asia-Pacific.[10] The sea routes flowing from the mouth of the Red River (Hanoi) through the Malacca Straits to Sri Lanka and India and the Persian Gulf, Red Sea and the Mediterranean facilitated trading systems between the Indian Ocean and Southeast Asia since ancient times. Srivijaya was a maritime empire, which controlled two key narrows on the Indian Ocean trade routes, i.e. the Straits of Malacca and the Sunda Straits. As a result, all goods traded among China, India, Arabia and other parts of the world along these routes had to go through Srivijaya. By the 11th century, it controlled points of the Philippines. Besides, Malacca was an important port of call for traders and sailors including China's Admiral Zheng He and early Portuguese explorers like Diogo Lopes de Sequeira.

In recent history, this commercial importance has continued for the maritime superpowers concerned with this region. This common interest and the geographic location of the Indian Ocean play a dominant role in the contemporary international relations. Despite their smaller size, Indonesia, Malaysia and other countries in Southeast Asia are expected to grow rapidly and make significant contributions to regional growth. Southeast Asia's cumulative economic, political and demographic weight is growing. With a combined population of 600 million, these countries have embarked on a drive, through the ASEAN, towards regional integration and connectivity by 2015.[11]

Currently several challenges have tested ASEAN solidarity and its way of dealing with a number of unresolved bilateral problems among members as well as the multilateral disputes in the South China Sea. Nevertheless, ASEAN has gained considerable acceptance as a regional grouping; major powers of the world recognize the role of ASEAN and its members in many

---

10 Emrys Chew, Southeast Asia And The Indian Ocean: Maritime connections across time and Space, ASEAN and Indian Ocean, The Key Maritime Links, *RSIS Policy Paper 2011*, p.15.

11 Australian in the Asia Century, (2012) White Paper, Australian Government. http://asiancentury.dpmc.gov.au/white-paper.

regional and global issues. The US appointed an ambassador to ASEAN in March 2011 followed by China in 2012. Currently there are 70 non-ASEAN member state ambassadors to ASEAN including India and Japan. ASEAN has succeeded in persuading its top trading partners such as China, US, Japan, India, Australia and New Zealand to start negotiations on the Regional Comprehensive Economic Partnership (RCEP) to create the world's largest trading bloc that will comprise more than three billion people and with a combined GDP of US\$ 15 trillion. Besides, ASEAN partners have established the ASEAN Free Trade Area with China, Japan, Korea and India, as well as Australia and New Zealand.

ASEAN is also poised to become a security community by 2015 based on the three key characteristics, i.e. a rule-based community of shared values and norms; a cohesive, peaceful, stable and resilient region with shared responsibility for comprehensive security; and a dynamic and outward-looking region in an increasingly integrated and interdependent world.[12] ASEAN strengths as a collective diplomatic voice and as a convening and organizing power of many regional initiatives in the maritime ambit such as the ASEAN Regional Forum, ASEAN Defence Ministers' Meeting Plus, ASEAN Maritime Forum have attracted non-members to be part of the process. The ADMM Plus forum serves with partners such as the US, Russia, India, China, the Republic of Korea, Japan, New Zealand and Australia to strengthen cooperation, and ensure regional security and stability.

In recognition of the fluid geopolitical dynamics and the emerging concept of the Indo-Pacific, it is timely for ASEAN to move beyond the context of regionalism to explore opportunities in the Indo-Pacific realm. The major challenges for ASEAN will be to balance its relations with the major powers in Indo-Pacific as the interests of the countries expand and overlap and there will be elements of competition and rivalry among nations. The expanding maritime interests and naval ambitions of China and India appear as a sign of a growing strategic competition that significantly converge in the Indo-Pacific. As suggested in *The Indian Ocean: A Future of Uncertainty (Looking out to 2020)*[13] the interrelations

---

12 Muthiah Alagappa (2013). Is Asean the cornerstone of Malaysia's foreign policy? The Edge. http://www.theedgemalaysia.com.

13 Leighton G. Luke & Tas Luttrell, Indian Ocean: A Sea of Uncertain Future Directions International, Future Directions International Pty Ltd, 2012.

of great power and possible rivalry between the three major powers of India, China and the US will continue to evolve in complexity, heightened by the possible rise of India and China and a perceived decline of the US power in the region. The convergence of strategic expansion will require governments in Southeast Asia to review and assess future strategic and security challenges in the Indo-Pacific to safeguard their interests.

Strategic Convergence in the Indo-Pacific Region and Implications for Malaysia

Malaysian Prime Minister's speech during the 10th IISS Asia Security Summit at the Shangri-La Dialogue, Singapore, in June 2011 provides a clear vision of Malaysia's stand on the geopolitical discourse in the coming years.[14] China and the US are Malaysia's trading partners, and Malaysia values her relations with other nations such as Russia, India and EU states. Malaysia and other member state of ASEAN share the values and aspirations of the major powers in the 21st century. In essence, Malaysia's stand is not to take sides in her relations with the major powers in the Asia-Pacific or in Asia. Although yet to incorporate the concept of Indo-Pacific in her foreign policy considerations, Malaysia acknowledges that multilateralism is the way ahead in the post Cold War era. However, the Indo-Pacific region has some significant flash points mainly in maritime domain. Economic connectivity across the region depends largely on maritime links for trade and energy supplies. As such it is significant for Malaysia to take cognizance of the fact that issues such as the overlapping claims in the South China Sea and the security of Straits of Malacca will converge in the Indo-Pacific region.

The arguments in this chapter will focus on three issues of concern to Malaysia as a member state of ASEAN, i.e. (a) the emergence of strategic attention in the Indian Ocean; (b) increasing China's assertiveness in the South China Sea; and (c) the US 'pivot' to Asia. Actions and reactions on these three interlaced issues will converge in the geopolitics of the Indo-Pacific. The Straits of Malacca and the South China Sea are at the crossroads of the Indian and Pacific Oceans and the chapter will focus on this nexus.

---

14 Najib Tun Razak, (2011) Keynote Address, The 10th IISS Asia Security Summit The Shangri-La Dialogue, Singapore.

The Indian Ocean

The Indian Ocean has emerged as the focus of strategic manoeuvrings among the great powers. The multifaceted security challenges including India-China rivalry, the ever increasing interest of maritime powers such as the US and its allies and major military nations such as France will intensify the geo-political dynamics in the region. As one of the major littoral states in Southeast Asia and the Indian Ocean and straddling the Indian Ocean and the South China Sea, Malaysia has keen interest in protecting its maritime domain in the region. Its interests in the Indian Ocean are dominated by the critical need to guarantee the freedom of passage for international shipping through the approaches to the Straits of Malacca.

Malaysia's National Defence Policy (NDP) has demarcated the geographical areas of Malaysia's vital interests. Located in the northeast edge of the Indian Ocean, the Andaman Sea narrows to form the Strait of Malacca, one of the most important shipping lanes in the world. The Andaman Sea's link to the northern sections of the Straits of Malacca is one of Malaysia's maritime domains that are within its strategic areas of interest that need to be protected. The Indian Ocean does not constitute a major source of strategic threat to Malaysia's interest at sea as compared to securing the sea lines of communication in the Straits of Malacca and Malaysia's claims in the South China Sea. Nevertheless, the Andaman & Nicobar Islands proximity to the northern entrance to the Straits of Malacca opens the sea area to the possibility of extra-regional players extending their influence in the region, thus, making the area vulnerable to both conventional as well as non-conventional threats.

Studies on the Indian Ocean often refer to Mahan (1840-1914) who believed that whoever attains maritime supremacy in the Indian Ocean would be a prominent player on the international scene. More recently, in his book "Monsoon: The Indian Ocean and the Future of American Power", Robert Kaplan described the Indian Ocean as the true nexus of world power and conflict in the coming years.[15] For the littoral states, the Indian Ocean has assumed increasing and growing importance for trade, social-economic and strategic interests. Hence, historian and naval

---

15 Robert D. Kaplan, Monsoon, The Indian Ocean and Future of American Power, Random House Trade Paperbacks; Reprint Edition, September, 2011.

strategists of the 19th to the 21st century have acknowledged the strategic value of the Indian Ocean and this has become more evident in the current geo-strategic confluence in the maritime domain. The following section describes the strategic importance of the Indian Ocean for the United States, China and India.

United States

The US Navy's maritime strategy, unveiled in October 2007, seeks a sustained, forward presence in the Indian Ocean and adjacent western Pacific, and less in the Atlantic. Moreover, the US Marine Corps' vision and strategy statement, unveiled in June 2008, covering the years to 2025, also describes the Indian Ocean and its adjacent waters as a central theatre of conflict and competition.[16] The US is currently operating at the UK's Diego Garcia military base in the Chagos Islands, which is leased to the US. Apart from US military assets located further north in Japan and South Korea, only Diego Garcia and Guam remain as purely dedicated Western military bases nearest to China's oil supply routes from the Middle East, through the Indian Ocean, the Straits of Malacca, the Nan Hai and from other oil sources in Africa.

Diego Garcia serves as primary hub for the US power projections in the region and is one of the most strategic US bases in the world. In October 2012, USS *George Washington* and USS *John C. Stennis* Carrier Strike Groups (CSGs) steamed into the Andaman Sea and conducted integrated flight operations while also practicing surface and anti-submarine drills.[17] Both CSGs conducted forward presence operations and port visits in the Asia-Pacific region; however, according to the US Navy, having two aircraft carriers operating together in the Andaman Sea is unusual. Further, the US and Indian navies conducted exercise Malabar during the latter part of 2012, a bilateral exercise designed to demonstrate cooperation between the US submarine rescue system and Indian submarines.[18]

---

16 A Cooperative Strategy for the 21st Century, U.S. Maritime Strategy, October 2007. http://www.navy.mil/maritime/MaritimeStrategy.pdf.

17 Washington, Stennis Carrier Strike Groups Operate in Andaman Sea U.S. 7th Fleet Public Affairs 10 December 2012. http://www.navy.mil/submit/display.asp?story_id=70103.

18 US and Indian Navies Demonstrate Submarine Rescue Operations During Indiaex-2012 Off The Mumbai Coast, Defence Now, October 26, 2012. http://www.defencenow.com/news/990/us-and-indian-navies-demonstrate-submarine-rescue-operations-during-indiaex-2012-off-the-mumbai-coast.html.

China

China has demonstrated its interest in the Indian Ocean region for some time. As the second largest consumer of oil in the world, China relies more and more on imported oil to sustain its economic growth. Much of this oil flows from the Arabian Sea through the Straits of Malacca and the South China Sea. It is anticipated that China may lead the demand for oil tankers of the Very Large Crude Carrier (VLCC) variety as its energy needs rise in the next five years. Assuming the increased tonnages are sourced from the Arabian Gulf, it could, according to estimates such as those published by consulting firm Poten & Partners,[19] create demand for an additional 80 VLCCs to meet Chinese oil demand by 2015. VLCC tankers will soon transport 80 per cent of China's oil.

China has thus placed added importance on safeguarding these sea lines of communication (SLOCs) to ensure its economic survival leading to China's growing role in the Indian Ocean. For example, China's new naval strategy of "far sea defence" is aimed at giving Beijing the ability to project its power in key oceanic areas, including and most significantly the Indian Ocean.[20] It also prompted an increased naval presence in the region. To achieve this, China is seeking to set up bases and outposts across the globe, strategically located along its energy routes, to monitor and safeguard energy flows. The strategy describes the manifestation of China's rising geopolitical influence through efforts to increase access to ports and airfields, develop special diplomatic relationships and modernize military forces that extend from the South China Sea through the Straits of Malacca, across the Indian Ocean and in to the Arabian Gulf.

Chinese aid and commercial investments in Sri Lanka have increased through the US$ 1 billion Chinese-funded Hambantota Port Development Project in southern part of Sri Lanka.[21] Hambantota is a strategically vital gateway for securing access to SLOCs in the Indian Ocean. The new port is only six nautical miles from major SLOCs between the Bay of Bengal and Arabian Sea. China has further modernised or constructed ports belonging

---

19 Ibid.

20 Harsh V. Pant, Chinese military bases are about more than just naval supplies and protecting trade routes, The Japan Times, 3, 2012. http://www.japantimes.co.jp/text/eo20120103a1.html.

21 David L.O. Hayward, China's Dependence Upon Oil Supply, First published as an RUSI Defence Research Paper & republished as a, SAGE International Special Study, 2012.

to Maldives (a naval base at the port of Marao, close to the Laccadive Sea at the tip of India), Seychelles and Madagascar.

India

The use of the term "Indo-Pacific" is a clear indicator of India's growing role and influence in Asia and no country can ignore addressing the role of India in the geo-strategic analysis. The Indian Ocean is of special interest to India. The control of its coastal waters is viewed as critical to India's defence policy while the importance of the Indian Ocean from the economic, political, legal and military perspectives is significant. Along its 7,500 km coastline, India depends on the unhindered access to 11 major ports and the security of 2 million square kilometres of its Exclusive Economic Zone (EEZ) and 500 island territories.[22] India relies heavily on offshore resources to meet its energy needs as well as the free conduct of sea trade. Additionally, India's quest for regional dominance in South Asia hinges on control of the Indian Ocean.

The Indian Ocean is also seen as India's backyard and it is both natural and desirable for India to function as the leader and the predominant influence in this region - the world's only region and ocean named after a single state. India occupies a strategic position in the Northern Indian Ocean, potentially allowing it to control the key SLOC to and from the Suez Canal, the Persian Gulf and the Straits of Malacca. Besides, India's security perimeter extends from the Straits of Malacca to the Strait of Hormuz and from the coast of Africa to the western shores of Australia. Thus, India has to play a larger role (in the Indian Ocean) if the prospects for peace and cooperation are to grow. The Indian Maritime Doctrine states that "by virtue of geography, we are ...in a position to greatly influence the movement/security of shipping along the sea lines of communication in the Indian Ocean".[23] Indian aspirations to become a predominant power in the Indian Ocean underpin its security ambitions in Southeast Asia. Over the last two decades, the Indian Navy has played an active role in extending India's influence throughout the maritime Southeast Asian region.

---

22 D. Nandakumar & M. Muralikrishna, Mapping The Extent Of Coastal,Regulation Zone Violations Of The Indian Coast, National Fishworkers Forum Valiathura, Thiruvananthapuram, 1998.

23 Indian Navy, 2004, p. 64) in James R. Holmes And Toshi Yoshihara China And The United States In The, Indian Ocean an Emerging Strategic Triangle?, Naval War College Review Summer 2008, vol. 61, no. 3 (2008).

In July 2012, the Indian Navy opened a new naval air station in Campbell Bay (INS Baaz) its southern most naval air station in the Andaman and Nicobar Islands[24] allowing for increased ability to monitor the vital maritime channel specially the Straits of Malacca. The new base, about 300 nautical miles from Port Blair, will also include an upgraded airbase and will soon be operating heavier military planes like the just-inducted Hercules C-130J Super Hercules meant for Special Forces operations. India already operates naval bases at Port Blair and Car Nicobar in the Andaman and Nicobar Islands chain. The unique Tri Services Command is also present in Andaman and Nicobar islands.

India's Look East policy and her relations with Southeast Asian nations

India's Look East policy has gained acceptance from Southeast Asian countries and India has significant commercial and trade interests in the Asia Pacific. India and ASEAN are committed to achieving a trade target of US$ 70 billion in 2012, up by 40 per cent to US$ 50 billion in 2016.[25] Malaysia's trade with Indian Ocean Rim – Association for Regional Co-operation (IOR-ARC) member countries represents close to 31 per cent of the country's total trade.[26] Trade with IOR-ARC member countries amounted to US$ 89.4 billion for the period January to August 2011, an increase of 13.1 per cent over the corresponding 2010 period.

The major difference of India's Look East policy is that, pre-1992 it was more on a bilateral basis and post-1992 the policy was towards multilateral level. In 1995, India became a full dialogue partner of the ASEAN Regional Forum (ARF) and the East Asian Summit (EAS). However, the relations have been basically on politics, ideology, non-alignment and anti-racial. Post-1992, the major thrust of the policy shifted from politics to economic and strategic relations. There were three major phases in India's Look East policy between the period from 1992 to 2003 in which the focus was on economics and India's role as a dialogue partner. During this period,

---

24 Naval air station opened in Campbell Bay, The Hindu, 31 July, 2012. http://www.thehindu.com/news/national/article3707955.ece.

25 Vision Statement ASEAN India Commemorative Summit, 21 December 2012. http://www.asean.org/news/asean-statement-communiques/item/vision-statement-asean-india-commemorative-summit.

26 Richard Riot, Deputy Minister of Foreign Affairs Malaysia, IORC-ARC 12th Meeting of the Council Ministers, Gurgoun, India, November 2012.

ARF was the only international body apart from the United Nations (UN) of which India was a member. However, India did not gain much economically from the Southeast Asia countries as the focus of the region at that time was America-centric and India was not part of it. India's pro-Soviet tilt in her foreign policy divided Southeast Asia nation's views on India. Malaysia, Indonesia, Thailand, Singapore and the Philippines were strongly anti-communist and this resulted in a poor reception for India's proposal for a security regime in the region.

The second phase of India's Look East policy from 2003 to 2010, saw significant developments. India also signed the Treaty of Amity and Cooperation (TAC) at the India-ASEAN Summit at Bali in October 2003; this was seen as a shift from economic-political relation to a Strategic Partnership. India also signed a framework agreement on Comprehensive Economic Co-operation with ASEAN in 2009 with Singapore in 2005 and a free trade agreement with Thailand in 2003. The most recent initiative on CECA, between India and Malaysia, was signed in 2011.[27] During this period India's position in the eyes of Southeast Asian countries changed and they began to accept India as part of Southeast Asia and the region became Indo-Pacific rather than Western-Pacific centric. India began its naval diplomacy conducting several military exercises with some of the countries in the region. In 2005, India became a member of the EAS. At this juncture, several Southeast Asian countries such as Thailand, Singapore and Indonesia were determined to push for India to become an active member in this region. This was due to the ambiguity among the countries in the Asian region on China's peaceful rise and India was seen as a balancing power in this region. India's advantage is that it does not have territorial claims and no historical baggage in its relations with ASEAN.

The third phase of India's Look East policy is largely focused on a maritime stance and there was a major shift in India's approach towards the Southeast Asian countries. In March 2010, during the Delhi Dialogue, India was criticized for not coming forward in a big way and India-China relations were a constraint and a detrimental factor in India's approach

---

27 Ready Reckoner for Indian And Malaysian Businesses on comprehensive Economic Cooperation Agreement (Ceca) Between India and Malaysia 2011. http://www.indianhighcommission.com.my/pdf/Comprehansive%20Economic%20Cooperation%20Agreement%20%28CECA%29.pdf.

towards Southeast Asian countries.[28] India on the other hand does not want to be seen as too active in this region.

US Pivot to Asia

Despite the geographic distance, the United States has been inextricably linked with the Asia Pacific region and particularly at the beginning of the 21st century. According to former Secretary of Defence Panetta, this has determined the US military presence and partnership in this region for more than six decades. The Asia-Pacific region, home to the world's largest populations, has the fastest growing economies of China, India and Indonesia, and the largest military budgets with a defence spending surpassing that of Europe in 2012, and is expected to continue increasing in the future.

President Barack Obama projects a larger role for the US in this region over the coming decades, not as a distant power but as part of, and working closely with, the nations in the Asia Pacific. The objective is to confront common challenges and to promote peace, prosperity and security. In 2010, Secretary of State Clinton outlined the US refocus on the Asia-Pacific, emphasizing diplomacy, trade and development as the key areas in their engagement. Now, the US military service is focused on implementing the president's mandate and the outline provide by the US leadership to make the Asia-Pacific a top priority. These were some of the central remarks made at the 2012 *Shangri-La Dialogue* in Singapore.

The US Asia-Pacific strategy involves a smaller and leaner, but more agile and flexible US military that is quickly deployable and employing cutting-edge technology. While the US military will remain a global force for security and stability, it will nonetheless tilt towards the Asia-Pacific region *vis-a-vis* maintaining its presence throughout the world. By 2020, the US Navy will shift its forces from a balance of 50/50 to 60/40 between the Pacific and the Atlantic oceans

Series of Meetings with Southeast Asian Leaders

Panetta held a series of bilateral and trilateral meetings with allies of the US such as Japan, South Korea, the Philippines, Australia, Singapore and

---

28 Baladas Ghoshal, International Affairs Forum on 'India's Look East Policy: From Economic Integration to Strategic Stakeholder in Asia-Pacific Region', Institute of Strategic and International Studies, Malaysia (ISIS) and 18 July 2012.

Thailand on the sidelines of the *Shangri-La Dialogue,* signifying the US strategy in the region and the strong value of its presence. The United States idea was to work closely on an expanding range of political, economic, environmental and security-related issues. In the Malaysian context, the US is looking forward to strengthening the US-Malaysia military-to-military relationship including expanding multilateral exercises. The US and the Philippines are collaborating on regional issues, emphasizing the importance of the Mutual Defence Treaty of 1951 to regional peace and security, the US is expected to help the Philippines improve its maritime presence. Both sides reiterated their respective national interests in the right to freedom of navigation and their support for a collaborative and multilateral diplomatic process to resolve any territorial disputes peacefully in accordance with international law.

Vietnam and the US have also increased their bilateral cooperation on defence and maritime issues. In September 2011, the US and Vietnamese defence officials signed a memorandum of understanding designed to bring the two militaries closer for developing high-level exchanges, cooperation in the maritime area, search and rescue efforts, humanitarian aid and disaster relief programmes and in peacekeeping operations. The US Department of Defence particularly would like to work with Vietnam on critical maritime issues including a Code of Conduct focusing on the South China Sea.[29]

The US and Singapore affirmed their close and long standing bilateral defence relationship and the shared strategic perspectives between both sides. The two countries signed a Strategic Framework Agreement (SFA) in 2005 for deepening bilateral defence cooperation. The forward deployment of Littoral Combat Ships (LCS) to Singapore on a rotational basis fits in the framework intended to strengthen the US engagement in the region through regional port calls, and engagement of regional navies through activities such as exercises and exchanges. The US and Singapore are working towards increasing the complexity of existing bilateral exercises, such as the incorporation of navy elements into Exercise Commando Sling, a bilateral air force exercise. Besides, they are working towards enhancing joint training opportunities, including the use of the Murai Urban Training

---

29 U.S. Department of Defense Office of the Assistant Secretary of Defense (Public Affairs) News Transcript, Media Availability with Secretary Panetta in Cam Ranh Bay, Vietnam, June 03, 2012.

Facility in Singapore for more regular joint training by the US Marines and the Singapore Armed Forces (SAF) from 2013 onwards.

The US Asia Pivot

There are three issues this section highlights with regard to the declared rebalancing strategy by the US in the Asia-Pacific. The first is whether the strategy has an undue military bias that will have an adverse impact on regional stability especially on the territorial issues in the South China Sea. The US FY 2013 budget for military rebalancing to Asia is quite modest; nevertheless, over time, it does seem likely to be significant as it includes six aircraft carriers, a majority of cruisers, destroyers, LCSs and submarines. The US Marine Air-Ground Task Force which is capable of rapidly fanning across the Asia-Pacific region will also be deployed. The US conducted 172 military exercises in 2011 in the Asia-Pacific region and the numbers are expected to increase considerably in the near future. It is worth recalling that the US service had split its submarines almost evenly between the Atlantic and Pacific keeping 60 per cent of its submarine in the Atlantic as a deterrent to the Soviet Union during the Cold War. The new US strategy seems to indicate that there will be a large military deployment in the Asia-Pacific, though not centrally targeting the South China Sea. At present, up to 60 of the 287 US Navy ships operating in the Pacific are in the South China Sea and the new strategy of 60/40 is not a major shift towards South China Sea. Overall, the deployment of her assets will have to be spread among Northeast Asia and the ASEAN region, as well the Indian Ocean. Thus the US pivot to Asia cannot be linked *per se* with China's rise or to South China Sea issues.

The second issue is whether the strategy is aimed at containing China. China's Anti-Access Area Denial (A2/AD) strategy (the capability to attack transportation, military bases, and other facilities and systems to defend its sovereignty and interests) has engaged the attention of US military planners. In response, the US outlined the Air Sea Battle strategy as a new concept to manage these threats, an approach that has gained credence among the security community since the QDR 2010 (Quadrennial Defence Review) was published as a means by the US to confront the A2/AD challenge. China's development of A2/AD capabilities is seen aimed at restricting the freedom of action of the US forces and other regional militaries, as well as creating challenges for global shipping. China termed the South China Sea as its "core interest," echoing the language used for Tibet and Taiwan and signifying its willingness to explore all options including resorting to force to defend it. China's emergence as a regional power with robust A2/AD capabilities could, in the view of external powers, check the US power projections into the Western Pacific. Although US rebalancing to the Asia Pacific is said to be not targeted at China, its actions at renewing and strengthening relationships with ASEAN or some of its members such as Vietnam, Singapore and the Philippines is seen as designed to constrain, if not contain, China.

The third issue is the possibility of a naval arms race as the great powers flex their positions in the region. China's military modernisation, the US rebalancing in Asia, increased regional arms procurements and the unresolved territorial disputes in the South China Sea present the stark possibility of an arms race in the region. Though the global financial crisis has forced a reduction of US defence spending in acquisition accounts and procurement, the defence budget for the Asia-Pacific will not be affected.[30] This is because China's advanced naval capability including the use of asymmetric capabilities, electronic and cyber warfare, ballistic and cruise missiles, advanced air defences, mining, and others pose serious challenges to US naval supremacy in the Pacific. As such, the US will continue to expend itself militarily to ensure its ability to operate effectively in an A2/AD environment. This will include implementing the Joint Operational Access Concept, promoting air-sea battle capacity, sustaining undersea capabilities, developing a new stealth bomber, improving missile defences, and continuing efforts to enhance the resilience and effectiveness of critical space-based initiatives.

China: Adventurism and Assertiveness in the South China Sea

Disputes in the South China Sea have been a source of conflict among the claimants namely Brunei, China, Malaysia, the Philippines, Taiwan and Vietnam for the past 30 years. The rapid development of China and the efforts of the People's Liberation Army to modernize its military forces have generated a great deal of disquiet in the region. China's rise has dynamically

---

30 See Panetta Announces Fiscal 2013 Budget Priorities. http://www.defense.gov/news/newsarticle.aspx?id=66940 According to Panetta, "The budget maintains the current U.S. focus in the Central Command region and increases American commitment to the Pacific Command area of operations. The request looks to maintain the Navy's current 11 aircraft carriers and 10 carrier air wings. It will also maintain the current Marine and Army posture in the Asia-Pacific region, and will base littoral combat ships in Singapore and Bahrain".

reshaped the region's economics as well as its security; nonetheless China's military rise and the emerging disputes seem to have a significant impact on the security environment in the region.

Given the territorial disputes and its geographical significance, the South China Sea will present a continuing challenge in the decades to come. Ever-increasing sea borne trade, expansion of navies and geopolitical rivalries are issues of concern to the South China Sea claimants. The increasing assertiveness of China in its claims over the South China Sea as well as the interest of outside powers such as the US wanting to play a bigger role, will contribute to regional instability. As pointed out by Rory Medcalf, Asia's most complex theatre of maritime security tensions, in the South China Sea, is not narrowly an East Asian problem but supposedly external players from the United States to Europe, India, the Middle East and Australia all have stakes in some of the world's busiest shipping lanes.[31]

To add to the cauldron of great power rivalry are the long-standing claims in the Spratly Islands in the South China Sea that have been a major impetus to naval modernisation among the claimants including Malaysia, Vietnam and the Philippines. The naval expansion however is only an action to a reaction and does not have the elements of a systematic and concerted arms race. Nevertheless, China's moves to strengthen its land, sea, air, space and cyber strategies and the enhancement of her deterrence and counter attack moves that include A2/AD, and the US strategy of Air Sea Battle may see the increased deployment of ships in the Pacific and the stirrings of an arms competition as nations strive to preserve the balance of power in the region.

Since 2010, the South China Sea geopolitical interest changed the entire game of this region. China's assertive actions and the responses from the other claimants made the region unstable and territorial disputes in South China Sea have become a long-term threat to the peace in the Asia. Some Southeast Asian countries have invited the US to play a bigger role to act as a balance to Chinese power projection. With the combined interest of the major powers like the US, interested powers like Japan and India, and middle powers like Australia and Indonesia it could be suggested that the Indo-Pacific concept could be a balance to great power hegemony

---

31 Rory Medcalf (2012) Pivoting The Map: Australia's Indo-Pacific System Strategic & Defence Studies Centre ANU College of Asia & the Pacific, The Australian National University.

in the Asian Region. However, in the South China Sea geo-politics, the confluence of interest of many powers would complicate the issues due to fact that China is the dominant factor that has not subscribed to Indo-Pacific concept.

Conclusion

Malaysia's policies have yet to incorporate the emerging concept of the Indo-Pacific although it may not be completely discounted in the future. The geographical reality of Malaysia (straddling the Straits of Malacca and South China Sea being strategic SLOCs that connect the two oceans) and her priorities on the Straits of Malacca and South China Sea require her to participate in this Indo-Pacific geo-political theatre. However, since Malaysia's foreign policy is not to take sides in relations with the major powers in the context of the Asia-Pacific or in Asia, her participation in the Indo-Pacific Region has not been forthcoming. To have a balanced system in the Indo-Pacific Region, it may require China's support as a major stakeholder in the South China Sea and due to the importance of Straits of Malacca for China maritime trade.

Economic, environment and security issues interact in the Indian Ocean in dynamic and challenging ways. Similarly, the Indian Ocean has emerged as one of the most important and critical seas of the world. Straddling three major choke points, i.e. the Strait of Hormuz, the Straits of Malacca and the Suez Canal, the security of the Indian Ocean as a critical SLOC has assumed even greater significance than ever and it is faced with a daunting number of conventional and non-conventional maritime security threats. Malaysia should place importance on the challenges engendered by the geo-strategic developments being played out by naval powers which will see the sea being used more intensively in the years ahead, which in turn will pose multifaceted security challenges to stakeholders. Developments related to India-China rivalry and the ever increasing assertions of interests by maritime powers in the Indian Ocean will see more manoeuvrings in the sea that will shape the geopolitical landscape in the region.

The South China Sea is of growing strategic interest as well as a region of various maritime disputes between China and other littoral countries. Issues of the Indo-Pacific may complicate the existing order since it encompasses both the interest of China and India, and the continued strategic presence of the United States in Asia. Should Malaysia and other

ASEAN countries subscribe to the Indo-Pacific vision, it may appear that their policies are more aligned towards the "Strategic Partnership" of the US and India and other middle powers to balance the rise of China in Asia. In the theatre of large power players, small nations such as Malaysia and others in ASEAN cannot afford to adopt the Indo-Pacific concept and all its ramifications, at least or until individual countries are assured that the converging and expanding interests of major powers will not destabilize this region. As it stands, from plain analysis this is too far a reach for smaller nations.

6

ASEAN and the Indo-Pacific Region

Chan Git Yin

This chapter provides a Southeast Asian perspective on the concept of Indo-Pacific region. It addresses a sub question of what are the possible responses and options that the Association of Southeast Asian Nations (ASEAN) would bring, which begs a further question of whether ASEAN and its members of Southeast Asian states are ready to immerse and integrate within this larger and emphatically more complex construct.

The Indo-Pacific Region – a relatively new geographical construct essentially referring to a wider geopolitical perimeter – extends beyond the Asia-Pacific to now include the Indian Ocean region. Presently at the Asia-Pacific front, debate is still ongoing on the US pivot or the rebalancing strategy to Asia, and its implication towards regional balance of power. This new construct arguably evokes a considerable change in mind set, which further complicates the current strategic discourse.

Raja Mohan posited that as a consequence of the rise of Asia, in particular of China and India, it makes sense to reconceptualise traditional geopolitical notions, to conceive of a wider Indo-Pacific region that includes their respective spheres of influences.[1] The sustainability of the stellar economic performances of these rising nations will depend largely on the reliability of maritime links across the Indo-Pacific region. As it stands, the Indo-Pacific region will likely be riddled with insecurity and strategic instability. The Indian Ocean has its fair share of border issues, acts of transnational crime, overlapping maritime claims, which will only

---

1   C. Raja Mohan, *Samudra Manthan: Sino-Indian Rivalry in the Indo-Pacific*, Carnegie Endowment For International Peace: Washington, 2012, p. 212.

add towards the existing Asia-Pacific spreadsheet of significant flashpoints.

Against the backdrop of a macro-region, i.e. Indo-Pacific - the Indian Ocean region (IOR) in itself is a focus of intensifying strategic and political attention. Much of the world's trade in energy originates in the IOR and crosses the Indian Ocean. With widespread concern for the security of sea lines of communication (SLOCs) across the ocean, this largely explains the renewed interest of extra-regional countries in the IOR.

This chapter argues that ASEAN should take a steady step forward to first establish, where it has, vital linkages with the IOR, before starting to consider an institutional role in the wider Indo-Pacific region. The chapter also seeks to examine the capacity of ASEAN, an embattled regional organization whose institutional cohesion and political relevance have been tested of late by South China Sea related concerns, to effectively deal with regional maritime challenges whilst seeking to engage and established vital maritime links with the IOR.

Primarily a summary of an RSIS Policy Paper of similar title co-edited by the author,[2] this paper supports the proposals in the Policy Paper for enhanced institutional building, to engender regional stability and cooperation, to promote cooperative initiatives to counter illegal activities and non-traditional security threats, and to establish effective management of regional waters. These efforts and initiatives should be seen as vital building blocks towards an expansionary view of regional boundaries.

Maritime Southeast Asia

Sitting astride key SLOC between the Indian and Pacific Oceans, Southeast Asia is a distinctive maritime region, hosting major straits such as the Straits of Malacca and Singapore, the Lombok/ Makassar Straits, the Sunda Strait and the Philippines Straits. Its strategic location coupled with the high volume of seaborne trade passing through regional waters, are both economically and strategically vital to the emerging economies of Asia. Southeast Asia's westward maritime links, to the IOR, should be as strong as they currently are with East Asia.[3] Maritime related issues and concerns have a major influence in inter-state dynamics between regional

---

2   Sam Bateman, Jane Chan and Euan Graham, "ASEAN and the Indian Ocean: The Key Maritime Links", *RSIS Policy Paper,* 2011.

3   Bateman, Chan and Graham, "ASEAN and the Indian Ocean", p. 7.

countries and in relations between these countries and the rest of the world. These issues include concerns over safety and security of SLOCs with a focus on seaborne trade and energy supply, increasing emphasis on maritime platforms in defence capability, and the attention given to offshore sovereignty and maritime jurisdiction. Some ASEAN members are critically dependent on SLOCs across the Indian Ocean and most are heavily exposed to the various non-traditional security threats, such as people smuggling, drug trafficking, severe weather events and piracy.

Unfortunately, ASEAN has given little attention to the IOR as a whole, notwithstanding existing strong bilateral relations between ASEAN and India, and between individual ASEAN and IOR states. Since its inception, ASEAN has looked primarily to the east and north with its strong economic and trading links with Northeast Asia, and the United States as the major regional strategic and military power. Several ASEAN members are IOR countries (i.e. Myanmar, Thailand, Malaysia, Singapore and Indonesia), and trade between ASEAN and the IOR has been increasing over the years. Although trade between the two areas fell by over a quarter between 2008 and 2009 during the global financial crisis, nevertheless, the compound growth rate in the trade between 2003 and 2009 was significant.

This chapter proposes that ASEAN and individual Southeast Asian members to start making inroads into the IOR. ASEAN has developed norms and principles, which dictates its interaction with one another, and provides a model for cooperation that could usefully be applied in its interaction with the IOR. The 'ASEAN Way', which relied mainly on consensus, non-confrontational approaches and the principle of non-interference in domestic affairs, is often acceptable in the new partnership. Although many had argued that the 'ASEAN Way' has been ineffective in times of need,[4] and proved to be rather tedious and at times clumsy, as exemplified in existing ASEAN led regional institutions.

Southeast Asia has strong historical roots in the IOR. For much of history, the trade, politics and culture of Southeast Asia was driven by maritime links with the Indian Ocean.[5] The focus of the region on the Pacific is a relatively recent construct shaped by post-colonial factors and

---

4 Sheldon Simon, "ASEAN and Multilateralism: The Long, Bumpy Road to Community", *Contemporary Southeast Asia*, vol. 30, no. 2 (2008), p. 267.

5 Emrys Chew, "Southeast Asia and the Indian Ocean: Maritime Connections Across Time and Space", in Bateman, Chan & Graham, "ASEAN and the Indian Ocean", p. 15-18.

superpower rivalries. For ASEAN now to look more to the west would reflect the new ways of thinking about the links between the Pacific and Indian Ocean. Infrastructure developments with roads, rail and pipelines across Asia from the east to the west suggest a different orientation to the concept of maritime Asia based on the SLOCs across the Indian Ocean through Southeast Asia and along the coast of East Asia. Perhaps in the long term, there is a risk that Southeast Asian countries may become marginalised economically and strategically as the direct continental links between East and West Asia expand. However, given the existing gaps in land connectivity, the bulk of trade between the IOR and East Asia is likely to remain seaborne for the foreseeable future, including most of the oil and gas exported from the Middle East.

Geo-Political Change

The geopolitics of the IOR has evolved considerably since the end of the Cold War. Impending change to regional and global distribution of power will likely bring about structural adjustment in the IOR. As these changes are slowly unveiling, ASEAN will have to be steadfast in reinforcing a comprehensive regional framework, and in focusing on common interests to ensure peace and stability in this sea of change.

Southeast Asia stands between the overlapping interests of China and India. Major shipping routes between the Pacific and Indian Oceans pass through the region, and any strategic competition between China and India would play out in regional waters. China with its deep concern for energy security is seeking greater influence in the region.[6] It is contributing to the building of new ports in many IOR countries, and providing extensive development assistance to African countries. China's trade with Africa has grown exponentially in recent years.

India, Australia and South Africa are other littoral countries that have sought to play a leading role in the IOR. In a speech in November 2010, the Australian Minister for Foreign Affairs said that "... now Australia must look west, to the great challenges and opportunities that now present themselves across the Indian Ocean region."[7]

---

6 Lee Jae Hyung, "China's Expanding Maritime Ambitions in the Western Pacific and the Indian Ocean", *Contemporary Soutehast Asia*, vol. 24, no. 3 (2002), pp. 552-553.

7 The Hon Kevin Rudd MP, Australian Minister for Foreign Affairs, Speech at the University of Western Australia: Australia's foreign policy looking west, 12 November

While traditional security risks are evident in the IOR, the region also faces extensive non-traditional security threats, notably climate change, transnational crimes (particularly drug and arms trafficking and people smuggling), food shortages and famine, and major maritime natural hazards, such as Tsunamis, cyclones and floods. Arguably, it took the proliferation of non-traditional maritime security threats, notably modern day piracy that put the Indian Ocean at the centre stage of the 21st century challenges.[8]

IOR littoral countries hold about 62 per cent of the world's proven oil reserves and 48 per cent of the proven gas reserves.[9] The Middle East is the source of much of the world's reserves of oil and gas, and other IOR countries provide many of the strategic minerals required to fuel the rapidly growing economies of Asia. Southeast Asia waters are one of the world's most important trans-regional oil supply chain, hosting major energy transit states, where a significant proportions of oil supplies from the Middle East to the rising powers in the East.[10] Energy is a key component of geopolitics in the contemporary IOR. The struggle over energy is a potential source of tension in the IOR where both large suppliers and the interests of rising consumers are concentrated. The 'power shift' between the established hegemony of the United States and the rising challenge of China has significant implications for the energy market.[11]

A high volume of oil is carried by sea through the narrow straits in the northwest and northeast of the Indian Ocean. The Straits of Hormuz are the world's most important oil choke point. The US, in particular, attaches great strategic importance to the security of the Straits of Hormuz, as well as to the security of the Straits of Malacca, as the key choke points leading in and out of the Indian Ocean. These and other choke points are also of major strategic interest to Northeast Asian countries, as well as to ASEAN.

2010.

8   Kaplan, Robert, 'Center Stage for the Twenty- first Century', *Foreign Affairs*, vol. 88, no. 2 (Mar/Apr 2009), pp. 16-29.

9   BP Statistical Review of World Energy 2009, www.bp.com.

10 Allison Casey and Mattew Sussex, "Energy transit states and maritime security in the Malacca Strait: the case of Singapore", *Australian Journal of Maritime and Ocean Affairs*, vol. 4, no. 1 (2012), pp. 26-27.

11 Rajesh Basrur, "Energy and Geopolitics in the Indian Ocean Region", In Bateman, Chana and Graham, "ASEAN and the Indian ocean", *RSIS Policy Paper* (2011), pp.32-35.

The safety and security of shipping are requirements that potentially provide the basis for maritime cooperation in the IOR.[12]

Nuclear issues are another major component of the geopolitics of the IOR. Much of the growth in the global consumption of nuclear power is concentrated in the region.[13] The illicit transportation of nuclear technology or materials by sea in the IOR is a related security concern.

Maritime Security Concerns

Threats to maritime security are very evident in the IOR and the wider Indo-Pacific region. They include the risks of interstate conflict,[14] non-traditional/ transboundary security concerns, e.g. maritime terrorism, piracy, illegal, unreported and unregulated (IUU) fishing, trafficking in drugs, arms and people, marine natural hazards and climate change. Energy security, food security and even the spread of infectious disease are all major issues with significant maritime dimensions. There is a multitude of common interests, particularly in the maritime domain, that will facilitate the cultivation of vital links between ASEAN and the IOR.

Piracy and armed robbery at sea are a significant maritime security problem in the IOR. While most recent attention has focused on the area around the Horn of Africa, attacks on ships also occur elsewhere down the East African coast and in ports in the Indian subcontinent. Data from International Maritime Bureau (IMB) and the Regional Cooperation Agreement on Combating Piracy and Armed Robbery against Ships in Asia (ReCAAP) Information Sharing Centre shows that the situation with piracy and armed robbery against ships worldwide has improved in 2012 compared to 2011.[15] In large part this has been due to the improved situation in Somalia, the South China Sea and the Straits of Malacca and

---

12 Rumley D, Chaturvedi S, Yasin MT (eds.) 2007. The security of sea lanes of communication in the Indian Ocean region, Maritime Institute of Malaysia, Kuala Lumpur.

13 Ibid.

14 According to the Heidelberg Institute for International Conflict Research Conflict Barometer 2008 at hiik.de/en/konfliktbarometer/index.html, 146 of the world total of 345 conflicts, or 42.3per cent, are in the IOR. They include six of nine wars and a considerable proportion of the world's high intensity conflicts.

15 International Maritime Bureau (IMB), *2012 Annual Piracy Report*; ReCAAP Information Sharing Centre, *Piracy and Armed Robbery against ships in Asia – Annual report for 2012*.

Singapore.[16] However, there was a marked increase in attacks in Indonesian waters in comparison with the previous four years, from 21 actual incidents in 2008, 14 in 2009, 37 in 2010, 47 in 2011 and 65 in 2012.[17] Most attacks in Southeast Asia targeted vessels at anchor, in port or entering or leaving a harbour. These attacks are usually of a minor nature and are best countered by more effective policing by port authorities, including active patrolling of ports and anchorages. In contrast, steaming vessels were often attacked in the IOR. The modus operandi is also vastly different from those in Southeast Asia, as most of the attacks involved the vessels and crews being kidnapped for ransom.

Maritime terrorist attacks are a threat in the IOR due to the presence of extremist groups and the incidence of piracy in the region. The terrorist attack in Mumbai in November 2008 demonstrated the risks of terrorist attack from the sea if coastal waters are not secure. Key access routes to the Indian Ocean, such as the Malacca and Singapore straits, the Strait of Hormuz and Bab el Mandab, have dense shipping traffic where potential targets are readily available to terrorists. The risks include terrorist attacks at sea and the use of the sea by terrorist groups for movement of personnel, arms and other materials.

The sea is the preferred medium for the illegal movement of goods and people. Larger quantities of cargo can be shipped at sea generally with less risk of detection. Illicit shipments can also be transshipped at sea and brought into a country in a vessel, such as a local fishing boat, without raising the suspicions of local authorities. Illegal trafficking in arms, drugs and people are all evident to some extent in the IOR, as well as trafficking in other contraband, such as liquor, cigarettes and wildlife. Most of this illegal trade is conducted by sea. These activities are all manifestations of transnational organised crime, and dealing with them requires cooperation between regional countries.

Human trafficking is a highly profitable business.[18] South Asia and Northeast Africa are major points of origin for refugees and asylum seekers in the IOR, while many victims also originate from Southeast

---

16 Ibid, p.13.

17 Ibid, p.12.

18 Centre for NTS Studies, "Transnational Organised Crime in Southeast Asia: Threat assessment", NTS Alert July 2010, Issue 1, p. 6.

Asia, particularly women and children.[19] Human trafficking from South to Southeast Asia might increase in size and scope given its geographic proximity, maritime environment and the high economic growth rates experienced by several ASEAN countries. Much of this trafficking occurs by sea.[20]

Illegal drugs are widely available across much of Southeast Asia, and this region has the largest number of drug users in the world.[21] Most illegal drugs used in the region originate from the IOR. The manufacture and trafficking in methamphetamines ('ice') and other amphetamine-type stimulants have increased substantially and pose a major problem in East and Southeast Asia. The dual uses of precursor materials make it difficult to suppress the manufacture of 'ice'. India, for example, is a major exporter of precursor chemicals and is unlikely to support export controls over those materials.[22]

IUU fishing is a serious problem in the IOR. Increased demand and the depletion of fish stocks elsewhere in the world have led to more fishing in the Indian Ocean and an increasing presence of fishing vessels from outside of the region. The involvement of these vessels is facilitated largely because there is no effective regime for regional fisheries management. The Indian Ocean Tuna Commission (IOTC) is notoriously ineffective.[23] Major links have also been found between international fishing vessels and transnational crime, including human trafficking.[24]

Marine natural hazards arise through climate change, tropical storms, Tsunamis and other severe oceanic conditions. Southeast Asia and other parts of the IOR are prone to these hazards, and scientific findings suggest that the intensity and frequency of disasters arising from these hazards is

---

19 Centre for NTS Studies, "Responding to Transnational Organised Crime in Southeast Asia: Case Study of Human Trafficking and Drug Trafficking", NTS Alert July 2010, Issue 2, p. 1.

20 Pau Khan Khup Hangzo, 'Non-Traditional Security Challenges in the Indian Ocean Region', in Bateman, Chan and Graham (eds), "*ASEAN and the Indian Ocean*", pp 28-31.

21 Centre for NTS Studies, "Transnational Organised Crime in Southeast Asia", p. 2.

22 Centre for NTS Studies, "Responding to Transnational Organised Crime in Southeast Asia", p.5.

23 Bateman and Bergin, Our western front, p. 29.

24 Rumley D, Chaturvedi S, Sakhuja V (eds) 2009. Fisheries exploitation in the Indian Ocean: threats and opportunities, Institute of Southeast Asian Studies, Singapore.

increasing.[25] According to the Asian Disaster Reduction Centre, Asia is the most disaster-affected area in the world.[26] This was demonstrated by the Indian Ocean Tsunami in December 2004 and the impact of cyclone Nargis in Myanmar in May 2008. Other areas of the region are vulnerable to cyclones, including islands in the Southwest Indian Ocean, and the associated impacts of storm surges and flooding. Sea-level rise poses a potentially existential threat to low-lying states in the region, such as the Maldives. Many IOR countries are relatively ill-equipped to deal with the problems posed by natural hazards, and potentially this is an area where ASEAN might help with capacity building.[27]

In 2007, Geoscience Australia undertook a hazard risk assessment of the Asia-Pacific region for AusAID, covering earthquakes, volcanic eruptions, Tsunamis, cyclones, floods and wildfire hazards.[28] This found that the northern part of the Bay of Bengal was the most dangerous area for large Tsunamis and that, of individual countries, Indonesia has the highest population threatened by tsunamis, followed by Bangladesh and India. The higher frequency of extreme weather events will have a great impact on low lying coastal areas, such as Bangladesh.

Improved oceanographic knowledge of the Indian Ocean would markedly improve predictions of severe weather events, as well as weather forecasting generally in littoral land masses. The Indian Ocean Dipole is a particular feature of the ocean. This is a system of temperature fluctuations in the eastern and western parts of the Indian Ocean. In its negative phase, the dipole system brings heavy rains to Southeast Asia and drought to the Arabian Sea region. In its positive phase, water temperatures are reversed and less rain falls in Southeast Asia, while the Arabian Sea region has heavy rains. Better ability to predict movements in the Dipole would benefit

---

25 Centre for NTS Studies, "Regional Support for Southeast Asia Disaster Preparedness", NTS Alert November 2009, Issue 2, p. 5.

26 Asian Disaster Reduction Center (ADRC) 2006. Natural disasters data book 2006: an analytical overview, ADRC. www.adrc.or.jp/publications/databook/DB2006_e.html.

27 Lee Cordner, " Maritime Security in the Indian Ocean Region: Compelling and convergent agendas", *Australian Journal of Maritime and Ocean Affairs,* vol. 2, no. 1, 2010, p. 17.

28 Simpson A, Cummins P, Dhu T, Griffin J, Schneider J 2008. 'Assessing natural disaster risk in the Asia–Pacific region—supporting international development through natural hazard risk research', AUSGEO News, 90:1–8. www.ga.gov.au/ausgeonews/ausgeonews200806/disaster.jsp.

agricultural output in East Africa, South Asia and Australia.

Promoting Links: Regional Cooperation

The ASEAN Regional Forum (ARF) has sought to apply ASEAN's norms and principles to the wider Asia-Pacific region, and has become the principal forum for security dialogue in Asia.[29] However, so far it has not turned its attention to the Indian Ocean and has been hesitant about addressing hard security issues. It has not brought the IOR into its geographical ambit despite the clear overlapping interests that exist with the Asia-Pacific. The fundamental nature of these common interests, including the key strategic issue of energy security creates a compelling logic for closer cooperation. Mutual benefits would flow to both ASEAN and the larger IOR from the development of inter-regional links.

Many have argued that Southeast Asian countries have long had the preference for collective action through various regional frameworks and initiatives.[30] The first desirable outcome is to do more to institutionalize the process of regional cooperation for good order at sea. ASEAN and the ARF have made some first steps in this regard but the process should be speeded up, including both "top down" initiatives that might come out of the ARF and ASEAN and "bottom-up" steps using existing processes as "building blocks" to further the process of cooperation. To facilitate this process, it is important that regional countries move quickly to ratify relevant international conventions rather than just paying "lip service" to their existence. Outstanding maritime boundaries should also be resolved as soon as possible.

At a "top down" level, the ASEAN Maritime Forum, the ARF ISM on Maritime Security, and the ASEAN Defence Ministers Meeting Plus (ADMM Plus) Expert Working Group on Maritime Security offer possible frameworks under which regional cooperation for good order at sea might be developed. The ASEAN Maritime Forum (AMF) was first mooted at the ASEAN Foreign Ministers' meeting in Jakarta in June 2004. The 3rd AMF meeting in Manila in 2012 was held back to back with the 1st Expanded

---

29 Ralf Emmers and Sam Bateman, "ASEAN's Model of Conflict Management: Lessons for the Indian Ocean Region", in Bateman, Chan and Graham, "ASEAN and the Indian Ocean", p. 24.

30 Simon, Sheldon, 'ASEAN and Multilateralism: The Long, Bumpy Road to Community', *Contemporary Southeast Asia,* vol. 30, no. 2(2008), pp. 265-268.

ASEAN Maritime Forum (EAMF), an offshoot of the AMF initiative, convened in response to the statement of the ASEAN Leaders, as well as the Leaders of the East Asia Summit (EAS), in Bali, Indonesia in November 2011, who encouraged a "dialogue involving EAS participating countries to utilize opportunities and address common challenges on maritime issues building upon the existing AMF." [31] The EAMF is also seen as an avenue for Track 1.5 diplomacy on cross-cutting maritime issues that are of common concern to the EAS participating countries. The ARF ISM on Maritime Security on the other hand, involves only government officials and has had four meetings thus far, currently co-chaired by Indonesia, South Korea and United States. The ARF Work Plan on Maritime Security contains three priorities for 2011-2013, i.e. (a) exchange of information, intelligence, and best practice; (b) confidence building-measures; and (c) capacity-building of law enforcement agencies. ASEAN Defence Ministers agreed at the very 1st ADMM-Plus convened in Hanoi, in October 2010, to establish Experts' Working Groups (EWGs) to promote cooperation in five identified areas including maritime security.[32] Australia and Malaysia are co-chairs of the EWG on maritime security.

At a "bottom up" level, the Information Fusion Centre (IFC), inaugurated in April 2009, aims to provide actionable information on maritime security threats in the wider Indo-Pacific waters, in order to obtain early warning by its partners, to contribute to the regional knowledge repository on MARSEC, and to enhance the collective maritime awareness, info-sharing and sense-making capabilities in the region. One of the key propositions of the IFC is the International Liaison Officers (ILO) initiative, where various agencies and countries that have established linkages with the IFC are represented. Both the ASEAN and non-ASEAN ILOs play key roles at the IFC, and both groups are cognizant of their purpose and the value they bring to the table. The ILOs are thus able to serve both their national and the wider regional interest in the same breath. IFC is also host

---

31 Chairman's Statement, 1st Expanded ASEAN Maritime Forum Manila, 9 October 2012. (The full statement is available at: http://www.asean.org/news/asean-statement-communiques/item/1st-expanded-asean-maritime-forum-manila).

32 Chairman's Statement of the First ASEAN Defence Ministers' Meeting-Plus: "ADMM-Plus: Strategic Cooperation for Peace, Stability, and Development in the Region" Ha Noi, 12 October 2010. (The full statement is available at: http://www.asean.org/communities/asean-political-security-community/item/chairman-s-statement-of-the-first-asean-defence-ministers-meeting-plus-admm-plus-strategic-cooperation-for-peace-stability-and-development-in-the-region-ha-noi-12-october-2010).

to the ASEAN Information-Sharing Portal (AIP), launched in July 2012, to facilitate real-time exchange of information between various operation centres and operational commanders in the ASEAN region.[33]

Another example is the ReCAAP, which offers potential for the development of initiatives that would promote good order at sea. ReCAAP has many strengths, including its identification of focal points in participating countries and its capacity-building programme. Despite the limitation that Indonesia and Malaysia are not parties to ReCAAP at present, it provides a useful "building block" for a more integrated approach to good order at sea.

Non-traditional security threats, particularly in the maritime domain, remained a common concern both within ASEAN and in the wider IOR. However, there is a lack of a common threat perception that could create the impetus for heightened levels of cooperation. Collaborative measures to deal with these threats offer a good vehicle for the engagement of ASEAN and nations within the IOR. Not only will such cooperation and collaboration help mitigate the impact of some of these threats on Southeast Asia, it will engender trust and confidence.

Conclusion

As it looks west, ASEAN might play a role in moves to dampen down regional security uncertainty, including using its links with China and India to moderate the risks of tension between these two key regional players. Both China and India participate in the ARF, but these rising powers not entirely respect the norms and principles developed by ASEAN and may be reluctant to have their bilateral relationship discussed within that forum.

The safety and security of SLOCs across the Indian Ocean and major chokepoints are strong common interests for most IOR and ASEAN states, as well as extra-regional stakeholders. Whilst detail measures to counter specific maritime security threats and illegal activities might differ according to the relevant peculiarity, in broad terms, cooperation and collaboration amongst all stakeholders is required to ensure safety and security of SLOCs and regional waters. Existing initiatives such as the Indian Ocean Naval

---

33 Spearheaded by the Republic of Singapore Navy (RSN) and the Indonesian Navy (TNI AL), the ASEAN Information-Sharing Portal (AIP) features two notable functions: a real-time chat module with a translation function and a downloadable mobile application.

Symposium (IONS), the IFC ought to be supported as key platforms to promote confidence and capacity building in the region. It is unlikely that the requisite level of cooperation with maritime policy will be achieved merely through naval cooperation. Taking into consideration the issues and challenges would generally require constabulary enforcement, more suited for maritime law enforcement agencies rather than the navies.

Strategic uncertainty is evident in the IOR due to the motivations of extra-regional countries in securing energy supplies, conflict in Afghanistan, the ongoing tension between India and Pakistan, and competition for regional influence between India and China, as well as to perceptions that the United States might be losing its ability to play a moderating role in the region. Inevitably by virtue of geography and the presence of key shipping choke points, Southeast Asia is enmeshed in this uncertainty as the spheres of influence of the rising naval powers of China and India, as well as other extra-regional powers, overlaps within its geographical limits. As Raja Mohan posited, "Put simply, ASEAN now needs a 'two ocean' strategy to ensure its own security.[34]

The mitigation of the risks arising from strategic uncertainty requires more attention to preventive diplomacy and maritime confidence and security building measures, including greater transparency with regard to naval operations and exercises. There is a need for preventive diplomacy in the region, but at present there is no effective forum in the region to carry initiatives forward. There is a potential for ASEAN, as a regional association, to be more active in helping to mitigate the risks of strategic uncertainty and bring more certainty to the IOR. If successful, will establish ASEAN as a key player in the wider Indo-Pacific region.

---

34 C. Raja Mohan, "Contemporary Strategic Environment of The Indian Ocean Region: An Overview", in Bateman, Chan and Graham, "ASEAN and the Indian Ocean", p. 22-23.

7

The Indo-Pacific Region or India's Rise in Asia-Pacific?: A View from Russia

Evgeny Kanaev

In recent times, the term 'Indo-Pacific region' has become part of international discourse at the political and expert levels.[1] Currently, the term still lacks specificity with regard to its geographical boundaries, institutional format and key projects. Nevertheless, its emergence may reflect, or anticipate, pending shifts in relations between powers shaping the strategic landscape in the Pacific and Indian oceans.

In Russian expert community, the term 'Indo-Pacific region' is not a popular topic; serious attempts to conceptualize it are just beginning to appear.[2] It is hardly surprising given that the key parameters of this hypothetical region have not yet been laid down. Because of this, in practical terms 'the Indo-Pacific discourse' may be currently seen mostly as New Delhi's quest to increase its profile in the 'traditional' region of the Asia-Pacific. At the initial approximation, this may be welcomed. This assessment is based on the evidence provided by two factors: serious imbalances being accumulated in Asia-Pacific and India's considerable potential to give impetus to the cooperative development paradigm of this region.

---

1 See, for instance: Chacko P. India and the Indo-Pacific: an Emerging Regional View. Indo-Pacific Governance Research Center Policy Brief. Issue 5. November 2012. http://www.adelaide.edu.au/indo-pacific-governance/policy/Chacko_PB.pdf; Hillary Clinton lauds India's role in Indo-Pacific region, urges for increased participation. *India Today* 14 November, 2012. http://indiatoday.intoday.in/story/hillary-clinton-lauds-indias-role-indo-pacific-region-talks-china-breifly-in-australia/1/229136.html.

2 Лукин А. На смену АТР идёт ИТР? (Lukin A. An Emerging Trend: Indo-Pacific instead of Asia-Pacific? (In Russian)) // http://russiancouncil.ru/blogs/dvfu/?id_4=328.

The chapter is divided into three parts. The first part analyses major economic, political and strategic imbalances in Asia-Pacific, and the second part gives insights into achievements of and prospects for India's Asia-Pacific policy and assesses its congruence with Russia's regional priorities. The third part offers a likely scenario resulting from India's increased future role in Asia-Pacific. The conclusion summarizes the foregoing analysis.

Asia-Pacific Imbalances

When the Cold War was coming to an end, Asia-Pacific state and non-state actors began to consider possibilities to create a system of multilateral cooperation in order to give a strong impetus to their economic development, and devise qualitatively new mechanisms of regional checks and balances based on new understanding of the term 'security' and ground-breaking approaches to ensure it. In the course of time, however, this multi-faceted and multi-dimensional system designed to mitigate pressing regional economic, political and military contradictions began to dissatisfy both big and small members. The root cause seems to lie in serious and constantly widening imbalances between Asia-Pacific development goals, mechanisms and institutions.

The key development goal repeatedly stressed in the Pacific leaders' statements and declarations of multilateral and bilateral settings is to maintain regional peace and stability, create an integrated, resilient and prosperous region which is in the vanguard of global growth and able to effectively cope with current and emerging challenges.[3] In order to achieve it, the potential of two mechanisms is exploited – the bilateral and multilateral cooperation; the latter falls within development institutions.

The goal stated above is laudable in all respects, especially along with expectations that in the years to come, the future of global economic and political processes will be shaped in Asia-Pacific. However, regarding the mechanisms and institutions aimed at materializing this scenario, ample evidence suggests that they may not be fully fit for it. Several points bear relevance in this regard.

---

3 Such statements have been made in overabundance, so references don't seem to be strictly necessary. Nevertheless, see: 2011 Leaders' Declaration. The Honolulu Declaration - Toward a Seamless Regional Economy. Honolulu, Hawaii, United States, 12 - 13 November 2011. http://www.apec.org/Meeting-Papers/Leaders-Declarations/2011/2011_aelmaspx; Dmitry Medvedev's article, "Integrate to Grow, Innovate to Prosper". 28.01.2012. http://eng.news.kremlin.ru/transcripts/3370 and others.

First, bilateral relations between main Asia-Pacific actors are far from contributing to the win-win cooperation. For instance, Sino-American relations; after the US' "coming back to Asia", Washington offered Beijing a model of "responsible leadership" with an intention to make China a "responsible shareholder" under the American "benign supervision". This project logically failed, not in the least because of differences, and in many respects, opposing attitude to the responsibility to international community adopted by Washington and Beijing. The former sees its responsibility in, figuratively speaking, "external terms", in combating the threat of international terrorism, preventing the proliferation of weapons of mass destruction and the like,[4] which means unrestricted access to any part of the globe. The latter takes a different view, i.e. the Chinese leadership must, first and foremost, be able to tackle domestic issues,[5] which attaches a paramount importance to defending national sovereignty.

This clash of visions predetermined a new wave of escalation of the South China Sea issue, the essence of which has changed since the Obama administration came to power. Before 2009, the contradictions concentrated, first and foremost, upon the issue of sovereignty over the disputed islands. Since the early 2009, the Sino-American geopolitical rivalry in the maritime Asia-Pacific and the South China Sea as its "strategic heartland" has come to the forefront of Asia-Pacific politics. The key lines of contradictions are as below.

An admissibility to violate the letter and spirit of Declaration on Conduct of Parties in the South China Sea (DOC) signed by China and the ASEAN states in 2002. China emphasizes that, according to the provisions of Declaration, all existing and potential problems are to be solved by sovereign states directly concerned and drawing up Code of Conduct of Parties in the South China Sea instead of DOC is to be based on consensus. Otherwise, in case 'letter and spirit' of the 2002 Declaration are not respected, the idea to find an internationally recognized legal framework in which the issue may be resolved can be discredited for many years ahead. Washington stresses that the international community, including

---

4   See, for instance: World at Risk. The Report of the Commission on the Prevention of WMD Proliferation and Terrorism. – New York, Toronto, 2008. http://www.absa.org/leg/WorldAtRisk.pdf.

5   A Changing China in a Changing World. Address by H.E. Yang Jiechi, Minister of Foreign Affairs of the People's Republic of China, at the Munich Security Conference. Munich, 5 February 2010. http://www.fmprc.gov.cn/eng/wjdt/zyjh/t656781.htm.

itself, should play a more prominent role in maintaining stability in the South China Sea, and speed up the Code on Conduct of Parties instead of the 2002 Declaration.

An admissibility of intelligence gathering activities in China's Exclusive Economic Zones. China and the US disagree on the interpretations of Articles 19, 25 and 30 of the UNCLOS which specify passage of foreign military vessels in a state's Exclusive Economic Zones. Nevertheless, the reasons behind this argument are easily discernible as both countries are jostling for influence in the Western Pacific. China is planning to establish its naval predominance within "the first island chain" which, in geographical terms, coincides with its claims in the South China Sea. In this context, the development of China's maritime programs doesn't make sense unless the operational space of the PLANavy is expanded.[6] The US, strives to maintain the current status quo in Asia-Pacific waters, which means, among other things, unimpeded freedom of naval activity as Washington sees it necessary.

An admissibility to explore the resources of the South China Sea. It is China's position that the South China Sea falls within its internal waters and its "core interests". Consequently, any attempts by other actors to explore the resources of the South China Sea, no matter, states or non-state actors, should be authorized by Beijing. In its turn, the US stresses that the South China Sea and its resources are part of global commons, and these resources can be developed by any interested party, be it oil companies (Exxon Mobil, BP, Shell, Chevron and Murphy), or fishermen of littoral states.

At the bilateral level, the South China Sea issue causes deep disagreements not only in Sino-American, but also in Sino-Vietnamese and Sino-Philippine relations. The way things developed in 2010-12 leads to an obvious conclusion: the South China Sea claimants are neither able nor ready to solve emerging problems on the basis of win-win cooperation, mutual trust and respect. This is contrary to numerous statements repeatedly pronounced by their governments. In this connection, the assessment that the issue, given its depth, complexity and emotional sensitivity, will generate further contradictions in relations between the claimant states in

---

6 A detailed assessment of this trend is found in: Buszynski L. The South China Sea: Oil, Maritime Claims, and U.S. – China Strategic Rivalry. The Washington Quarterly. 2012. vol. 35. no. 2, pp. 139-156.

the years to come seems to be more than realistic.

The bilateral dimension of relations also includes the factor of nationalism which reveals itself in both escalation of territorial issues and pursuing individual interests at the expense of collective good. In the former case, suffice it to recall disputes in the East China Sea and the Sea of Japan, along with increased economic cooperation and plans to raise trade, investment and technological exchanges between the Northeast Asian countries to a qualitatively new level. Concerning the latter, the way the Southeast Asian states are moving towards the ASEAN Community reveals that Southeast Asia as an internally cohesive and integrated geo-economic region will long remain a catchy policy slogan rather than a realistic and attainable goal.

Finally, bilateralism as a mechanism of development includes differing – and, which is much more important, conflicting approaches to cooperation with the US and China, in terms of depth, scale and spheres this cooperation embraces. Since the US has been "back in Asia" and has made steps to strengthen its leadership in the Pacific, this "divergence of minds" has been on the rise. This also contributes to an increased polarization of relations between countries and territories of Asia-Pacific and hampers its cooperative development paradigm.

The multilateral dialogue in Asia-Pacific, in spite of many institutions designated to build confidence, prevents conflicts and, in the final analysis, contribute to the win-win cooperation, is also facing hard times. The key imbalances which this system is encountering are outlined below.

Multilateral dialogue platforms: rise in number vs. conservation in substance. The existing institutions like ASEAN Regional Forum, ADMM Plus and East Asia Summit can be rightfully regarded as brave ASEAN attempts to create a viable system of strategic checks and balances in Asia-Pacific. Nevertheless, progress in resolving urgent regional issues has been hampered by ASEAN institutional minimalism and its principles of cooperation based on consensus and a pace comfortable to all participants. As a result, these institutions are growing in number, as well as seriousness of the problems being discussed – but no tangible results are in sight.

Issues and approaches: complication vs. stagnation. With the passage of time, challenges which the region is encountering have undergone a profound transformation. It has already been pointed out that the essence of the current contradictions on the South China Sea issue has very little in common with what existed ten or even five years ago. Nevertheless, up to now the ASEAN-centric multilateral platforms have been unable to respond to the changing situation, first and foremost, at the conceptual level. In practical terms, this means conservation of the instruments of conflict resolution rather than making them forward-looking, able to adapt to changes and therefore, effectively cope with current and emerging regional threats.

Trans-Pacific vs East Asian vector of multilateralism. At present, there are two parallel tracks of economic regionalism in the Pacific, the Trans-Pacific manifested by APEC and the US-led initiative Trans-Pacific Partnership (TPP), and the East Asian, exemplified by free trade and investment regimes being developed by East Asian countries. In many respects, these initiatives have proved to contradict rather than compliment to the cooperative paradigm of Asia-Pacific. Suffice it to say that the TPP is at variance with ASEAN prospective planning – to establish ASEAN Economic community scheduled for 2015 – and a subject of China's sharp criticism. The Free Trade Area of Asia-Pacific as the key APEC project doesn't seem to be realistic owing to many obstacles it is encountering. As for the most recent undertaking, the Regional Comprehensive Economic Partnership (RCEP), it still has to prove its utility to its members. Nevertheless, given that the US is not part of RCEP, a scenario under which RCEP will compete with TPP cannot be excluded.

All this is unfolding simultaneously with Asia-Pacific emergence as the main global powerhouse and the cutting edge of the future world order. Under these circumstances, the situation can be rectified, first and foremost, by efforts taken by established global powers with stakes in Asia-Pacific. One of these powers is India.

India in Asia-Pacific: A Power to Reckon with

The key economic, political and strategic trends currently developing in Asia-Pacific provide ample evidence for arguing that India is the *de-facto* key regional power whose influence upon the future evolution of the region will inevitably be growing. Evidence to confirm this assessment appears to be strong and overwhelming.

First, economic relations between India and the countries of Northeast Asia, Southeast Asia and South Pacific are on the rise. For instance, trade between India and ASEAN jumped from less than US$ 10 billion in early 2000s to US$ 79 billion in 2012. Given that in late 2012 India and ASEAN finalized their free trade agreement (FTA) in services and investments, to achieve the target of US$ 100 billion by 2015, as it has been scheduled,[7] seems to be a realistic task. Even assessments that mutual trade may have increased to US$ 200 billion by 2022,[8] are not beyond the realm of the 'possible'. In Northeast Asia and South Pacific, ambitious plans to expand economic cooperation with India are harboured by China, Japan, South Korea and Australia. Investment, technological and human resource exchanges between India and Asia-Pacific states have also intensified and hold good growth potential for the years to come.

In relations between India and ASEAN, it is especially important that they embrace many directions which correlate with ASEAN's prospective planning and in which the Association is particularly interested. Among them, of note is *connectivity* not only land connectivity, but also maritime and air connectivity. At present, infrastructure projects with India's contribution loom large in ASEAN's order of priority. In this light, the fact that ASEAN-India Partnership has recently been elevated to the strategic partnership is neither unexpected nor surprising.

Second, India is strengthening its defence and political ties with many Asia-Pacific countries. For instance, in Southeast Asia defence dialogue between India and Indonesia, Vietnam, Myanmar, Thailand and the Philippines is being actively developed. India seems to be using to the fullest potential, its strategic advantage. Given the traditions of non-alignment in its foreign policy, it is neither feared nor associated with a quest for hegemony. In Northeast Asia and South Pacific, of note are Australia's and Japan's plans to inject new vigour in their defence ties with India. But the most significant example is provided by the Australian leadership's readiness to raise the status of relations with India to that of

---

7 India, ASEAN Finalise FTA in Services, Investments. The Hindu. 20.12.2012. www.thehindu.com/business/Economy/india-asean-finalise-fta-in-services-investments/article4222052.ece.

8 India Harapkan Peningkatan Hubungan Ekonomi Dengan ASEAN. Antaranews.com. 20 Desember 2012. http://www.antaranews.com/berita/349477/india-harapkan-peningkatan-hubungan-ekonomi-dengan-asean.

the US, Japan, China, South Korea and Indonesia.[9]

These perceptions are explicable not in the least because India is paying close attention to developing its defence-industrial complex. Special emphasis is placed on upgrading the R&D potential of the national defence industry. Various forms of state support to enterprises as well as financial incentives in order to attract promising human resources are under consideration. Ways to optimize cooperation between defence and civil industry sectors are being elaborated. In this regard, urgent priority is attached to developing naval programmes; suffice it to mention that 16 per cent of the US$ 80 billion allocated for defence needs is designated to the Navy. In qualitative terms, the naval modernization emphasizes acquisition and domestic production of technologically advanced weapons, among which aircraft carrier and submarine programs are given priority.[10] All this will enable India to project its naval power beyond Indian Ocean, with the Pacific Ocean being a very likely direction.

Third, India has enough capabilities to influence upon important Asia-Pacific security challenges, first and foremost, in Southeast Asia. For instance, the South China Sea is important because Indian oil and gas company, Oil and Natural Gas Corporation (ONGC) is engaged in oil and gas exploration with TNK Vietnam and Petro Vietnam. A possible deployment of Indian warships to protect the country's interests in the South China Sea[11] will make the Indian factor in the South China Sea much more conspicuous than it is at present. Apart from the South China Sea, the Mekong issue deserves mentioning. In case Mekong-Ganga Cooperation Ministerial Meetings are held at the annual basis and new areas of cooperation are explored, as suggested by India in 2012,[12] this might produce an overall stabilizing effect upon the Mekong issue given that confidence between the Mekong actors will be growing. Also, this is

---

9   Australia plays catch up in India. East Asia Forum. 23.10.2012. // http://www.eastasiaforum.org/2012/10/23/australia-plays-catch-up-in-india/.

10 For details, see: India's Naval Acquisitions I: Defense Ship-Building in India. Thought Leadership Series. December 2011. // http://www.aviotech.com/pdf/Aviotech_Thought_Leadership_Series_Naval_Shipbuilding_December_2011.pdf.

11 See: Pandit R. Ready to Tackle China Sea Threat: Navy Chief. The Times of India. 4.12.2012. // http://articles.timesofindia.indiatimes.com/2012-12-04/india/35594081_1_south-china-sea-accordance-with-international-laws-vietnam-coast.

12 6th Mekong Ganga Cooperation Meeting. 6.09.2012. // http://thecalibre.in/in-depth-current-affairs/6th-mekong-ganga-cooperation-meeting/092012/?p=1214/.

very important given the Mekong issue will with a great degree of certainty become the key Southeast Asian security challenge in the near future.

Last but not least, India is an influential participant of the key East Asian and Trans-Pacific multilateral dialogue platforms. For instance, India has been in EAS, ADMM Plus Eight and the Expanded ASEAN Maritime Forum since their inception and joined ASEAN Regional Forum a short time after it was established. Currently, another possible undertaking is catching observers' attention: India, together with Australia and New Zealand, may become part of the Chiang Mai Multilateral Initiative. This step is considered to bring about profound favourable repercussions for that financial safety mechanism.[13]

On the whole, India's influence in Asia-Pacific is on the rise. In future, this trend is likely to continue due to a number of reasons. In the economic realm, many East Asian states seem to be eager to both avoid being in the epicentre of the unfolding Sino-US geo-economic competition and develop promising alternative partnerships. This is more so since in economic terms, the options which have been and are being offered to these countries by the US and China turn out far from being as attractive as they could have seemed initially, no matter what Washington and Beijing may claim. For instance, the TPP has not too many economic benefits to offer to its Asian participants, while the results of China-ASEAN Free Trade Area are mixed at best. Under these circumstances, the diversification of economic ties becomes an urgent priority of many Asia-Pacific nations. In light of this, of note is the quote from a Hitachi representative regarding the company's prospective planning: "Japan in the past, Thailand now, India in future".[14]

Furthermore, given an eye-catching trend towards trade in services liberalization, it will be in India's interests to capitalize on its many highly developed service sectors. According to the Strategic Global Outlook-2030, a research project carried out by the leading Russian think-tank IMEMO in 2011, in the next two decades, India's service sector is expected to be

---

13 See, for instance: The Next Steps in ASEAN+3 Monetary Integration. Research Institute on Economy, Trade and Industry. 27.05.2012. // http://www.rieti.go.jp/en/special/p_a_w/015.html.

14 Japanese companies keen on investing in India but want stable policy. 24 01.2013. // http://post.jagran.com/japanese-companies-keen-on-investing-in-india-but-want-stable-policy-1359003017.

developing at an increasing tempo.[15] In this regard, one shouldn't forget that along with the free trade boom in East Asia, in many countries' service sectors remain underdeveloped. This gives India a strong competitive advantage.

Third and finally, in geopolitical terms ASEAN, the locomotive of the key multilateral dialogue platforms in the Pacific, is likely to welcome a more active Indian contribution to strengthening regional peace and stability. The reason is clear – in the unfolding Sino-American geopolitical competition ASEAN fears regional destabilization and regards India as an influential power in whose interests is to prevent this scenario.

All this is unfolding simultaneously with Russia's move eastward. In this connection, a logical question arises: how should Moscow see it? The answer is as follows: the current and expected rise of India in Asia-Pacific is not against Russia's interests. Of course, a long history of friendly and constructive relationships plays its role. But much more important is another factor, i.e. currently, Russia and India have very close strategic priorities in Asia-Pacific.

This assessment is substantiated by strong evidence. In fact, both India and Russia are established global powers trying to assert themselves in Asia-Pacific. Neither India nor Russia is interested in the polarization of the region as a result of Sino-American confrontation. Both see a peaceful regional milieu as the vital prerequisite to maintain economic development. Both share the same historical experience as not to take sides in geopolitical games played by other powers. Last but not the least, both have sufficient economic capabilities to pursue independent foreign policies.

No less significant is a convergence of Indian and Russian interests at the global level. Russia and India share the view that the new world order must be polycentric and inclusive. The latter point means that within this emerging global equilibrium, China must be one of big but not a dominant power. Also, both parties agree that current global issues cannot be effectively settled without a more active participation of developing countries in global trade, investment and financial exchanges, and that

---

15 Брагина Е.А., Володин А.Г., Лунев С.И., Мачавариани Г.И. Индия и Южная Азия. Стратегический глобальный прогноз 2030. Расширенный вариант / под ред. акад. А.А.Дынкина. – М., 2011. – С. 407. (Bragina E., Volodin A., Lunev S., Machavariani G. India and South Asia. Strategic Global Outlook 2030. Extended Version. /Ed. by Alexander A.Dynkin. – M., 2011. – P. 407. (in Russian)

these countries can and should become the driving force of global growth.[16] Given that at present Asia-Pacific issues are rapidly globalizing, the role of this factor cannot be underestimated.

With all this in view, India's intention to raise its profile in Asia-Pacific does not run counter to Russia's priorities in this part of the world. On the contrary, points of convergence ultimately prevail.

What Will India's Future Rise Bring to Asia-Pacific?

To construct future scenarios is always an enviable task as many factors which cannot be foreseen are constantly growing in number. Nevertheless, along with the rise of India in Asia-Pacific, the overall regional situation will probably become more stable and cooperative. Before going into details, some preliminary remarks are necessary. In the early 2010, key political, economic and defence trends suggest pending shifts in Asia-Pacific equilibrium. Among the factors that will shape the parameters of the emerging regional order. Among these two are particularly noteworthy.

First, contradictions between China on the one side and the US and its Asia-Pacific allies on the other will probably be growing. To substantiate this point, it is important to have a look at shifting naval balance in the Asia Pacific. Although Washington is trying to reinvigorate its regional partnerships and harbours ambitious plans to increase its presence in these waters, ample evidence suggests that the US potential has reached its maximum. Owing to budgetary constraints, a modest supply network and a necessity to disperse energies to directions other than Asia-Pacific, are just a few factors. Against this, PLANavy's capabilities are on the rise, given massive financial injections which resulted in China testing its aircraft carrier and upgrading it submarine fleet. Although still at an initial stage, but in due course of time, these processes can significantly alter regional strategic balance. Other examples include conflicting schemes and initiatives of economic regionalism, Sino-American contradictions relating to the US' missile-defence system in Asia-Pacific, and the like. Under these circumstances, for many states of the region, an uncomfortable prospect to

---

16 Soviet and Russian experts have traditionally paid very close attention to the bilateral vector of relations between USSR/Russia and India. The most recent assessment can be found in: Тезисы о российско-индийских отношениях: рабочая тетрадь № III, 2013 /Гл. ред. И.С.Иванов. – М.: Спецкнига, 2013. (Theses about Russo-Indian Relations. Working Paper № III, 2013 /Ed. by I.S.Ivanov. – M.: Spetskniga, 2013. (In Russian)) // http://russiancouncil.ru/common/upload/wp_russiaindia_313.pdf.

choose between Washington and Beijing is becoming very real.

The second trend is an increasing prominence of trans-national infrastructure projects, mainly in transport and energy sectors, are priorities of Asia-Pacific countries. It is exemplified by Master-Plan on ASEAN Connectivity, ASEAN Strategic Transport Plan, railways and motorways from China to Indo-China, the idea of the trilateral trans-Korean projects – the railway, the gas pipeline and the transmission lines from Russia to ROK via DPRK – which is still alive in spite of an awful state of inter-Korean relations. Needless to say in case implemented, this large-scale construction may make invaluable contribution to strengthening regional stability.

In sum, Asia-Pacific is currently facing a "bifurcation point" and the balance between the key trends influencing upon the future evolution of the region is very fragile. India can play a significant role in strengthening the cooperative paradigm of Asia-Pacific. The expected consequences are as follows:

First, this may have a positive influence upon regional stability. This is predetermined by the already mentioned India's economic potential combined with its independent foreign policy and non-alignment traditions. It should be stressed again that under the current trend towards the "globalization" of Asia-Pacific affairs, this stabilization will be possible by exploiting the potential of established global powers. This cohort includes India.

Second, economic cooperation between Asia-Pacific states will receive a strong impetus. In future, as bilateral free trade regimes and the project RCEP are developed, India factor will be increasingly felt in the Pacific.

At this juncture, of note are ASEAN's plans to use India's and China's contribution to finance infrastructure projects in Southeast Asia. Currently, the Association is elaborating on turning ASEAN infrastructure fund into Asia Infrastructure Fund.[17] For ASEAN, this may be helpful in moving towards ASEAN Economic Community given very high costs it evokes. But with regard to China, apprehensions exist that it might have plans to

---

17 ADB to tie up with India and China for ASEAN Infrastructure Fund. Business Standard. 21.01.2012. // http://www.business-standard.com/article/economy-policy/adb-to-tie-up-with-india-and-china-for-asean-infrastructure-fund-112012100078_1.html.

develop a kind of "China – Indo-China connectivity"[18] which will compete with ASEAN vision of regional connectivity. In India's case, this perception is absent.

Third, no matter how unexpected it seems, India factor may positively influence upon the situation in the South China Sea. Currently, the South China Sea issue is rapidly globalizing, and to place it in its previous China-ASEAN framework is impossible whether or not some parties may like it. Given this trend, it is not appropriate to use the potential of India, a country with entrenched peaceful traditions of foreign policy and non-alignment thinking, to have its say in order to make the situation in this maritime area more cooperative than it is now? Based on the assumption that India's strategic interests are best served by achieving greater regional stability and reckless steps are out of the question; this idea deserves attention.

All this appears to be in congruence with Asia-Pacific priorities of the Russian Federation. Currently, Russia, at least at the expert level, is exploring the niche of a great non-allied Pacific power whose interests is to prevent the aggravation of Sino-US geopolitical rivalry and maintain the stable regional milieu. The latter is seen as the key prerequisite for successful economic modernization of Russia's Siberia and Far East.[19] Also, infrastructure development is occupying one of the top priorities in Russia's Pacific objectives and in this context it is useful to recall the agenda of the APEC Summit-2012.[20] Last but not the least, Russia is developing a balanced and problem-solving approach to the South China Sea issue. This approach is premised on the assumption that Russia should dissociate itself from any developments that can provoke tensions and more actively implement projects which may lessen contradictions, strengthening energy security, develop alternative transportations routes, etc.[21] At this juncture, a

---

18 This point is elaborated in: Wade G. ASEAN Divides. // Regional Outlook. Southeast Asia 2011-2012. Ed.by Montesano M., Lee Poh Onn. – Singapore: ISEAS, 2011. P. 18-21.

19 For more details, see: Sino-American Rivalry in Asia: Conclusions for Russia. // Security Index. 2012. Vol. 18. N. 4(101). P. 45-62.

20 Sumsky V., Koldunova E., Kanaev E. Russia's Interests in the Context of Asia-Pacific Region Security and Development. Report. RIAC/RSC APEC/Ed.by I.S.Ivanov. – Moscow: Izdatelstvo Prospect, 2012. // http://russiancouncil.ru/en/inner/?id_4=684#top; APEC-2012 Priorities. // http://www.apec2012.ru/docs/about/priorities.html.

21 See, for instance: Kanaev E. Russia and the South China Sea Issue: in Search of a Problem-Solving Approach. IMEMO Comments. 15.11.2011. // http://www.imemo.ru/en/comments/151111_Kanaev.pdf; Kanaev E. The South China Sea Issue: a View from

scenario that has a positive influence upon the globalizing South China Sea issue will be exerted by concerted efforts of responsible regional powers, with India and Russia being among them doesn't seem to be unrealistic.

In sum, there is enough evidence for arguing that India has enough resources, political, economic and reputational, to play the role of an Asia-Pacific "stabilizer", non-aggressive, responsible, and strengthening cooperation and compromise thinking. The position that other Asia-Pacific states, including the Russian Federation may only welcome.

Conclusion

It has become a commonplace to argue that the centre of gravity in the global economy and politics is shifting to Asia-Pacific. If so, in the same direction are also moving unresolved global contradictions. Evidence to substantiate both points is in overabundance. In case the latter trend grows, which is a likely scenario; further polarization of Asia-Pacific seems imminent, which is the most upsetting for its countries and territories. Contrary to the Cold War era, this time their new "economic miracles" are very likely to be out of the question.

The situation is aggravated by a widening imbalance between Asia-Pacific development goals, mechanisms and institutions. At present, this process is just increasing its tempo, but with a lapse of time it will undermine the existing trends towards mutually beneficial cooperation and compromise thinking.

Under these circumstances, to give a fresh impetus to the cooperative evolutional paradigm of Asia-Pacific becomes a pressing necessity. It seems that India, an established and respectful global power whose significant economic potential is underpinned by independent foreign policy and entrenched non-alignment traditions, has good chances to achieve this goal. This will be appreciated by other Asia-Pacific nations for a very simple and obvious reason: it is exactly what most of them expect from New Delhi.

Russia. ASEAN – Russia: Foundations and Future Prospects/ ed. by Sumsky V., Hong M., Lugg A. – Singapore: ISEAS, 2012. – P. 97-109.

8

Indo-Pacific Region: Perspectives from Russia

Ekaterina Koldunova

> *"Nations come and go – why shouldn't regions?"*
>
> - Donald Emmerson[1]

Despite globalization tendencies, the contemporary world is far from being uniform. Moreover, the key drivers of world political changes seem to increasingly originate from regional transformations which produce new forms of cooperation, various regional integration patterns and also new types of contradictions and conflicting behaviour and yet unclear implications for regional-global nexus (Buzan and Weaver 2003, Nel, Nabers and Hanif 2012, Godehard and Nabers 2011).

For the past decade the world has been witnessing an emergence of new regional centres of power, some of them collectively defined as BRICS (Brazil-Russia-India-China-South Africa), and hence new regional and interregional constellations in the making. For instance a growing net of interactions, primarily in the economic sphere, and the rise of China made many experts claim that Northeast Asia and Southeast Asia are getting 'closer' together and potentially may merge in one regional entity or become much more interconnected than they used to be just several decades ago (Voskressenski 2010, Buzan and Weaver 2003). At the same

---

1 Emmersond, Donald (1984) Southeast Asia: What's in a Name? Journal of Southeast Asian Studies XV(I), March, 1984, p.20.

The paper is prepared with the support of Russian Foundation for Humanities (grant project № 12-03-00538a).

time the region-building intellectual exercise became increasingly popular among some, first and foremost, US policy makers and experts willing to use the spatial constructions for justifying or achieving certain political goals by governing regional transformations. Thus, the concepts of Greater Middle East or Greater Central Asia, however disputable they are, came into being (for debatable issues of these concepts see Roy 2005, Ottaway and Carothers 2004). The former related to the countries prone to preserving non-democratic regimes with the deficits of 'freedom, knowledge and women's empowerment' (Al-Hayat 2004). The letter urged Central Asian states and Afghanistan to 'drift' economically and politically towards South Asia, away from Russia and post-Soviet space (Boucher 2006; Starr 2005).

As the previous examples demonstrate the objective and subjective reasoning for defining new spatial construction often mingle not speaking of political, economic or security concerns. This seems to be the case for the new spatial concept of the Indo-Pacific region as well.

For quite a long time the Indo-Pacific area used to be more of a biogeographical or natural science notion rather than a political or strategic one. Indeed the confluence of Indian and Pacific oceans creates a unique and naturally interconnected area. Geo-economically and politically, however, for the past decade Russian academic community more actively discussed such concepts as Greater Eastern Asia or East Asian macro-region in the making (Voskressenski 2010).

Internationally, the studies of East Asian regionalism tended to indicate formal and, more importantly, informal mechanisms which were forging new macro-regional entity (Dent 2008, Hatch 2010). The drivers for this kind of regional transformation were multiple. The Japanese economic diplomacy and expanding region-wide production network contributed to a specific form of East Asian market-driven integration. ASEAN 'functional' expansion due to the mechanism of dialogue partnerships as well as ASEAN+3, ASEAN+6 and East Asian Summit mechanisms created the institutional framework for expanded regional cooperation. The economic rise of China and its intensively growing trade with Japan, South Korea, ASEAN member states, India and Russia became another key factor which made both regional and extra-regional actors think how to get accommodated to China's growth through regional mechanisms. Indian economic dynamism and Look East policy initiated in the 1990s made India yet another prominent economic and political actor in the regional processes.

From the late 1990s, Russia also undertook gradual efforts to get more actively involved in East Asian regional affairs at least at the institutional level. In 1996 it became ASEAN's dialogue partner, in 1997 – an APEC member and in 2010 joined East Asian summit. Russia's economic ties with the region at that time were based primarily on the cooperation in the energy sphere and Russian academic community was actively discussing the possibilities of using energy factor as an economic means of Russia's integration in Greater Eastern Asia (Voskressenski 2006, Torkunov 2007). The overall economic situation and modernization aims set for Russian regions of Siberia and the Far East in the first decade of this century made Russia more compatible with East Asian regional agenda for economic development than it used to be in the early 1990s (Sumsky 2011).

Thus, the geo-economic core of Greater East Asian macro-regional entity comprised China, Japan, South Korea, ASEAN member states with India, Australia, US, Russia being the actors also actively involved in the regional affairs. There were also noticeable efforts to match this new regional entity with the corresponding identity making. The idea of East Asian community, and its manifold interpretations (some based on the ideas of the Asia-Pacific regionalism and some on pan-Asianism), became an important reference point both for regional experts and policy makers like Malaysian ex-prime minister Mahathir Mohamad, Australian ex-prime minister Kevin Rudd, Japanese ex-prime minister Yukio Hatoyama and others (He, 2010).

The idea of the Indo-Pacific region emerged in the end of the first decade of this century seems to have different underpinnings. However, the important geo-economic explanations of this spatial construction may be the core considerations for defining this region lay in the strategic sphere, putting it more precisely – in the sphere of the control over the sea routes in the Indian and Pacific oceans amidst growing economic, political and strategic competition in this area and China's bid for maritime presence (Khurana 2007, Yoshihara 2013). Another important consideration for framing the Indo-Pacific area appears to be the significance of India, but also Australia and Japan for the US to counterbalance China at times when the United States cannot afford economically costly rising military presence in this part of the world but still need to support its rebalancing movement to the Asia-Pacific. In this case a gradual emergence of a self-sufficient intra-Asian security network within which American regional partners will be building a closer cooperation among themselves present a certain answer to American economic and security dilemmas (Cronin et al. 2013).

Moving beyond geostrategical considerations makes one pose a question what can make the Indo-Pacific region a viable construction? So far there have been two attempts to answer this question and integrate the notion of Indo-Pacific into the official international political discourse – one has come from Australian defence establishment and another one from Indonesian diplomacy.

In 2013, Australian Defence White Paper defined the Indo-Pacific area as an emerging macro-region situated at the crossroads of trade flows from the Middle East to South, Southeast and Northeast Asia. Australia, as the document stated, has an 'enduring strategic interest' in this region for security and economic reasons (Defence White Paper 2013: 13, 25). The strategic concerns originate from the necessity to secure the energy and trade routes in the region, while economic ones imply the need to reconcile the economic growth of China and India. Putting strategic concerns aside, this concept also seems like an Australia's attempt to play a more prominent role in the region or to show its unique regional stance (Medcalf 2012), a task which could have been much less possible under the macro-regional framework of East Asia or Greater Eastern Asia. Being geographically close to East Asia, Australia nevertheless can hardly constitute the core of this region. Not so long ago Australia's efforts to make its contribution to the process of regional identity shaping through Kevin Rudd's Asia-Pacific community project were not very successful, not least of all because it could diminish ASEAN's core role for regional institutional-building efforts for the benefit of larger regional actors.

One may find another, normative, vision of the Indo-Pacific region in the recent Indonesian proposal of the Indo-Pacific treaty. In May 2013, Indonesia suggested concluding the Indo-Pacific Treaty of Amity and Cooperation which should duplicate Treaty of Amity and Cooperation in Southeast Asia but in a broader regional scale (The Straits Times 2013). The idea came as a reaction to the aggravated tensions over disputed Spratly and Paracel Islands and growing internationalization of this problem. Indonesian proposal implied to remind all regional actors of the international legal norms which should first and foremost govern their behaviour in the regional disputes. According to Indonesian Minister of Foreign Affairs Marty Natalegawa, this treaty should have three key aims. The treaty will enhance mutual strategic trust in the region. It will help the regional players to manage territorial disputes and regional transformations in general. Looking beyond these aims one may add that should the parties involved conclude such a treaty it will put ASEAN in the centre of new regional construction of the Indo-Pacific.

Director for Program and Research at The Habibie Centre Dewi Fortuna, Anwar speaks in favour of ASEAN as a core mechanism for a wider regional cooperation. She argues that nowadays ASEAN represents the only dialogue platform acceptable to all regional players regardless of their status and interests[2]. The logic of this approach is to balance external players one by another and engage them as far as possible in various forms of regional cooperation which is beneficial for ASEAN Member States. The precedents of Australian and Japanese concepts of East Asian and the Asia-Pacific community demonstrate that ASEAN will hamper any idea which stresses the predominance of a certain regional power at the expense of the Association itself.

Looking at other reasons for singling out the Indo-Pacific region one should definitely not overlook the Indian factor. So far the geo-economic implications of India's rise seem to be less conceptualized from the academic point of view than that of China. However for India itself, obviously, the concept of the Indo-Pacific region may bring new benefits. At the current level of India's economic development the traditional geographical framework of South Asia is proving to be too narrow for India. The success of regional integration in South Asia has been quite limited so far. Small regional actors are not ready for a full-scale integration while Pakistan is a troublesome neighbor with looming large economic and security problems. Thus, the regional integration in South Asia does not add a multiplicative effect for India's economic rise and will inevitably push this state towards closer cooperation with East Asian/ Asia-Pacific partners. India's strategic partnerships with Japan, South Korea and Australia as well as strategic dialogue with Vietnam add a security dimension to India's ties with East Asia.

---

2 Russia-ASEAN Relations and East Asian Regional Dynamics (ASEAN Centre roundtable, MGIMO-University, Moscow, 15.05.2013).

However, India cannot be the only driving power for the Indo-Pacific region-building. The significant part of Southeast Asian and East Asian states' trade is still linked mainly to China, while the most important investment flows come to Southeast Asia mainly from the EU (17 per cent), Japan (11.7 per cent) and the USA (9.6 per cent) (ASEAN 2013). China is the number one ASEAN trading partner. In 2012, its share equaled to almost 13 per cent of the Association's total trade (for comparison India's share constituted 2.9 per cent) (ASEAN 2013a). In 2012, about 21 per cent of Japan's and about 18 per cent of Australia's import also were coming from China (World Trade Organization 2013, 2013a).

India's model of development differs from East Asian export-oriented model and so far India and East Asia does not have critically high complimentary interdependence. Besides it is likely that China will proceed with its strategy of building a stronger economic link with Southeast Asia. Recent Chinese economic proposals made by President Xi Jinping during his visit to Indonesia in October 2013 demonstrates China's wish to smoothen the South China Sea tensions by expanding economic cooperation with ASEAN. Taking into account American pivot to the Asia Pacific, China will definitely avoid any confrontation with the US at the global level, but will strive for domination at the regional level, first and foremost through economic means.

For Russia any strategic changes in East Asian/Asia Pacific region will be of critical importance since Russia is trying to expand its presence in this part of the world and promote the idea of inclusive regional security architecture instead of one built on bilateral security arrangements (Lavrov 2013, Chongkittavorn 2013). The attempts to proceed with the development of Siberia and the Far East will make Russia search for new forms of cooperation with East Asian partners while avoiding meddling in regional disputes and taking any sides in these disputes. Thus the idea of the Indo-Pacific region, in case it retains its strategic and geopolitical orientation, may not be conducive for Russia's regional economic and political agenda. However, Russia's strategic relations with China and India are more of global significance for Russia rather than of merely regional or macro-regional. Consequently it will not be in Russia's interests to get involved in the competition of macro-regional projects, the contours of which has just started to gleam ahead for the Indo-Pacific/East Asian/Asia-Pacific region.

Conclusions

The concept of the Indo-Pacific region does capture some important strategic changes in Asia. These changes include not only China's rise, but also other actors' rise, first and foremost India's. A growing strategic importance of Indian and Pacific oceans and the area of their confluence imply a necessity to secure trade flows and energy flows, which fuel regional economic growth. Strategic considerations of China, the US, India, Australia, ASEAN member states towards the Indian and Pacific oceans actually underpin the recent academic attempts to proceed with the conceptualization of the Indo-Pacific region.

However, this process of conceptualization also brings to the forefront some serious questions. Who will be the driving forces behind this new kind of regionalization? How such region-building powers as ASEAN, Japan and China will perceive this regional framework? How to accommodate players like Russia which has political and economic interests in the Asia Pacific and is trying to promote an inclusive idea of regional security architecture?

The concept of the Indo-Pacific region, at least some of its variations, seems to reproduce the classical geopolitical antagonism of sea power versus land power with all due consequences. The economic potential of this framework, if any, is still in its initial phase and may be easily overshadowed by military-security concerns if strategic understanding of the Indo-Pacific region will dominate over other, namely, normative, institutional and geo-economic visions.

As for now, the concept of the Indo-Pacific region creates much room for the debate. Though no one can deny the importance of strategic considerations for regionalization such considerations alone cannot make a region. Moreover a framework, which engages some players while leaving others outside, even implicitly, may not work well for this economically boosting but politically not very pacific region.

REFERENCES

Al-Hayat (2004) G8 Greater Middle East Partnership *Al-Hayat*, 13 February 2004.

ASEAN (2013) Top Ten ASEAN Trade Partner Countries/Regions, 2012, http://www.asean.org/images/2013/resources/statistics/external_trade/2013/table20.pdf(accessed January 2, 2014).

ASEAN (2013a) Top Ten Sources of Foreign Direct Investment Inflow to ASEAN, Cumulative Annual: 2009-2011, http://www.asean.org/images/2013/resources/statistics/Foreign%20Direct%20Investment%20Statistics_/Table%2027.pdf(accessed January 2, 2014).

Buzan Barry and Weaver Ole (2003) *Regions and Powers: The Structure of International Security*, Cambridge: Cambridge University Press.

Boucher Richard (2006) Richard A. Boucher, Assistant Secretary of State for South and Central Asian Affairs Statement to the House International Relations Committee Subcommittee on the Middle East and Central Asia *'U.S. Policy in Central Asia: Balancing Priorities (Part II)'* Washington, D.C., April 28, 2006 URL: http://commdocs.house.gov/committees/intlrel/hfa27230.000/hfa27230_0f.htm (accessed December 31, 2013).

ChongkittavornKavi (2013) China, Russia Respond to US Pivot to Asia, The Straits Times, 17.07.2013.

Cronin Patrick, Fontaine Richard, Hosford Zachary, MastroOriana Skylar, Ratner Ely and Sullivan Alexander (2013) *The Emerging Asia Power Web: The Rise of Bilateral Intra-Asian Security Ties*, Washington DC: Center for a New American Security.

Defence White Paper 2013 (2013), Australian Government, Department of Defence, URL: http://www.defence.gov.au/whitepaper2013/docs/WP_2013_web.pdf (accessed December 31, 2013)

Dent Christopher (2008) *East Asian Regionalism*, Abington: Routledge.

Godehardt Nadine and Nabers Dirk, eds. (2011) *Regional Powers and Regional Orders*, Abington: Routledge.

Hatch Walter (2010) *Asia's Flying Geese: How Regionalization Shapes Japan*

(Ithaca: Cornell University Press).

He Baogang (2004) 'East Asian Ideas of Regionalism: A Normative Critique' *Australian Journal of International Affairs*, Vol.58, Iss.1, pp.105-125.

KhuranaGurpreet (2007) 'Security of Sea Lines: Prospects for India-Japan Cooperation' *Strategic Analysis*, Vol.31, Iss.1, pp.139-153.

Lavrov Sergei (2013) 'Towards Peace, Stability And Sustainable Economic Development in the Asia Pacific Region', http://www.mid.ru/brp_4.nsf/0/D19A0531B380362544257BFB00259B9E (accessed January 2, 2014).

Medcalf Rory (2012) 'Indo-Pacific: What's in a Name?' The Interpreter, 16.08.2012,http://www.lowyinterpreter.org/post/2012/08/16/Indo-Pacific- Whate28099s-in-a-name.aspx(accessed January 2, 2014).

Nel Philip, Nabers Dirk and Hanif Melanie (2012) 'Introduction: Regional Powers and Global Redistribution' Global Society Vol.26, No.3, pp. 279-287.

Ottaway Marina and Carothers Thomas (2004) 'The Greater Middle East Initiative: Off to a False Start' *Carnegie Endowment for International Peace Policy Brief*, 29 March 2004, URL: http://carnegieendowment.org/files/Policybrief29.pdf (accessed December 31, 2013).

Roy Olivier (2005) The Predicament of 'Civil Society' in Central Asia and the 'Greater Middle East' *International Affairs* 81:5, pp. 1001-1012.

Starr Frederick (2005) *A 'Greater Central Asia Partnership' for Afghanistan and its Neighbors* (Washington, D.C.: Central Asia-Caucasus Institute and Silk Road Studies Program).

Sumsky Victor (2011) 'East Asian Summit and Russia: Long-awaited Invitation' Security Index, Vol.17, No.2 (95), pp. 63-68.

The Straits Times (2013) Indonesia FM seeks new Asia treaty to curb conflict. 17.05. 2013. http://www.straitstimes.com/breaking-news/se-asia/story/indonesia-fm-seeks-new-asia-treaty-curb-conflict-20130517 (accessed January 2, 2014).

Torkunov Anatoly, ed. (2007) *Emergeticheskiyeizmereniyamejdunarodny hotnosheniyibezopasnosti v VostochnoyAzii [Energy Dimension of*

International Relations and Security in East Asia], Moscow: MGIMO-University.

Yoshihara Toshi (2013) 'The US Navy's Indo-Pacific Challenge' *Journal of the Indian Ocean Region*, Vol.9, Iss.1, pp. 90-103.

World Trade Organization (2013) Country Profile: Japan, http://stat.wto.org/CountryProfile/WSDBCountryPFView.aspx?Language=E&Country=JP(accessed January 2, 2014).

World Trade Organization (2013a) Country Profile: Australia, http://stat.wto.org/CountryProfile/WSDBCountryPFView.aspx?Language=E&Country=AU(accessed January 2, 2014).

Voskressenski Alexei, ed. (2010) *Bol'shayaVostochnayaAziya: mirovayapolitikairegional'nyetransformazii [Greater Eastern Asia: World Politics and Regional Transformations]*,Moscow: MGIMO-University.

Voskressenski Alexei (2006) '*Bol'shayaVostoshnayaAziya: mirovayapolitika ienergeticheskayabezopasnost' [Greater Eastern Asia: World Politics and Energy Security]*, Moscow: Lenand.

9

Indo-Pacific Region: Perspectives from the US

Daniel P. Leaf

This chapter addresses the terminology choice of Indo-Pacific versus Asia-Pacific from a practical approach. The positive future of the world is in Asia or the Indo-Pacific. The responsibilities of the US Navy then and now were totally focused on avoiding conflict. They were not about conquest, they were not about competition, but for making the Asia-Pacific region a safer and a more stable place. This is the perspective of the US military in general, but also of the diplomats.

It will be useful to understand the historical view about the rebalance, or the pivot. It is also a common knowledge that the US never left the Asia–Pacific region. The first President to speak seriously and relatively comprehensively about Asia-Pacific was Millard Fillmore who served in 1850-1853, so it is not a return.

Further, it is important to emphasize that the message of the rebalance, the strategic shift, the focus on Asia–Pacific is both internal as also external and is lost in the discussion sometimes. So, when the President and the Secretaries of Defence and State felt compelled to say that their communities look up from Iraq and Afghanistan and look West or East, depending on one's perspective, because that's where the future is, not totally, not exclusively, but largely and importantly. So, the rebalance is not a return. There is great debate about whether or not it is rhetoric or it is real; it is in fact real. How does one make a rebalance real? Also, those who doubt the rebalance should take a look at the investments made by the US in the Asia–Pacific region. Some of its best and brightest Generals,

Admirals and Diplomats are being put on the job to a larger degree. That makes it real.

What is this rebalance about? Is it about containing China? No. If it is not then what is it about? First, the idea that it is either possible or in the US interest to contain China is ridiculous or the interdependence of our two nations and economies, the size and natural power, of China. It is incorrect to think that the US could or would want to contain China. So, if it is not about that, what it is about? The question is that the United States, after the initial statements, did not answer particularly well, did not say clearly what it is about. The US activities in the Asia–Pacific are about creating or sustaining a peaceful, stable and prosperous region. The US pronouncements on why the Asia–Pacific is important, is because of its economic interests, the five treaty allies, the many partnerships, the emerging economies and the emerging democracies; but the higher purpose really is for everybody in the region, a peaceful, stable and prosperous region. That is in the United States interest, and it is in everybody's interest. But for the US presence in the Asia–Pacific and influence over the past several decades, it is likely that South Korea, Japan and Taiwan would be nuclearized! Now, how would that be for China? Not so good. The US presence and the rebalance in the Asia-Pacific are good for China. It is argued that the rebalance does have a military component; the shifting of some forces is for legitimate role for military deterrence to prevent, deter, aggressive action by whomever, it is a balance; and it is a necessary force in the region. The US does not seek conflicts; it does not try to provoke conflict, and the US interaction in regards to the discussions recently in the South China Sea and with regard to the Diaoyu-Senkaku disagreement, the US is seeking a rule of law solution and avoiding open conflict. Nothing is worse for the world than conflict between US and China, which can have broader negative effects. No matter how small it begins or if it stays small, it would be tremendously destructive and there is a reason to have a deterrent presence that is carefully placed and properly postured to avoid conflict from blossoming.

There is more opportunity than risk in the region. It is a peaceful region and regional organisations are thriving even though they face challenges through varying reports on the state of ASEAN; but when one looks at what has been accomplished regionally and sub-regionally and what has not happened, Asia-Pacific or Indo-Pacific region is largely a peaceful region and can provide the foundation for the modern world. Because of more opportunity, Myanmar's (Burma) emergence into the modern world is a very positive trend. The development of governments and economies throughout the region is generally positive. The US has a role to play to enable it and support it, but not control it. However, the situation in North Korea is of concern. These are not ordinary times on the Peninsula.

The US rebalance is positive and this is a real effort that involves the entire US government and that there is a positive place for all of the regional players, such as India, China and others. The US has made its strategic choices and choices does not mean they are in control, neither the US nor the Chinese can control this vast and a very diverse region. But as China makes strategic choices about its core interests, and decides how it will approach conflict and resolution of disputes and what approach it will take to the competition, it is naturally the key determinant of the Asia-Pacific or the Indo-Pacific future. The US is not trying to contain China or prescribe those decisions, but the 'rebalance' does seek to influence them in a mutually agreeable outcome because peace, prosperity and security in the region for China and the US and the global community are inextricably intertwined.

10

India and the Indo-Pacific Region

Hemant Krishan Singh

This chapter first makes a few observations on definitions and India's return to the Indo-Pacific and then cover some security and economic architecture aspects. On definitions, this chapter only assumes the fact that this is new terminology and what used to be called the Asia-Pacific or East Asia is gradually becoming known as the Indo-Pacific. It is not a grand strategic design, it is just a terminology. The US has not used it in its policy pronouncements, instead used the Asia-Pacific which they will continue to do so. This chapter is not about the Indo-Pacific, which stretches from Africa to America or the entire Indian Ocean littoral; it is basically going to be a sub-set of that, which will be defined in due course.

It is important to know about the Indo-Pacific, because this is the region which will be the driver of global growth between now and 2050; it re-emerges and reoccupies its historic position at the centre of the world's economy. Inevitably, the region will become the strategic centre of gravity in global geopolitics. India made a good start and India convened the Asian Relations Conference even before it became independent; but India was largely absent from East Asia for decades and it is the economic reforms of 1991 and the Look East policy thereafter which started the process of India returning to the region, to the historic space which India had occupied civilizationally. It was however not till India joined the East Asia Summit (EAS) in 2005 that it finally returned to this region. It is important for India to remember who its friends were, who brought it there and who opposed its entry into that forum. To discuss about the Indo-Pacific, if India had not joined the EAS, similar to its position in the APEC, this would have been a very different kind of discourse. This led to various other events including the Japanese Prime Minister declaring India to be part of broader Asia, bringing about a confluence of the seas and hence the Indo-Pacific.

Maritime domain matters, C. Raja Mohan and Robert Kaplan, in their respective books have defined how important maritime issues are going to be as the economies of the region surge and new powers rise. India is trying to reposition itself from a continental power to a growing maritime power. Its geographical location gives it a unique role in shaping developments of the future. In the IOR-ARC and the Indo-Pacific, one is looking at different zones, different type of architectures and open regionalism.

It is an unsettled region; there is an unprecedented period of historic transformations led by the ongoing economic interdependence and overlapping interests of regional and resident powers. There will be changes in power transitions within countries in the next two years as well. There are four major security concerns in the region – North Korea, East China Sea, South China Sea and the breakdown of ASEAN cohesion and these point towards the danger of strategic destabilization. To achieve its economic potential, Asia has a big challenge in creating regional institutions that address insecurity, reduce prospects for irrational conflict and promote collective action. Freedom of maritime commons is a critical necessity in this regard.

India on its part needs to be very clear about its goals to avoid the pitfalls of miscalculation and advance benefits from the Indo-Pacific. The first step in this direction would be to understand the implications of China's rise and craft an appropriate response. India must see China is a self-confident, assertive country today, reshaping the international order to serve its interests in the future. It does not endorse any multilateral regional architecture that it does not dominate including the EAS. It is no longer hiding its strengths and biding time. President Xi Jinping has announced his dream of a strong nation and a strong military by 2049. The military rise of China has been faster than its economic rise, which it is clear from the 11.8 per cent growth in its defence spending over the last 12 years.

China is also pursuing its 'core interests' based on its foreign policy on which there can be no compromise. To use the words of Xi Jinping, "will not abandon and absolutely cannot sacrifice", and his subsequent remarks in a press conference that resolving the India-China boundary issue won't be easy. Then there is the escalation of tensions between China and Japan which is partly a response to the US pivot; it is also meant to discourage countries from drawing strength from the US presence. The fundamental problem is whether Japan can accept China's expanding strength and what does it mean?

Redefining China's ties with the US as between two equal great powers is another element of the Chinese discourse. Asia-Pacific issues should be discussed and dealt with by the countries of the region themselves; there is another Chinese way of looking at things. It is clear that China is seeking a hierarchical redistribution of power in Asia and not multi-polarity, and India is yet to figure in this calculus. There are growing convergences between India and many other actors in the region, including the US, Japan, Indonesia; several ASEAN countries, desire for an Indo-Pacific architecture and common concern about the unresolved disputes and growing asymmetries with China.

By comparing Indian and US statements regarding the Indo-Pacific region, one will almost find no difference in what is being said. For example, India uses the following: 'balanced, inclusive, transparent, open architecture; ASEAN centrality, greater maritime security cooperation with ASEAN; freedom of navigation; and peaceful settlement of disputes under international law'. The US side uses similar words: 'strengthening regional institutions, stable security environment, economic openness, and peaceful resolution of disputes consistent with international law'. Ash Carter, the Deputy Defence Secretary, accurately defined the 'rebalancing' by saying that the rebalance mostly is a political and economic concept, and not a military one. The military rebalance will gradually come and there will be funding available for it. It will gain momentum but it is a long-term proposition. This is a huge accretion of the US power or addition to what is already in the region in the immediate future. The other element of US rebalancing is that now they view Northeast Asia, Southeast Asia and the linkages with India as one theatre and that is a new development. For India, American position is very clear; they accept India's rise and firmly support it. The US and Indian interest converge peacefully in the Asia-Pacific.

Finally, will the American pivot survive or not. Yes, it will because there is a clear indication that Obama will continue to attend the EAS summits year after year as part of his commitment to make this a premier political and security forum. India has no issues with the US security footprint covering East, and Southeast Asia; India also has no problems with the US recognition of India's role in maritime security and the importance of India's Look East policy. The increasing US engagement with ASEAN is similar to what India itself has been trying to do. Indonesia too is of utmost importance and there is very strong congruence of interests between India and Indonesia. It pursues a dynamic equilibrium, in which all EAS players are enmeshed in the overlapping institutions like EAS, ADMM, ARF and there is no single predominant power. Building new trust and norms holding China to the declaration on Code of Conduct of 2002 converting this into a code of conduct, and if one does not succeed in that, then building new binding principles based on the Treaty of Amity and Cooperation and the Bali Principles will be the road ahead.

To conclude, on the security side, India-ASEAN agree to no 'US-China rivalry' and 'no US-China condominium of power'. The US endorsement of ASEAN and its role in regional stability and EAS based security architecture, is similar to India's position. China's reluctance to advance EAS beyond a talking shop on soft security issues is quite evident. India could be making a strategic mistake to assume that what happens in the East and South China Seas will not impact it. It is important to note that, it will impact on its capacity to claim that it wants a balanced inclusive architecture, which it is pushing. If India pushes all these disputes down the road, there is a danger of confronting an even more uncompromising China in the future, and that is why ASEAN is struggling to convert DOC into a COC. Japan is a natural partner for India, and any hold back on that will cost India dear. A deeper and broader Indian partnership in the Indo-Pacific will make China more amenable to accommodate India's regional aspirations.

As far as economic challenges are concerned, there are four things happening. First, region's weight in the global economy will grow exponentially; second, the East Asian economic integration process will accelerate rapidly. India's largest economic opportunity lies in this region; trade with ASEAN jumped 41 per cent to almost US$ 80 billion. China has gone down in terms of bilateral trade. Trade liberalization is taking place outside the WTO, so both RCEP and TPP will confront India in the immediate future. Neither of these will be easy for India to join if it does not commit to further reforms. Finally, enhancing physical connectivity through Myanmar, taking advantage of services and trade with ASEAN, participation in the world's most advanced production networks, these have to be foremost priorities for India. India must focus on Myanmar connectivity issues and also improve the gateway infrastructure along India's eastern seaboard. It must start utilizing the Andaman & Nicobar Islands and not leave them as an unproductive backwater. On economic integration, RCEP and TPP are different concepts. The problem for India is that both are high standard and WTO+ at the end. So, either India joins the process and starts making these rules which will define the working of global markets in the future, or India will just have to sit aside and accept the fait accompli at the end. India will find difficulties and therefore the key will be more domestic reforms, more deregulation, more tariff liberalization, improved logistics infrastructure, and finally strengthening its own ICT networks to be able to be part of supply chains.

India cannot take its role in shaping East Asian security architecture and economic integration for granted. It really needs to shake off the inertia inherent in its references to benign power and display greater commitment. India must bolster its strategic autonomy by building partnerships that will enhance its power and influence. The Look East policy is largely an unfulfilled potential at the moment; it is losing ground on delivery and must address the issues of capacity as well as will. Given India's geographic location, it will be called upon to provide levels of regional public goods especially in security, and it must take decisions on that. Finally, India's greatest strength is its democratic pluralism; Japan pursues values-based diplomacy; Indonesia anchors the Bali democracy forum; but India habitually diminishes the power of its democratic example and this needs to be taken seriously by India.

11

Prospects for Economic Integration

Zhu Cuiping

This chapter analyses the Indo-Pacific region and the possibility and prospects for economic integration. The chapter is divided into four parts: first, necessity and concept of Indo-Pacific regional integration; second, economic growth in Indian Ocean region; third, economic interdependence between Indian Ocean region and Pacific region; and lastly the conclusion and prospects for economic integration.

It is a well known fact that evolution of globalization had made the world transform from mutually assured destruction to mutual economic dependence (MED) giving importance to economic integration. However, the economy will keep on struggling in the middle of crisis and the chance of slowing down still exists. While examining the integration of Indian and Pacific Oceans, it is obvious that there are a number of internal and external factors, but economic relation between nations is the primary factor for regional integration, because only from the perspective of economic integration can this be realized and thus, succeed to achieve a win-win purpose. But the question arises as to how these two Oceans can be combined. There are 38 countries alongside the Indian Ocean and the dilemma occurs as to how to extend to the Pacific. This chapter analyses these questions from the economic point of view. The Indo-Pacific construction itself is contested. Firstly, the Indian Ocean-Pacific region, including both the Indian Ocean and Pacific Ocean, are vast spaces of ocean. Secondly, the idea may be is to extend the West Pacific Ocean to the West Indian Ocean along the eastern coast of Africa. The regions start from the eastern edge of Bay of Bengal, encompassing India, Southeast Asia, China, Japan and the Korean Peninsula.

Most importantly then, how can the Indo-Pacific region be defined? First, that can be done by analysing the economic growth of Indian Ocean region. According to World Bank 2011 statistics, the economic growth rate of the region is 2.3 per cent, out of which the economic growth rate of the developed countries amounts to only 1.53 per cent, and that of the developing countries is 6.39 per cent, though the rates of economic growth in Indian Ocean economies has slowed down. But it has a stronger growth rate compared to the other regions; for instance the economic growth rate in South Asia is 6.48 per cent and Middle East together with South Africa is 5.19 per cent. If one looks at Gross Domestic Product of the Indian Ocean rim, South Asia, Southeast Asia, Africa and Australia exhibited an increase in the GDP, which is obvious. Moreover, India's GDP growth presents a good pattern, except for 2008 and for 2011 and 2012. If one looks at the trade volume between the five regions in Indo-Asian region in 2007, only Southeast Asia is seen as having a high rate but the other countries experienced low growth. If one examines the trade volume between middle powers and the 38 other countries in the Indian Ocean region in 2011, one finds that a number of countries which are the main stakeholders contributed a lot in the Indian Ocean region.

Third, to analyze economic interdependence between Indian Ocean region and the Pacific Ocean, one can find that interdependence from the Indian Ocean to the Pacific Ocean is higher than the Pacific Ocean to the Indian Ocean and is experiencing a trend towards a rise. If one analyses the East Indian Ocean and West Indian Ocean, one finds that interdependence for the East Indian Ocean to West Pacific is higher than the East Indian Ocean to the West Indian Ocean, and also from the East Indian Ocean to the East Pacific Ocean. To look at West Indian Ocean interdependence from West India to West Pacific is also higher than West India to East India, or from West India to East Pacific. So, from the perspective of economic integration, the West Pacific region and the East Indian Ocean can be said to be better than others.

As a country of the Pacific region, China's exports to Indian Ocean region kept rising in these years. Among the 12 countries in the Indian Ocean, one finds that India is rising rapidly. Also, China's imports from the Indian Ocean region are rising. There can also be another method to analyse trade intensity, which can also be used to express the dependency. If the figure is greater than one, it means larger reliance on the partner than expected. Accordingly, the trade intensity of the real economies to China is greater than one, which means, a greater degree of dependency, not to mention the fact that the trade intensity of China to the real economies has also been on a rise. Another method to look at the trade potential is to calculate trade complimentary index. By this calculation, one can find that the TCI of the real economies to China is rising, and also that the TCI of China to the real economies shows a good trend. Further, China-India foreign trade dependence showcases a highly positive trend.

Therefore, to conclude, firstly, the world economic growth rate seems to have slowed down, but economic dependence among countries has stayed intact, which means countries can come together in the future to mutually integrate. Secondly, the economic growth rate of the Indian Ocean region and the Pacific region is the greatest in the overall global economic growth. The third, with increasing economic and trade links, there is greater economic integration potential for the Indo-Pacific region. Fourth, while integrating two regions into one, the importance of India is self evident. But undoubtedly, keeping in mind the relations between major countries, especially Sino-India ties to promote economic integration of these two regions, along with the world, the centre of gravity can shift to Indo-Pacific. Lastly, if the major powers in the Indian Ocean region and Pacific region can make an effort to formulate a common idea and make efforts to utilize such an opportunity fully, it will not only benefit the Indo-Pacific integration but can also promote the overall peace and prosperity of Asia and the rest of the world, which is our ultimate common goal.

12

Indo-Pacific Region: Perspectives from Indian Ocean

Noellie Alexander

This chapter offer the Seychelles perspective of a small island developing state, a group of 150 dots somewhere in the Indian Ocean. Being small, its resources, except for its large seas are very limited. Indeed its human resources capacity is especially limited that relies on regional technical assistance in almost all sectors. In the Indian Ocean region, India is a key strategic player and partner in both economic and social development. India's population size and strategic location gives it a prominent voice in international affairs and its growing economic strength, military prowess, and scientific and technical capacity give it added weight, especially for Seychelles.

From a Seychelles perspective, cooperation with India and the Indian Ocean is centred through the provision of ITEC training, equipment and joint military exercises due to the scourge of piracy. Besides military assistance, India also offers training for civilians, technical assistance and scholarships. These are mainly in the areas of health, culture, information technology, trade, investment and civil aviation. Seychelles is also historically linked to India and it would be mutually beneficial to strengthen the future collaboration and linkages. From a general and global perspective, it is also worth mentioning that the Indo-Pacific region has become well known in the global financial arena as the much maligned global economic meltdown has had minimal impact on the region unlike the western hemisphere and in particular the European Union. The continued economic growth of

China in the wake of the crisis has propelled the region and others to Look East. This has had a magnetic effect and created an economic powerhouse in this region for business and trade activities to remedy the stifled growth and other economic setbacks. The Indian Ocean countries like Seychelles see this as an opportunity within its configuration, the pivoting centre which generates and facilitates trade and business. It must also be borne in mind that Africa, known for its abundance of natural resources, is currently regarded as the bread basket of the 21st century. All this helps to further fuel growth and most importantly sustainable development of this region. Thus, countries of the Indian Ocean region can only manifest in terms of improved connectivity and trade openings for their own specific socio-economic growth. The identity, therefore, will be consolidated rather than substituted as capacity building and infrastructural development, steps to respond to the needs of the trade and growth dimension around the concept under discussion. At a glance one can visualise infrastructural development such as better sea ports, airports, ICT development, roads and railway expansions.

The Integration Concept, already a buzzword, and work in progress globally, will be further improved in the region as connectivity gives impetus to greater interaction of people, institutions, movement of goods and services, and exchanges of ideas. Easy access, freedom of choices, and a certain degree of equilibrium to wealth distribution can be ascertained. Within this matrix there are more plusses than minuses. The recognition of the need to secure sustainable growth and economic development can in this connected age be better achieved and guaranteed in such a grouping using mutual synergies from close proximity and spring-board for other strengths such as improving and conserving the environment, political stability, cross-border trade, attracting foreign direct investment and capacity building. This can be achieved through harmonisation and establishment of a cohesive common ground. The political will to execute a commonly reached decision is important. The evolution of the concept of the Indo-Pacific will of course depend on the collective vision of member states including participation in decision making, good governance, observance of the rule of law, accountability and transparency, respect for individual government institutions within the configuration using the right balance approach for a win-win situation. Peace and stability within the Indo-Pacific concept can be achieved and can be upheld.

In conclusion, the domestication of the concept of the Indo-Pacific in all its dimensions must be owned by all member States for it to achieve fruition. The issue of sovereignty needs to be addressed and perhaps redefined in the context of the globalised sense. One has to take cognisance of the evolving realities of integration in its totality. The onus will rest on the respective leaders to spearhead the concept with a global mindset and to bring the virtues of regional unity of purpose to their individual member states; it is a question of looking at the bigger picture and considering the realism of the 21st century.

13

Indo-Pacific Region: Perspectives from Indian Ocean

M. R. Khan

In the map of the Indian Ocean one can see two prominent channels made from it, Red Sea and the Persian Gulf. These two channels have been the East-West communication channels since the dawn of history. Red Sea had the advantage that the distance to the head of the Red Sea from Europe was much shorter but the channel itself was difficult to navigate, the winds were poor, the ports were not developed, whereas Persian Gulf had the advantage that its ports were developed though the distance to the head of the Persian Gulf was much longer from Europe. But its ports were developed, the waters were imminently navigable, well charted and the winds were good. So, it has been the Persian Gulf which has been the prominent East-West channel. Besides the location of the region on the crossroads of three continents makes it a vital region and the empires of the past, irrespective of the period, this was always a contested region.

The emergence of the great Persian Empire and its extension into Asia Minor brought it face-to-face with Greece, and resulted in the Greeko-Persian wars. After Persia failed to subjugate Greece, it continued to control its Asian empire, and became a contested region between Romans and Persians. The region is also rich in history; four of the great civilisations were around the waters of the Persian Gulf, and the Red Sea, i.e. Egyptian, Mesopotamian, Persian and India was adjacent to it. When the cable came, it came through the Persian Gulf, when the air routes came those came over this, and it was part of the Silk Route. So, all in all this has been a vital region.

But, there is no denying the fact that today much of its importance is because of its enormous hydrocarbon reserves; Saudi Arabia has 266 billion barrels, Kuwait 98 billion barrels, UAE at 100 billion barrels, Iraq at 180 billion barrels, and Iran at 150 billion barrels. These enormous hydrocarbon reserves are the mainstay of the Gulf. Gulf also has about 13 million expatriates, 6 million of them from India, which remit about US$ 100 billion to poorer countries like Philippines, Pakistan, India and Bangladesh. Besides, Gulf states have accumulated around US$ 3 trillion in oil surpluses, which have been invested in Europe and United States. Gulf is now the 11th largest market; it imports about US$ 400 billion. So, the region is extremely important in the present context.

The Gulf region's links with Asia-Pacific were a bit hazy in the early part of history. Under three Kingdoms, China had sent emissaries, during the Han dynasty, later under Tsun dynasty, etc., to the Gulf region, but the real firm links were established around the 8th century when Caliph Mansoor established Baghdad. There were a number of ships leaving the Gulf ports– Kish, Rishar, Basra, Suhar, Muscat, Hormuz, Bandar Abbas, laden with goods unloading some of their goods in India, crossing Malacca, touching Indonesia, Malaysia, setting course for Canton and bringing back goods from China, Indonesia, India, returning to the Gulf and from there going to Europe.

China's trade with the Gulf continued for about 300-400 years. With the coming of the colonial powers, the Chinese trade began to decline. The first to appear in the region were the Portuguese; Bartholomew rounded the Cape around 1496 and Vasco da Gama came in 1498. Portuguese were the first to realise the importance of the Indian Ocean and General Albuquerque, wrote to the King of Portugal that Indian Ocean had certain choke points and whoever controlled these choke points would control the Indian Ocean and whoever controlled the Indian Ocean would control the world trade. Further, he noted that he would emulate Alexander the Great in his penetration to Ganges, and wrote to the King of Portugal asking for reinforcements so that he could control these choke points. They finally controlled Bab al Mandab, Hormuz, Malaccas and Trincomalee. Portuguese lasted about 150 years and by the 17th century it was the Dutch who were the dominant powers in the Gulf region. Later in the 17th century, British were virtually everywhere and they wrested control of all these chokepoints from the Portuguese, and some by war and some by political manoeuvring.

But the turning point in the history was in 1798 when an agreement between Imam of Muscat and the British was reached. Apparently this was to stop Napoleon's advance into India; but in reality it gave control of one principality after the other in the Gulf region and it was Pax Britannica from the 19th century onwards. Britain was not the only country, Ottomans were in Housa Coast, Kuwait and in Iraq, but without doubt it was Pax Britannica from the beginning of 19th century. The British did not relinquish this control till 1969 and that was because the empire was liquidated, the financial conditions had deteriorated and they decided to leave. At the time when the British left, Gulf was relatively a tranquil place and the Americans did not move in.

Between the wars, nobody had realised the potential of the Gulf oil at all. It was not considered as strategically important but it was only after the World War II that Gulf was considered important because it provided the only access to Central Asia and much of the supplies to Russia away from the Luftwaf were routed through the Gulf. That is why, Iran was occupied by two colonial powers, a reflection of which is seen today in Iran's distaste for any colonial power. In fact, Iran is the only country which has in its constitution that Iran will not give access to resources to any hegemonic power in the world. So, it was only after the World War II that this was realised.

The US did not import much of the oil; they were self sufficient in 1969. Though they considered it is as an important strategic region, but they could not move in despite the talk of vacuum in the Indian Ocean. The US could not intervene because of its preoccupation with Vietnam War; and they lacked resources for it. In 1972, to quote an anecdote, when Nixon visited Iran, and during a dinner he leaned over to Razashah Pehlvi and asked him to look after American interest. Razashah responded by saying that he would do, provided the US supply him enough arms. This started the biggest arms build up in the history of Gulf. From 1971 to 1973, US$ 20 billion worth of arms were imported by Iran and this region was managed in the so called twin pillar policy till 1979. But between 1980 and 1989 there were four events which are worth mentioning since they changed the complete strategic picture in the Gulf. First the Iranian revolution; second Afghanistan's invasion by Russia; third South Yemen invading North Yemen; and fourth preponderance of the Soviet Navy, the Gorshkov era in the Indian Ocean. The US suddenly realized that this strategic region needs to be looked carefully.

Under the Carter doctrine, a statement by President Carter in the State of the Union Address of 1980 January noted that the Persian Gulf was a region of vital importance to the United States and any attempt to take control of the region would be resisted by all means including force. Americans did not have the wherewithal and they did not have the power to do that. The lease of Diego Garcia was concluded, in Djibouti they had a base, followed by the Masera base and they started talking to the Gulf countries. It was Central Command which really started American footprint in the region and the Central Command in 1980-81 was under Florida Base Command. It was decided to have around 150,000 troops which were of course on call and since then the American footprint in the Gulf has increased continuously. This process continued after the First and the Second Gulf War.

There was another turning point in the Gulf. Throughout the colonial period, all connections to the Pacific Ocean from Indian Oceans were controlled by the colonial powers, and the British Navy. It was only after the World War II, in 1950s, Japan started industrializing and the Gulf connection became open. Japan became the biggest importer of oil from the Gulf region. Then came the rise of South Korea and Taiwan and the Gulf oil traffic increased towards East Asia, but it was the rise of China which changed the picture because China till about mid-1990s was self sufficient in oil but from the mid-1990s onwards it started importing oil and mainly from the Gulf. Today, China is the biggest importer of oil from the Gulf region amounting to about 3 million barrels oil annually. That also coincided with India's rise; India imports about 2.5 million barrels of oil from the Gulf region. Japan has now overtaken China because many of their nuclear plants have been closed down.

This is the biggest shift witnessed in geopolitical terms today and the trade of Gulf-East Asia has overtaken Europe. Though EU is still the second largest trading partner, but in terms of import of oil, EU is also importing oil from Africa as well as Russia and limited oil is coming from the Gulf. Yet, EU is the only trading partner which has a positive balance of trade with GCC, the reason being insatiable appetite of Arabs for luxury goods. Today, EU is the second largest partner for the Gulf region; Japan US$ 161 billion, EU US$ 156 billion, China US$ 150 billion, India US$ 148 billion, South Korea US$ 120 billion, Taiwan US$ 60 billion. If one looks at these figures, out of US$ 1 trillion worth of trade, nearly 70 per cent is from

East Asia, Pacific and India. India, next to EU, is the largest exporter to the Gulf region at about US$ 45 billion. But if one looks at the Gulf and the landed cost of goods in Gulf from India, one can see that the potential is enormous; it could increase to enormous amount because the landed cost of goods from India is minimum.

There is a talk of Strategic Partnership between Saudi Arabia and China. Chinese President Hu Jintao visited Saudi Arabia twice between 2008 and 2010. Premier Wen Jiabao followed it in 2011; Saudi Arabia and China even signed an agreement for nuclear cooperation. Saudi Arabia intends to set up 16 nuclear plants. Therefore, it is not only talk of trade but also about Strategic Partnership. Similarly, UAE has signed for four nuclear plants with South Korea at a cost of US$ 20 billion.

To conclude, today Gulf has become a battleground among Russia, China and United States. United States professed aims in the Gulf are (i) access to oil; (ii) its availability at market prices; (iii) security of Israel; (iv) war on terror; and (v) non-proliferation. But China and Russia are convinced that these aims are only for public consumption and United States considers this region as a vital region. Its pivot to Asia will be only partly true because the control of this region gives United States critical leverage in world affairs. So, it has much more than oil and the United States is unlikely to leave the region. This is the strategic picture and this explains why Russia and China were compelled to involve in this region that they would not allow the fall of Bashar-Al-Assad's government. They also believe that if the US succeeds in Syria, probably same game could be repeated in Central Asia where many authoritarian regimes are pro-Chinese and pro-Russian.

14

The Indo-Pacific Region: A European Perspective

Joachim Krause

In Europe, the term "Indo-Pacific region" is not commonly used. The European Union prefers to use established terms such as ASEAN (Association of South East Asian Nations) or South Asian Association for Regional Cooperation (SAARC). Informal terms such as "Asia-Pacific" or even "Indo-Pacific region" are treated with great reluctance. In official EU-documents they do not appear. In public and scholarly debates, the term "Asia-Pacific" (encompassing North East Asia, South East Asia, and the larger Pacific area) is, however, used quite often. The term "Indian Ocean Region (IOR)" is also in use, but mainly in connection with India only. In contrast, other areas, which are considered to be treated as a whole, are East Africa as well as the Gulf area. However, they are treated as separate regional entities. Yet, in public and scholarly debates in Europe, one will find hardly any source which uses the term "Indo-Pacific region."

The term "Indo-Pacific region" originates from the scholarly disciplines of maritime biology, ichthyology and other maritime sciences and usually circumscribes a maritime area, comprising the tropical waters of the Indian Ocean, the western and central Pacific Ocean, and the seas connecting the two in the general area of Indonesia.[1] The term has only been recently used in a few publications to describe an area of strategic interest.[2] So far, this concept has only a heuristic value, i.e. it is a concept

---

1 G. Helfman, B. Collette, and D. Facey, *The Diversity of Fishes* (London: Blackwell Publishing, 1997) pp. 274 – 276.

2 The first mentioning was by Gurpreet S. Khurana, "Security of Sea Lines: Prospects for India-Japan Cooperation", *Strategic Analysis*, Volume 31, No. 1 (2007) pp.139 – 153.

that needs to prove that it is needed. From a European perspective, such a concept will be used the very moment the states in this area use the term themselves in a regular way in order to describe their state of affairs.

Furthermore, one might ask oneself whether the concept "Indo-Pacific region" makes sense from a European perspective. It surely would be applicable in case there are strategic and political developments that would suggest conceiving of that area as an entity that is shaped by common economic and societal bonds (such as strong intraregional trade, tourism and mobility) as well as common political institutions. However, these conditions are not given so far. Intraregional trade is growing, but the strongest trade bonds are still with Europe and the US. The states of the region are making progress in developing regional identities and in discovering that there is value in intra-regional political approaches. So far, this can only be observed in a few countries and it is surely not a widespread common phenomenon.

However, from a European perspective, it might be reasonable to use the concept of the Indo-Pacific, because this space – encompassing various regions, such as East Asia, Southeast Asia, the Western Pacific area, South Asia, Australia, the Indian Ocean, East Africa, & the Horn of Africa, the Arab Peninsula as well as the Persian Gulf – is already characterized by a high degree of "strategic interaction". In other words: what happens in one region of this space has implications for other regions and *vice versa*. The growing demand of China and India for food, raw materials, petroleum and for natural gas, for instance, has implications for events in the Middle East and in the Persian Gulf as well as for Sub-Saharan Africa. Regional actors in the Middle East, East Africa or in South Asia are increasingly using the emerging Indo-Chinese rivalry as a means to find support for their causes as well as for balancing off Western influence. Additionally, one can find examples of cooperation within the Indo-Pacific space to manage trans-boundary problems, such as piracy.

Hence, it seems to be prudent for Europeans to look at the Indo-Pacific region (or space) as an area of strategic interaction, which might – in the mid-term – become an area of strategic relevance or a region of strategic concern. From this viewpoint, however, the concept of "Indo-Pacific region" makes only sense if it also covers – beyond East Asia, Southeast Asia, the Western Pacific, Australia, South Asia and the Indian Ocean – sub-Saharan Africa (at least the East African coastal areas of the

Indian Ocean) as well as the Arab Peninsula and the Gulf-Region. During the coming years, there will most likely be a shift in perception in Europe, according to which Europeans will have to conceive of this region as something that forms some kind of strategic unity. At least today there is a growing awareness in Europe that the whole Indo-Pacific area is subject to a dynamic development although many uncertainties are involved.

Europeans as Stakeholders

European governments as well as the institutions of the European Union consider themselves to be major stakeholders in both the Asia Pacific as well as the Indian Ocean area. This surely does not imply any repetition of colonial ambitions. Modern Europe has gone through a process of foreign policy pacification which is quite profound. There is a new sense within Europe to address international challenges, and this goes along with a preference for diplomacy and soft means, something Europeans call a civil-power approach.[3]

The main factor that makes Europe a major stakeholder in the Indo-Pacific region is the high degree of interdependence due to dense trade relations. Among the 20 largest trading partners of the EU, 11 are from the Indo-Pacific area. One of them (the Peoples' Republic of China) is the second largest trading partner of the EU (after the US). Japan is the 7th largest, India ranks as number 8, South Korea as number 10 and included in this list are also Saudi Arabia, South Africa, Singapore, Australia, the United Arab Emirates, Hong Kong and Taiwan. Almost 40 per cent of European Union trade is carried out with states from the Indo-Pacific region.[4]

---

3 The concept was originally devised by Francois Duchêne, "Europe's Role in World Peace," in: *Europe Tomorrow. Sixteen Nations Look ahead*, ed. by R. Mayne (London: Collins Publishers, 1972), p. 32 – 47; see also Mario Teló, *Europe a Civilian Power. European Union, Global Governance, World Order* (London: Palgrave, 2006); Charlotte Bretherton and John Vogler, *The European Union as a Global Actor* (London: Routledge 2002), Jan Orbie, "Review Essay: Civilian Power Europe – Review of the Original and Current Debates," *Conflict and Cooperation – Journal of the Nordic International Studies Association*, Vol. 41, no. 1 (2006), p. 123 – 128; Hanns W. Maull, "Civilian Power: The Concept and its Relevance for Security Issues," in: *Mapping the Unknown - Towards a New World Order*, ed. by L. Babic and B. Huldt (Stockholm: Swedish Institute for International Affairs, 1993), p. 115 – 131; for a critical assessment see Hedley Bull, "Civilian Power Europe – A Contradiction in Terms?" *Journal of Common Market Studies*, Vol. 21, no. 2 (1982), p. 149-170.

4 See EU Commission, DG Trade, *EU Bilateral Trade and Trade with the World*. Briefing

A similar picture can be found when looking at German foreign trade partners, which is in principle strongly focussed on Europe: Yet, among the 40 largest trading partners are China (rank 3), Japan (rank 14), South Korea (rank 22), India (rank 24), South Africa (rank 27), Australia (rank 30), Taiwan (rank 31), Singapore, (rank 32), the United Arab Emirates (rank 34) Malaysia (rank 35), Saudi Arabia (rank 36), Thailand (rank 39) and Hong Kong (rank 40). By the same token, the EU is the most important (or second most important) trading partner for most economies from the region. For many of them, the relative importance of the European Union as a trading partner is much higher than their relevance for the EU. They are more often closely connected with the EU through trade than with regional neighbours. However, this trend is changing since trade relations within the Indo-Pacific region are growing fast.

In addition, Foreign Direct Investment (FDI) of European sources in the Indo-Pacific region had grown considerably before 2008. The crisis that began in 2008 has left its mark, but FDI is going to catch up again, although the levels of 2007 and 2008 have not been reached so far. The European Union is currently the largest source of Foreign Direct Investment in the world (more than US$ 550 billion dollars in 2011), of which more than 15 per cent go to the Indo-Pacific region. While China (including Hong Kong) continues to be the largest recipient of FDI, the states of South Asia are catching up, in particular India. For India, the EU has been the most important source of FDI inflow. Again, these figures demonstrate that there is a growing degree of interdependence between the regions. Also, FDI by Japan, India, China, Hong Kong, Singapore, Malaysia, Saudi Arabia and others in the EU are growing as well.

As a corollary to this high degree of economic interdependence in the trade and FDI area, the security of the transport routes between the EU and the Indo-Pacific region is of paramount importance.[5] Most trade takes place by way of ship traffic; hence the security of international sea routes is a topic that is increasingly being focused upon in Europe and where European interests and those of the states of the Indo-Pacific region coincide. The sheer number of maritime choke points is somewhat

---

Paper issued Brussels 23 April 2013, http://trade.ec.europa.eu/doclib/docs/2006/september/tradoc_113366.pdf.

5   Jean Paul Rodrigue, "Straits, Passages and Choke Points", *Cahiers de Géographie du Quebec*, Vol. 48, no. 135 (decembre 2004), p. 357 – 374 [http://people.hofstra.edu/jean-paul_rodrigue/downloads/CGQ_strategicoil.pdf].

disturbing, in particular since the relevance of maritime traffic will increase significantly.[6] They include:

(a) The Suez Canal, which is currently not a problem, but given the uncertainties over the future of Egypt and the unstable situation on the Sinai Peninsula it might become one.[7]

(b) The Bab el Mandab is one of the most important straits connecting Europe and the Indo-Pacific region. Its security is being threatened by piracy as well as by the domestic situation in littoral states such as Yemen, Eritrea and Somalia.[8]

(c) The Strait of Hormuz is even more important for the supply of Europe as well as of the littoral states of the Indo-Pacific region. Its security is increasingly endangered by the efforts of the Iranian leadership who threaten to close the strait by using asymmetric military means. A look at their military preparations reveals that this is a threat which has to be taken seriously.[9]

(d) The Straits of Malacca is being bedevilled by piracy and is, at the same time, considered by China as well as all other states in the region to be of paramount importance for international trade.[10]

(e) The Singapore Strait, the Sunda Strait and the Lombok Strait are of similar relevance for international naval traffic in the region. Again, piracy is among the main concerns for all states in the region.

(f) The South China Sea is important both for unrestricted international naval traffic as well as for the exploitation of raw

---

6 QinetiQ/Lloyd's Register, and University of Strathclyde Glasgow, *Global Maritime Trends 2030* (London: Lloyd's Register, 2013), p. 56 – 81.

7 Tamim Elyan, "Insight: In Sinai, militant Islam flourishes – quietly," *Reuters News Agency* (1 April 2012), [http://www.reuters.com/article/2012/04/01/us-egypt-sinai-idUSBRE83006120120401].

8 Jennifer Steil, "Yemen: descending into despair", *World Policy journal*, Vol. 28, no. 3 (Fall 2011) , p. 62-72.

9 Jeremy Binnie, "Gulf Guerillas: Iranian naval forces," *Jane's Defence Weekly*, Vol. 50, no. 6 (6 February 2012), p. 34 – 40.

10 P. K.Gautam, "Mapping Chinese Oil and Gas Pipelines and Sea Routes," *Strategic Analysis*, Vol. 35, No. 4 (July 2011), p. 595 – 612.

materials and petroleum. For decades it has been subject to conflicting international claims concerning the sovereignty over small islands and the extension of Exclusive Economic Zones. These conflicting claims have the potential of leading into a major regional conflict drawing in regional and extra-regional powers.[11]

(g) Also the Western part of the Indian Ocean, i.e. the Arab Sea (in particular the sea area off the coasts of Somalia and Yemen), has to be considered as a problem area. Here the interplay of state failure, poor governance, over-fishing by Europeans and Asians as well of piracy, Islamist extremism and regional ambitions form a dangerous mixture for international naval traffic.[12]

All these chokepoints and problem areas have one thing in common: due to political factors (poor governance, failing state institutions, revolutions, regional ambitions of individual states, regional rivalries among states, piracy, etc.) there is a growing demand for international cooperation, including cooperation between the EU and states of the Indo-Pacific region.

The closer both regions become the more common interest must be acknowledged in order to cooperatively deal with problems that could have a negative impact on naval traffic between them. As we may have observed during the recent attempts to fight piracy in the Indian Ocean waters, such a sense of cooperation was present. The European Union, through its Operation Atlanta, bore the brunt of international efforts to secure ships in the Western Indian Ocean against piracy.[13] There were cases of fruitful cooperation with naval units from India, Japan and China as well. Fighting piracy will continue to be an important area of cooperation between Europe and the Indo-Pacific Region and it needs to be extended.

---

11 See Sarah Raine and Christian Le Mière, Regional Disorder. *The South China Sea Disputes* (London: Routledge, 2013); for an earlier analysis see Marc Valencia, *China and the South China Sea Disputes. Conflicting Aims and Possible Solutions in the South China Sea* (Oxford: Oxford University Press, 1995).

12 Ruchita Beri, "Piracy in Somalia, addressing the root causes," *Strategic Analysis*, Vol. 35. No. 3 (May 2011), p. 452 - 464.

13 Marianne Riddervold, "Finally flexing its muscles?, Atlanta – the European Union's naval military operation against piracy," *European Security*, Vol. 20, No. 3 (September 2011), p. 385 – 404.

But it is not only piracy that endangers sea routes. There are further problems that have to be addressed as well:

(a) One problem is the future path of the societal and political movements in the Arab world, formerly called the "Arab Spring". In Egypt, Tunisia, Libya, Yemen and, in particular, in Syria, the influence of radical Salafist movements is growing and might turn these countries into hotbeds of crisis and civil war. Developments in these countries could, as was mentioned above, endanger the freedom of passage through the Suez Canal as well as the Red Sea

(b) Another problem is Iran, which is not only constantly threatening to shut down the Strait of Hormuz, but which is posing a much broader challenge to international stability. The leadership in Tehran has become a principal problem for international security because of its nuclear programme and its military and revolutionary involvement in the internal affairs of other states in the region. It depicts itself as the prime challenger of the alleged Western dominance of the world, yet Iran is increasingly being perceived as a source of concern and irritation in the region and beyond.

(c) Political instability in the Horn of Africa and in Yemen might spell further trouble for the freedom of sea routes.

(d) The continuing dispute over who is controlling the South China Sea (in particular the Spratley Islands) is a further source of concern for the international freedom of maritime routes.

Energy and Raw Materials

Besides the freedom of sea routes, there are other issue of concern in which, from a European point of view, the Indo-Pacific region is gaining in terms of relevance. In particular, both regions need energy sources (mainly crude oil, natural gas) and access to raw materials. Both energy and raw materials might become scarce commodities in a not so distant future, even if the recent "fracking revolution" might ease the problem to a considerable degree. In principle, competition over scarce commodities must not lead to conflict. It is better solved by international cooperation, in particular if new technologies are involved.

The European Union has discovered energy as a major issue of its foreign relations only quite recently.[14] However, until now EU initiatives have focussed on Russia, Ukraine, the Mediterranean states, the Gulf States and Central Asia. Extending cooperation towards the Indo-Pacific region is necessary. Such cooperation must be different from the collaboration that is practiced with Russia or other Central Asian states. The main focus must be placed on three elements:

(a) To agree on principles and rules which allow states to operate as competitors for energy and raw materials without resorting to force or "unconventional" ways of securing energy or raw materials. This could be of critical importance in Sub-Saharan Africa. It is not to propose a specific format for such cooperation, but a dialogue between the EU and governments of the Indo-Pacific on such issues might be a good starting point.

(b) Much could be gained through political cooperation in the field of conflict management in regions whose stability is crucial for international energy security. The Gulf Region is the most salient one. It is also not to suggest specific proposals, but as a matter of fact, it is often the European Union (or individual European states together with the US) who take active interest in the security of the Gulf area. So far, there have not been many positive actions by states of the Indo-Pacific region with the intention to contribute to a peaceful stabilization of the Gulf region, although states of the Indo-Pacific region are much more dependent on petroleum supplies from the Gulf than the states of Europe. Any fruitful initiative by governments of the region would be welcomed in European capitals.

(c) An important factor will be technological cooperation between the EU and states of the Indo-Pacific region. The more the states of this region gain a status in which they are involved in cutting-edge technologies, the more cooperation with the other sources of high technology, such as Europe and the United States, becomes imperative in areas relating to energy production, consumption, and, in particular, to renewable energy.

---

14 Energy challenges and policy. Commission contribution to the European Council of 22 May 2013 http://ec.europa.eu/europe2020/pdf/energy2_en.pdf.

Furthermore, the Indo-Pacific region is both a challenge and a chance for Europe. It is a challenge, because this region is catching up in terms of economic growth and modernization. It is full of economic competitors, who do make life hard for European companies (unless they spread their activities around the world). On the other hand, it is a growing market where European companies can discover new opportunities. The dynamic economies of the Indo-Pacific area also pose a challenge to the encrusted European welfare systems; however, it is too early to determine what is better: to either slow down economic progress by a costly welfare state, or to speed up economic growth and risk social unrest.

Conclusion

So far, the concept of the Indo-Pacific region is, from a European perspective, nothing more than a heuristic, analytical instrument, whose value still needs to be proven. It will become a commonly accepted concept the very moment the societal, economic and political bonds within this region become denser and the more the Indo-Pacific region is viewed as forming a space of strategic interaction. But until the states forming the Indo-Pacific region come to a consensus about belonging to this common space, the European Union will be hesitant in using the concept "Indo-Pacific region" in international documents.

The European Union has a long and fruitful tradition of cooperating with other regional (or trans-regional) institutions in a very open and pragmatic way, such as with the Association of South East Asian Nations (ASEAN), the South Asian Association for Regional Cooperation (SAARC), the African Union (AU) or with the Southern America Common Market (MERCOSUR). But as a fundamental principle, the European Union builds relations only on the basis of established regional entities which reflect the common volition of the states involved.

15

Indo-Pacific Region: Perspectives from Indian Ocean

Hoseana B. Lunogelo

In a way to some extent Africa is very passive in terms of leading the agenda on what it wants out of the engagement with the rest of the world. This chapter attempts to explore on how Africa and rest of the world can work further. Even some of the programs, which are progressing in Africa, are more a product of UN systems rather than out of African efforts. This passive attitude of Africa on geopolitical analysis has persisted despite historical background that personalities such as Jawaharlal Nehru, Mahatma Gandhi, and others tried to build or at least to set the pace for Africa to find a place in global or world politics.

In recent years, Africa has not yet increased trade and engagement with BRICS, India and China in particular, as a source of raw material but also as a market for products on both sides. It is a learning experience trying to understand and absorb how Africa should really position itself. The choice of Africa or the inevitability of Africa dealing with the geopolitics of the day stems from several factors. In the face of the natural gas discoveries in the Indian Ocean off East Africa coast, there is a need to make sure that it can be seen from two perspectives: first, Africa has geopolitical dispensation in response to internationally crafted obligations and therefore it needs to constantly keep on engaging and understanding its role in the region. But, as part of the long-term obligation internationally, drawing back or tracing back 40 years ago when the UN Conference on the Least Developed Countries in 2011 and Istanbul Plan of Action makes it very clear on the need for developing countries and also among the least developed countries to cooperate. Therefore, Africa cannot avoid and try to understand the different scenarios in terms of geo-politics of the Indian Ocean and of course extending to the Pacific.

So, it is an important way for bringing things with the proposition to collaborate with the Asian and the Pacific States. There are four factors which should drive Africa's agenda for East Asian collaboration; first is the historical connection; the second is the emergency of lawless parts of the world, and for example, East Africa has witnessed population prone migration at the same time. These are interesting issues and the Indian Ocean provides a route for that. At the end the discovery of huge stocks of non-renewable resources on shore and also off-shore added to it.

As far as the historical connection is concerned, Africa has a population with origins in Asia and also is the islands in the Indian Ocean which actually draw their descent from both sides, from African continent and also Asian subcontinent. It makes sense for Africans not to abandon the agenda of trying to understand the geopolitics of the region. The fragile state of Somalia and most of the literature defines the role of collaboration in terms of assuring security in the Indian Ocean and the Pacific as well. In recent years, countries like Kenya are also participating to bring peace in the region. But nation states also gain from joint navy operations or territorial ventures like the Kenyan army had done.

With the growth of the migrating population, it is important to understand the dynamics which are driving African population to migrate. In recent years, Africa has emerged as a transit route for migrants of middle and lower middle income class in pursuit of greener pastures in the US and they use the Indian Ocean and Pacific Ocean as part of their transportation system. Migration also has its own benefits. There are opportunities for Africa to understand the source of xenophobia among the transit countries like Republic of South Africa. At the end of the day it is due to the consequences of global economic crisis and tightening of job opportunities in the transit countries.

The discoveries of stocks of non-renewable resources onshore and offshore, especially in the East Coast of Africa stretching all the way from Ethiopia, Kenya, Mozambique and Tanzania is noteworthy. The International Energy Agency is defining this era as the golden age of gas. To understand, for example, how Asian or Indian companies can extract gas and oil exploration, but also given the economic and business merits to export the gas through offshore facilities will mean that security in the Indian Ocean and the Pacific, bring China and Japan into picture to transport gas in tankers. The issue of security cannot be ignored. Under the Indo-Africa capacity building programme, the Indian government offers about 1000 scholarships each year and several others in specialised areas. It is important to define the priority areas for building capacity especially in developing skills for extraction, cooperation in energy and other petroleum products.

In conclusion, the discovery of huge stocks of gas and oil in Africa demands more dedicated studies on how geopolitics, trade, investment patterns and security concerns are addressed. The discoveries are most likely to shift to the internal politics, and geopolitics of the Indian Ocean go beyond what has been preoccupying most of the African countries, basically dealing more on poverty issues given the high levels of malnutrition, illiteracy, etc. More African countries will begin to assert their territorial claims in the Exclusive Economic Zones. Tanzania, last year, moved the UN to try to expand its claim because of the importance of the discoveries of gas.

In a nutshell, this is an opportunity for the African States to singularly and jointly develop strategies based on the imminent geopolitical dynamics of the Indo-Pacific region with special interest on India and China, as the next leading economic giants of the world in the 15 years to come. Africa, has to be proactive, has to set the agenda on how to engage with the Indo-Pacific region in optimising benefits from the Indian Ocean. India and the other States should continue commitments made by G20 and also under the UN LDC Framework. Based on this, Africa based scholarly networks should be encouraged to blossom. Asian and African countries and individuals should enhance their collaboration.

16

India in the Indo-Pacific: Maritime Stakes and Challenges

Raghavendra Mishra

"The waters of the world form one vast expanse. While land may be enveloped by the sea - and the Continents are so enveloped – the oceans are divided only by artificial boundaries".[1]

- Sardar KM Panikkar

The aforementioned quote, enunciated about 60 years ago, exemplifies a significant shift in the contemporary Indian strategic thought about maritime domain. The oceans are no longer considered a 'traditional frontier and barrier to be protected' complemented by a gradual emerging idea of the seas being 'an enabling medium'. This transformation from a hitherto continental mindset has been influenced by two major factors; the first being, the changing contours of Indian economy from an internal autarchic focus professed in the post-independence period which is now externally oriented since the initiation of liberalisation process of early 1990s. The linked effects of ever-expanding commercial linkages and footprint have mandated that the national economic focus should have an outward point of reference which has in turn led a 'tack to the seas' as a medium for leverage. The second factor is the gradual recognition of India's 'geo-strategic heft' in world order especially in the oceanic continuum, not only amongst the Indian policy makers but the global community as well. The robust and the rapid development of military maritime capabilities

---

1 KM Panikkar, *India and the Indian Ocean: An Essay on the Influence of Sea power on Indian History*, London: George Allen & Unwin, 2nd Edn, 1951, p. 18.

coupled with a national posture of abiding by internationally recognised behavioural norms have seen India being recognised as a 'provider of net security in the Indian Ocean and beyond'[2]. Indo-Pacific as a geo–spatial construct, for the purpose of this chapter is premised to extend from the Indian Ocean to the western Pacific Ocean besides encompassing the littoral states of Asia including the Middle East and eastern Africa.[3] The basic theme of this chapter is to argue that this geographic continuum with a predominant flavour is truly representative of Indian geo-strategic interests in terms of military-security and economic terms. It is in this context that this chapter aims to analyse India's maritime stakes and challenges in the Indo-Pacific, as they obtain today and how these are likely to shape in the future. The key areas addressed are: the correlation between maritime domain and geo-strategic salience; the maritime economics, energy and security dimensions of the Indo-Pacific; and, the present and future opportunities as well as challenges for India within the Indo-Pacific construct.

World at the Cusp of Radical Reorder

The new millennium has witnessed a fundamental redistribution of geo-strategic influence characterised by a relative decline of the West accompanied by a corresponding ascendance of the East.[4] While surprising to some, such a shift had already been predicted in the immediate aftermath of the Cold War characterised by confrontationist bipolar power politics.[5] Some scholars had also forecast this radical reworking of global order including the impending arrival of information age, great societal changes and the current economic downturn with accuracy.[6] Further, the long-

---

2   United States Department of Defense, *Quadrennial Defense Review Report 2010*, p. 60, available at http://www.defense.gov/qdr/qdr%20as%20of%2029jan10%201600.PDF, accessed February 08, 2013.

3   The cartographic limits of Indo- Pacific have been derived from the map appended at C Raja Mohan, *SamudraManthan: Sino- Indian Rivalry in the Indo – Pacific*, Washington D.C.: Carnegie Endowment for International Peace, 2012.

4   National Intelligence Council Report, *Global Trends 2025: A Transformed World*, 2008, US Government Printing Office, 2008, Executive Summary, esppgs vi – vii. Electronic version available at URL - http://www.isn.ethz.ch/isn/Digital-Library/Publications/Detail/?ots591=0c54e3b3-1e9c-be1e-2c24-a6a8c7060233&lng=en&id=94769, accessed on February 12, 2013.

5   Paul Kennedy, *The Rise and Fall of Great Powers: Economic Change and Military Conflict from 1500 to 2000*, London: Unwin Hyman, 1988, pp. 514 – 535.

6   Joshua S Goldstein, *Long Cycles: Prosperity and War in the Modern Age*, London: Yale

perspective theorists have derived 16 point logic to determine the signs of a cataclysmic systemic change in global politics. This logic, inter alia, takes into the instability and changes in international hierarchy, dominance of realpolitik syndrome in strategic discourse, serial crises in a particular region, multiple strategic and commercial rivalries, shifting economic hubs, destabilising innovations (Kondratieff Waves), and changes in energy use patterns, besides weakening of Kantian peace dynamics as the determinants of a systemic change in international architechture.[7] These symptomatic pointers when correlated with contemporary events, point to an era of upheaval, uncertainty and significant reordering of global architecture.

Maritime Context in Global Politics

The importance of sea power in global politics can be gauged from the findings of a study by two eminent theorists of 'long cycle school' which suggests that the pre-eminence of global great powers is intimately related to the relative degree of influence that the nations have been able to exert in the maritime commons.[8] The twin hypotheses analysed by this study that were found to be true through systemic documentation of the episodic rise and fall of maritime powers and the corresponding changes in geo-political architecture were:-[9]

(a) In the modern world system, world powers have been sea (or ocean) powers, exercising command of the sea.

(b) Changes in position of world leadership are associated with shifts in the distribution of sea power.

Further, this study also deduced that sea power was a superior medium and an optimal index for measuring global power status for the following reasons:[10]

University Press, 1988, p. 353 and the accompanying footnotes.

7   William R. Thompson(Ed), *Systemic Transitions - Past, Present, and Future*, New York: Palgrave Macmillan, 2009, p. 3. Michael P. Colaresi, Karen Rasler and William R. Thompson, *Strategic Rivalries in World Politics: Position, Space and Conflict Escalation*, Cambridge: Cambridge University Press, 2007, Chapter 2.

8   See George Modelski and William R Thompson, *Seapower in Global Politics, 1494-1993*, Plymouth: Macmillan Press, 1988 for a detailed exposition on this theme.

9   Ibid, pp. 16-17.

10 Ibid, p. 14, authors' emphasis.

(a) Confers greater mobility hence access to a wider variety of resources and experiences[results];

(b) Employs higher order technology, is more expensive, and generates greater innovation;

(c) Carries a larger information content, higher visibility and symbolic load [greater connect to the national strategic posture];

(d) Operates worldwide and at the global level.

The foregoing highlights certain key characteristics of maritime commons like the enabling features of extended reach and mobility on global magnitude and, more importantly, sea power being an indicator of the relative standing amongst the comity of nations in geo-strategic salience. In military-security parlance, maritime domain has also been identified as one of the key enablers to have shaped the contours of global geo-politics and its relevance has been amply proven in the recent conflicts like the Falklands War (1982), the First Gulf War (1990-91), Kosovo Crisis (1999), Operation Iraqi Freedom (2003-2011) and the ongoing Operation Enduring Freedom (OEF) in Afghanistan since October 2001. Therefore, by looking at a continuous historical precedent as well as the current environment dominated by an emerging Indo-Pacific with a macro-maritime orientation, it would not be amiss to posit that seas have been one of the key determinants of global power structure.

Emergence and Salience of Maritime Indo-Pacific

During the Cold War era, despite Indian concerns about the Indian Ocean turning into an area of intense bipolar completion, this realm was largely considered a strategic backwater by the two dominant ideological streams. West and Central Europe, North Atlantic, the Mediterranean and the North-Western Pacific were considered to be the centres of geo-strategic gravity during this period. With the end of the Cold War, based on then existing distribution of politico-military and economic strength, popularly known as the unique American unipolar moment, it was widely predicted that the next millennium would belong to the Western Hemisphere and termed as the coming Pacific Century.[11] However, the emergence of a new

---

11 Mark Borthwick, *Pacific Century: The Emergence of Modern Pacific Asia*, Colorado: Westview Press, 1998, Paperback Edn.

and more diffused economic order stretching across the Asia-Pacific region in the aftermath of 1997 Asian Financial Crisis along with the economic performances of India and China amidst a global downtrend, the 21st century was recast as the Asia-Pacific Century. While this phraseology does continue to find wide usage, a more inclusive geo-strategic paradigm of Indo–Pacific is now finding greater salience.[12] This southward shift and assemblage of thus far spatially distinct areas of geo-strategic significance in the post-Cold War period would be more apparent through depiction at Figure 1.

Figure 1: Shifting Centres and Assemblage of Geo-Strategic Salience

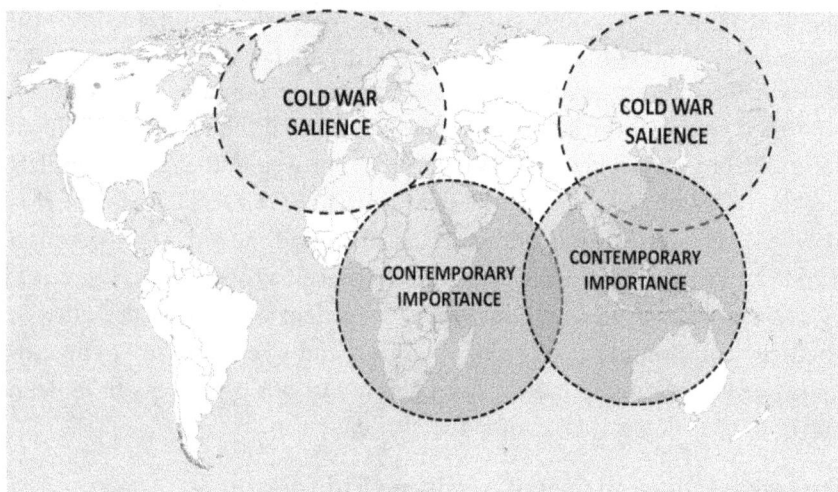

The significance of this emerging Indo-Pacific geostrategic concept has benign as well as adverse facets. On the positive side, it is resident to the emerging global economic powerhouses, an undisputed largest source of energy, rich natural resource base and witness to increasing societal affluence. However, the Indo-Pacific is also considered to contain the

---

12 Prior its usage in geo-strategic parlance, the Indo-Pacific, sometimes known as the Indo-West Pacific was used to describe a marine resource rich bio-geographic region comprising the tropical waters of the Indian Ocean, the western and central Pacific Ocean. The term 'Indo-Pacific' was first used in global strategic/ geo-political discourse in January 2007. See Gurpreet S. Khurana, *Security of Sea Lines: Prospects for India–Japan Cooperation*, Strategic Analysis, New Delhi: Volume 31, Issue 1, 2007, pp. 139-153. In this instance, the term was used to describe to the maritime space comprising the Indian Ocean and the western Pacific as well as the littoral states of Asia including the Middle East and eastern Africa.

seeds of global instability or conflict marked by widespread poverty and unequal development, religious extremism, fountain of trans-national terrorism, internal strife, seemingly intractable territorial disputes with emotive overtones, and not in the least, the future playground for Sino-US struggle for global pre-eminence.[13] The emerging power dynamic especially that of resurgent realpolitik anarchical scenarios is not new and has ample historical evidence as precedence.[14] It has also been surmised that the contours of this global shift are not likely to be smooth and India by its geographic positioning and expanded international footprint would inevitably get involved.[15]

Taking the discourse forward, this region for long has been considered as the focus of future geo-strategic instability and an area of increased military competition by the United States security establishment in post 9/11 scenario as an arc of instability tag that extends from North Africa running roughly eastwards across the extended Middle East to Afghanistan -Pakistan region and thereon to Southeast Asia.[16] The resultant concerted US focus is evident through the popular pronunciations of 'Rebalance towards the Asia-Pacific' by the previous US Defence Secretary Leon Panetta and that of an 'Asia-Pacific Century' by the Secretary of State, Hillary Clinton.[17] While these two recent postulations have captured the public imagination, the US military reorientation to the Indo-Pacific had

---

13 National Intelligence Council Report, *Global Trends 2030 - Alternative Worlds, November 2012*, esp Chap 2 titled 'Megatrends', pgs 7 – 38, available at http://www.dni.gov/files/ documents/GlobalTrends_2030.pdf, accessed February 24, 2013.

14 John J. Mearsheimer, *The Tragedy of Great Power Politics*, New York: W. W. Norton & Company Inc., 2001, Chap 2.

15 C Raja Mohan, *India and the Changing Geopolitics of the Indian Ocean*, Eminent Persons Lecture Series, National Maritime Foundation, July 19, 2010, available at http://www. maritimeindia.org/pdfs/EminentPersonsLectureSeries_RajaMohan.pdf,   accessed February 22, 2013.

16 United States Department of Defense, *Quadrennial Defense Review Report, September 30, 2001*, p. 4.

17 For the US foreign policy perspective see Hillary Clinton, *America's Pacific Century*, November 2011, available at http://www.foreignpolicy.com/articles/2011/10/11/ americas_pacific_century, accessed February 26, 2013. For the broad contours of United States realignment of military power to the Asia–Pacific see Leon Panetta, Secretary for Defence, *The US Rebalance towards the Asia-Pacific*, address at the Shangri la Dialogue 2102, Singapore on June 02, 2012, available at http://www.iiss.org/conferences/the-shangri-la-dialogue/shangri-la-dialogue-2012/speeches/first-plenary-session/leon-panetta/, accessed February 25, 2013.

commenced as early as 2005-06 during the process of formulating the 2006 Quadrennial Review Report, wherein, the deployment of six aircraft carriers and 60 per cent of nuclear submarine force on Pacific seaboard had already been set in motion.[18]

The emerging contours in the Indo-Pacific with its predominant maritime flavour have significant relevance for India. The first and the most obvious reason, as mentioned earlier, being the expanding economic linkages since the liberalisation reforms started in early 1990s. The second reason is the linked maritime context, the increasing importance of stability and security at sea as well as the littoral space for continued national development.[19] The next reason is the increased securitisation of geopolitical space not only at the regional level but at the global stage besides large accretion of military capabilities within this geographical construct.[20] This 'Maritime Dynamism of the Indo-Pacific' has attracted the global attention and is stated to be unprecedented in the history by any matrix of measurement both benign and adverse, in terms of container flows, shipping schedules, shipbuilding tempos, port development, energy flows, naval construction, coast guard activity, submarine acquisition, maritime terrorism and piracy attacks.[21] In addition, the rising military maritime capability accretion in the Asia-Pacific of major resident players such as India, China, Japan, South Korea and Australia, besides the greater focus of quasi/extra-regional players such as EU members as well as the US, have also been considered as a source of greater friction akin to the

---

18 United States Department of Defense, *Quadrennial Defense Review Report*, February 6, *2006*, p. 47.

19 A K Antony, Minister of Defence, India, *Protecting Maritime Freedoms*, address at the Shangri la Dialogue 2102, Singapore on June 02, 2012, available at http://www.iiss.org/conferences/the-shangri-la-dialogue/shangri-la-dialogue-2012/speeches/second-plenary-session/a-k-antony/, accessed February 27, 2013. For a foreign policy perspective see Nirupama Rao, *Maritime Dimensions of India's Foreign Policy*, Eminent Persons Lecture Series, National Maritime Foundation on July 28, 2011, available at http://www.maritimeindia.org/sites/all/files/pdf/Speech%20by%20Foreign%20Secretary%20Nirupama%20Rao.pdf, accessed February 27, 2013.

20 SIPRI Press Release, *Rise in international arms transfers is driven by Asian demand, says SIPRI*; March 19, 2012. http://www.sipri.org/media/pressreleases/rise-in-international-arms-transfers-is-driven-by-asian-demand-says-sipri, accessed February 27, 2013.

21 James A. Boutilier,'Maritime Dynamism in Indo-Pacific Region' in Rupert Herbert-Burns, Sam Bateman, Peter Lehr(Eds), Lloyd's MIUHandbook Of Maritime Security, Boca Raton: Taylor & Francis Group, 2009, pp. 271 – 276.

naval arms race during the Cold War era of 1970 to mid-1980s.[22] This has had profound impact on the strategic thinking at politico-military levels and animation amongst the strategic community which is evident by the greater emphasis on the maritime domain.[23] The last and the most important reason is the large coincidence between the geographical stretch of the Indo-Pacific and 'the areas of interest' defined by the Indian Navy in its doctrine. The primary and secondary areas of interests enunciated by the Indian Navy based on their relative importance are as follows:-[24]

Primary Areas

(a) Maritime Zones of India covering the territorial waters, contiguous zone and Exclusive Economic Zone (EEZ), up to 12 nm, 24 nm and 200 nm, respectively from the national baseline;

(b) The Arabian Sea and the Bay of Bengal, which largely encompass India's island territories and EEZ, and the littoral reaches;

(c) The choke points leading to, from and across the Indian Ocean, viz. The Straits of Malacca and Singapore, the Sunda Strait, the Lombok Strait, the Strait of Hormuz, Bab-el-Mandeb the Cape of Good Hope, the Mozambique Channel, the Six Degree Channel and the Eight/Nine-degree Channels;

(d) The Persian Gulf, which is the source of majority of our oil supplies and is also home to a considerable population of expatriate Indians;

(e) The principal International Shipping Lanes (ISLs) crossing the IOR and island counties located in their vicinity.

---

22 Geoffrey Till, *Asia's naval expansion: an arms race in the making?*,IISS Adelphi Series, (2012), 52:432-433, pp. 11-12, 14-26 and 241-243.AlsoToshi Yoshihara and James R. Holmes(Eds), *Asia looks seaward : power and maritime strategy,* Connecticut: Praeger Security International, 2008, pp.1-9.

23 Arun Prakash, "The Rationale and Implications of India's Growing Maritime Power" in Michael Kugelman(Ed), *India's Contemporary Security Challenges,* Washington, DC: Woodrow Wilson International Center for Scholars, 2011, pp 77-87. See also C. UdayBhaskar, *Pacific and Indian Oceans: Relevance for the Evolving Power Structures in Asia,* in *Queries,* Foundation for European Progressive Studies Magazine, Brussels: No 03(6), 2011, pp. 62-65.

24 Integrated Headquarters of the Ministry of Defence (Navy), *Indian Maritime Doctrine (INBR 8),* New Delhi, pp. 65-68.

Secondary Areas

(a) The Southern Indian Ocean Region, due to our interests in Antarctica, and the friendly littoral states in the continents of Australia and Africa;

(b) The Red Sea and its littoral states;

(c) The South China Sea, other areas of west Pacific Ocean and friendly littoral countries located therein;

(d) Other areas of national interest based on considerations of Diaspora and overseas investments.

Indo-Pacific region has certain geographic imperatives and their relevance to India needs to be reiterated. On similar lines as the Indian Ocean Region (IOR), this region is also geographically constrained, and access is only feasible through chokepoints, narrow and restricted waters surrounded by large landmass/islands. The classical oceanic sweep with multi-directional access, therefore, does not obtain in the Indo-Pacific. This makes this region more susceptible to adverse spill-over effects from the surrounding littorals. The emergence of piracy in the Horn of Africa (HOA) due to poor governance on land is a contemporary example. The concerns raised over energy flows through the Strait of Hormuz during the Iran-Iraq tanker war of 1980s and the same worries expressed during a future armed confrontation over the ongoing Iranian nuclear issue support this hypothesis. In a similar vein, the effect on global maritime commerce and energy flows in case the South and East China disputes were to deteriorate due to an aggressive behaviour by the involved parties' supports this proposition. However, the prime supporting evidence, now largely forgotten, can be traced to the global oil shock experienced post 1973 Arab–Israeli conflict precipitated by the closure of the Suez Canal. The relevance of energy for economic development for India and China can be gauged from the US Energy Information Administration (EIA) 2011 assessment which provides an understanding of the larger context:-

"Two nations that were among the least affected by the worldwide recession are China and India. They continue to lead world economic growth and energy demand growth …….. Since 1990, energy consumption in both countries as a share of total world energy use has increased significantly, and together they accounted

146

for about 10 per cent of total world energy consumption in 1990 and 21 per cent in 2008. Although energy demand faltered in many parts of the world during the recession, robust growth continued in China and India, whose economies expanded by 12.4 per cent and 6.9 per cent, respectively, in 2009. U.S. energy consumption declined by 5.3 per cent in 2009, and energy use in China is estimated to have surpassed that of the United States for the first time."[25]

A relatively more important issue is the transformation in maritime economics of the Indo–Pacific region. From being a littoral providing the majority of base or break bulk goods, be it minerals, ores and energy, this geographical entity in contemporary scenario is an equatorial pendulum that also transports the majority of value added goods connecting the Occident to the Orient. Therefore, in the current era of increasing economic meshing, the effects of events in this oceanic body create ripples that have global connotations.

Geography accords India a commanding position over the Indo-Pacific, but difficult relations with Pakistan and China do not accrue the typically Mahanian insular position that finds general mention in public discourse. However, the density and pattern of maritime trade[26]as well as the global energy flows[27] at Figures 2 and 3, respectively, which occupy a central theme being the engines of a developing economy, exemplify the salience of this region to India during peace, crises and conflict situations.

---

25 U.S. Energy Information Administration, *International Energy Outlook 2011*, Sep 2011, pp. 9-10. For a comprehensive review of the growing Indian and Chinese interest in the Middle East to secure seaborne energy supplies see, Geoffrey Kemp, *The East Moves West - India, China, and Asia's Growing Presence in the Middle East*, Washington, D.C.: Brookings Institution Press, 2010, pp. 174-228.

26 Compiled by Dr. Jean-Paul Rodrigue, Dept. of Global Studies & Geography, Hofstra University, New York, Source: Shipping density data adapted from National Centre for Ecological Analysis and Synthesis, *A Global Map of Human Impacts to Marine Ecosystems*. Available at http://people.hofstra.edu/geotrans/eng/gallery/Map_Strategic_Passages.pdf, accessed February 26, 2013.

27 Compiled by Dr. Jean-Paul Rodrigue& John Field, Dept. of Global Studies & Geography, Hofstra University, New York, Source: Adapted from *The International Tankers Owners Pollution Federation Limited & Energy Information Administration, World Oil Transit Chokepoints*, available at http://people.hofstra.edu/geotrans/eng/ch5en/appl5en/oiltransportation.html, accessed February 26, 2013.

Figure 2: Global Maritime Shipping Routes and Strategic Locations

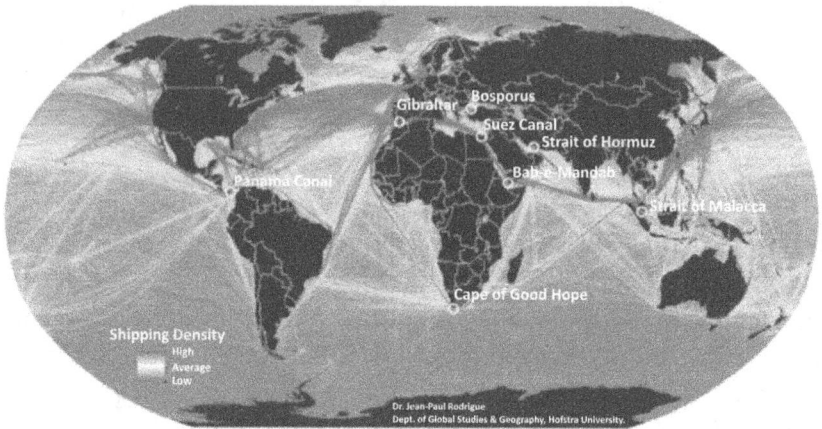

Source: Rodrigue, Comtois, Slack; Geography of Transport Systems, Routledge, 2009.

Figure 3: Global Major Oil Flows and Chokepoints, 2005-06

(Areas of Large Volume Energy Flows Highlighted)

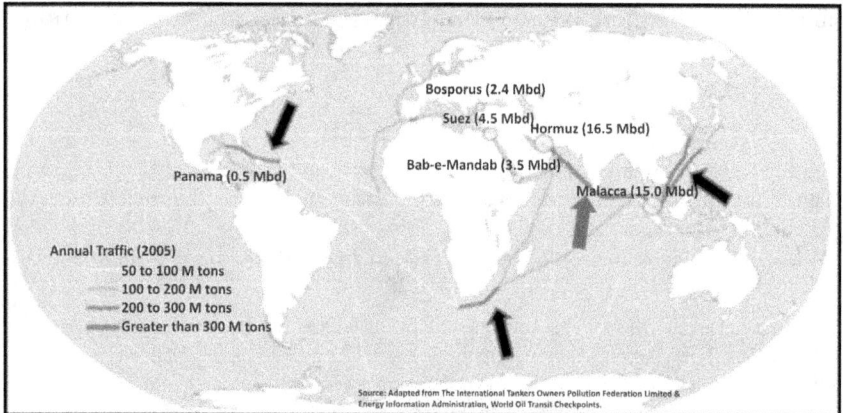

Source: Rodrigue, Comtois, Slack; Geography of Transport Systems, Routledge, 2009.

An increasing recognition of credible Indian military maritime capabilities, as already mentioned, has elevated it from the status of a 'Rule Follower' to a 'Rule Maker'.[28] In addition, some analysts have deduced that there are growing signs of congruence of interests and a trend of greater co-operation amongst India, Japan and the United States to improve stability in the serial-crisis ridden environment of the Indo-Pacific. This has been largely driven by the shared regional security interests of stability and adherence to the universally accepted norms of international behaviour. To a lesser degree, this loose amalgamation has also come about due to the significant Chinese naval capability accretion along with its increasingly assertive behaviour in South and East China Sea disputes.[29]Besides the Sino-US rivalry, another node of discord among the major regional power players is of competing interests between India and China. While on the politico-diplomatic front, the statements by Delhi and Beijing seem to convey the spirit of cooperative development; there seems to be mutual unease in bilateral relations driven by the long-outstanding territorial dispute, status of Tibet, seeming overlap between the respective spheres of influence and access to resource bases, besides ideological dissonance.[30]

Economic Stakes

The important role of maritime commerce and the criticality of maritime commons being the economic highway are well-known with 90 per cent of world trade by value and 95 per cent by volume being carried through the medium of the seas. The importance of Indo-Pacific would be readily apparent from the majority share that Asia occupied in the global maritime commerce in 2011. As per the latest UNCTAD report,[31]Asia and Oceania together, a rough equivalent to the Indo-Pacific, were the leading regional entity accounting for 50 per cent of goods loaded and 57 per cent of goods unloaded in tonnage terms (Figure 4).

---

28 Supra Note 2.

29 For recent comprehensive overviews of Chinese naval modernisation see Saunders, Phillip C. et. al.(Eds), *The Chinese Navy: Expanding Capabilities, Evolving Roles*, Washington D.C. : National Defense University Press, 2011. For the emerging informal trilateral see David Scott, The "Indo-Pacific"—New Regional Formulations and New Maritime Frameworks for US-India Strategic Convergence, Asia-Pacific Review, 19:2(2012), pp. 85-109.

30 Raja Mohan, Note 3, pp. 13-34.

31 United Nations Conference of Trade and Development, *Review of Maritime Commerce, 2012*, p. 10.

Figure 4: World Seaborne Trade by Region – 2011

(Percentage Share in Global Tonnage Terms)

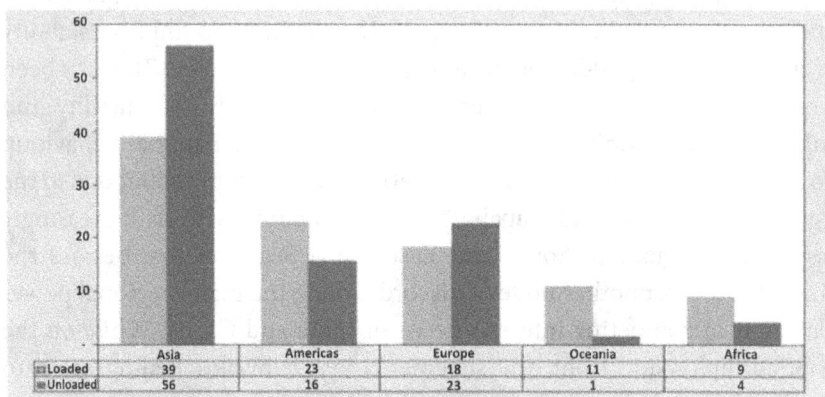

	Asia	Americas	Europe	Oceania	Africa
Loaded	39	23	18	11	9
Unloaded	56	16	23	1	4

Source: Compiled by the UNCTAD secretariat on the basis of data supplied by reporting countries, and data obtained from the relevant government, port industry and other specialist website and sources. Figure are estimated based on preliminary data or on the last year for which data were available.

Source: UNCTAD, Review of Maritime Commerce, 2012, p.12.

For India, maritime trade accounts for 90 per cent by volume and 70 per cent by value with the merchandise trade intensity of India's GDP below 30 per cent.[32] The divergence of figures in respect of India vis-a-vis global norms can be attributed to the services and agriculture sectors that comprise a significant share of national GDP of the order of 65 per cent and 17 per cent, respectively with industry constituting 18 per cent share.[33]

Despite the Indian economy being dominated by the service sector, certain key aspects considered are noteworthy:[34]

(a) India's total merchandise trade increased over three-fold from US$ 252 billion in Financial Year (FY) 2006 to US$ 794 billion in

---

32 Ministry of Shipping, Government of India, *Maritime Agenda: 2010 – 2020*, January, 2011, p. 7, available at http://shipping.nic.in/showfile.php?lid=261, accessed March 12, 2013.

33 Extracted from the CIA World Factbook 2012, *FIELD LISTING:: GDP - COMPOSITION BY SECTOR*, available at https://www.cia.gov/library/publications/the-world-factbook/fields/2012.html#in, accessed March 03, 2013.

34 Export-Import Bank of India, *Catalysing India's Trade and Investment*, p.2, available at http://www.eximbankindia.com/fore-trade.pdf, accessed March 12, 2013.

FY 2012 with both exports and imports having trebled during the period;

(b) Trade to GDP ratio has increased from 30.2 per cent in FY 2006 to 42.9 per cent in FY 2012 and Exports to GDP ratio during this period has witnessed an increase from 12.4 per cent to 16.5 per cent. In addition, share of India in world merchandise export was 1.67 per cent in 2011 with a corresponding 19th rank (up from 28th in 2006).

The importance of economic stakes and their maritime correlation can be gauged by an analysis of regional distribution of Indian trade, both in terms of imports and exports. Indian export destinations comprising ASEAN, Northeast Asia, West Asia (GCC and others), North and East Africa constitute 45.7 per cent and on the import front, these regional entities account for 42.9 per cent of total inward commerce.[35] The new millennium has also witnessed a radical shift southwards of Indian trade with a greater focus on Asia and Africa and indicates greater Indian economic interdependencies along the Indo-Pacific continuum accounting for even greater share of exports since 2000 (Table 1).[36] This trend is indicative of increasing diversification of Indian export basket and a shift in Indian economic focus that seems to be in congruence with the earlier discussed southward shift of global geo-strategic salience since the end of the Cold War. The aforementioned importance of Indo-Pacific for Indian economy is further reinforced by a comparative analysis of major exports and import trading partners. All ten leading export destinations and nine out of ten major import origins in the context of bilateral trade with India are littoral/island states.[37]

---

35 Department of Commerce, Ministry of Commerce and Industry, Government of India, *Export Import Data Bank,* region wiseexport and import dataavailable at http://commerce.nic.in/eidb/default.asp , extracted and arranged by the author, accessed March 12, 2013.

36 Ministry of Finance, Government of India, Economic Survey: 2012-13, p. 158.

37 Export- Import Bank, Op Cit, p. 4.

Table 1: Historical Trends in Indian Exports

Region	Percentage Share of India's Exports				
	2000-1	2005-6	2011-12	2012-13 (upto Nov)	Export Growth since 2000-01 in per centage terms
Europe	25.9	24.2	19.0	18.7	(-) 7.2
Africa	5.3	6.8	8.1	9.6	(+) 4.3
America	24.7	20.7	16.4	19.5	(-) 5.2
Asia	37.4	46.9	50.0	50.4	(+) 13.0
CIS & Baltics	2.3	1.2	1.0	1.3	(-) 1.0

Source: Ministry of Finance, Government of India, Economic Survey: 2012-13, p. 158.

Energy Dynamics, Energy Security and Security of Energy

On global scale, the changing pattern of fossil fuel production and consumption brings out that the Middle East is contributing an ever-increasing share of world production on one hand and Asia-Pacific has become the largest regional consumer of this commodity.[38]This would become more apparent through Figure 5.

Figure 5: Changing Pattern of Global Oil Production and Consumption

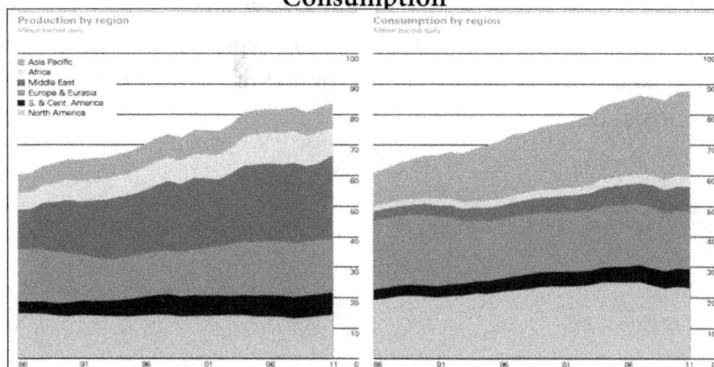

Source: BP Statistical Review of World Energy, June 2012.

---

38 BP Plc, *BP Statistical Review of World Energy, June 2012*, p. 12, available at http://www.bp.com/assets/bp_internet/globalbp/globalbp_uk_english/reports_and_publications/statistical_energy_review_2011/STAGING/local_assets/pdf/statistical_review_of_world_energy_full_report_2012.pdf, accessed on March 05, 2013.

The importance of maritime mode for transport of energy resources can be gauged from the statement that "Ships are and will likely remain the most cost effective means of transporting oil; the cost of transporting one barrel of oil over a distance of 1000 km (540 nautical miles), was estimated in 2007 to be $0.163 by tanker, $0.793 via pipeline and $7.190 by train."[39]It would thus be evident that the cost of transporting oil by pipelines is about five times more expensive as compared to the maritime mode and about 44 times more expensive, if transported by rail.

The importance of an extended Middle East within the Indo-Pacific being the leading energy resource hub, global energy flow pattern via the maritime medium and India's favourable geographical position has already been alluded to. While considerable research and investment is being undertaken to develop green and renewable energy technologies these developments remain in nascent stages. It would thus be a fair assessment that fossil fuels in contemporary and foreseeable scenario would remain the drivers of global economies. The criticality of Middle East oil plays an important part in the calculus of major Asian economies like China, India, and Japan (Figure 6).[40]

Figure 6: Dependence on Middle East Oil: Select Countries & Regions

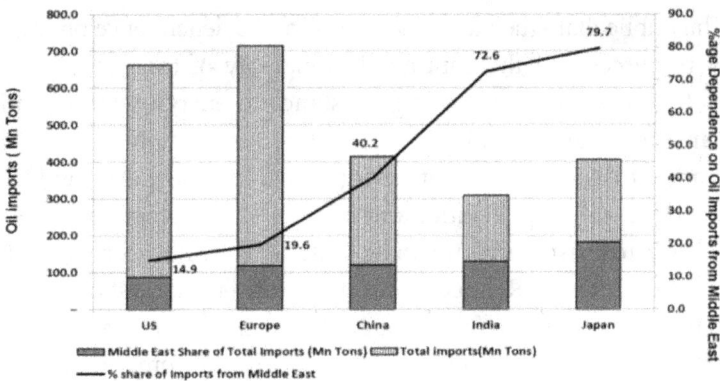

Source: BP Statistical Review of World Energy, June 2011.

---

39 Bernard D Cole, *The Great Wall at Sea: China's Navy in the Twenty First Century*, Second Edn,Annapolis: Naval Institute Press, 2012, p. 54.

40 BP Plc, *BP Statistical Review of World Energy June 2011*, p. 11, extracted and arranged by the author, available at http://www.bp.com/assets/bp_internet/globalbp/globalbp_uk_ english/reports_and_publications/statistical_energy_review_2011/STAGING/local_ assets/pdf/statistical_review_of_world_energy_full_report_2011.pdf, accessed March 11, 2012.

In addition, certain salient issues related to fossil fuel and derivatives based energy use with special relevance to India are: [41]

(a) India was the 4th largest importer of crude oil, LNG, feedstocks, additives and other hydrocarbons, totalling 164 million tons in 2010 after the United States, China and Japan. The imports account for about 70 per cent of total national consumption;

(b) It is the 10th largest producer of energy using oil accounting for 26 Terra Watt hour (TWh) which comprises 2.6 per cent of global capacity. It was ranked 9th in terms of LNG use for energy generation at 118 TWh constituting 6.1 per cent of global share;

(c) India is the 4th largest producer of refined oil products totalling 206 million tons (5.4 per cent of global share) after the United States, China and Russia. It is the 3rd largest net exporter of such products at 42 million tons in 2010 accounting for 8.9 per cent of global share. Based on 2011 data, India has the 5th largest crude distilling capacity of 4163 thousand barrels per calendar day (kb/cd) that constitutes 4.5 per cent of global share after the United States, China, Russia and Japan.

The public dialogue has focussed on India's dependence on imported energy resources and the continued availability of this resources being vital to the nation thus according substance to energy security with the attendant importance of SLOC. While this proposition is true, similar importance to the security of energy, that is, the ports and related infrastructure, refining facilities and offshore development areas that are located close to coast or in immediate hinterland are not accorded a similar space in the discourse. Refined oil products form the largest component of Indian export accounting for about 26.8 per cent by value among the top ten export commodities[42] and it could be stated with some confidence that while India imports 70 per cent of its crude requirements, it is as much of a major oil power in the export sense also.

---

41 International Energy Agency, IEA Key World Energy Statistics 2012, extracted and arranged by the author, available at http://www.iea.org/publications/freepublications/publication/kwes.pdf, accessed March 09, 2013.

42 Export- Import Bank, Op Cit, p. 5.

Maritime Security in the Indo-Pacific

The recent major shifts to have shaped the security paradigm are:

(a) The term *security* itself has assumed a different connotation from the Cold War era definition of a narrow politico-military construct to a more holistic approach in contemporary environment that includes societal, economic, cultural and human development issues;

(b) The lines between peace, crisis and conflict, traditional and non-traditional, regional and global, inter-state and transnational issues are increasingly getting blurred through the effects of information revolution as well as the horizontal and vertical proliferation of disruptive technologies.

As far as the military context is concerned, the complex scenarios demand an increasing requirement of capabilities that need to fulfil mutually paradoxical requirements of agility, responsiveness, fungibility and precision as against the needs of long persistence dwells to defeat time-sensitive opportunity threats. In addition, military response needs to be conducted under the scrutiny of pervasive media coverage which can sometimes provide a totally different spin to any event. These dilemmas are further accentuated by the ever-increasing cost of military capabilities that are rising at an annual rate of 10 per cent.[43] The inflationary effects are most pronounced on maritime forces which by their very nature and purpose are technology intensive, require a relatively longer time frame to be generated and, not in the least, are capital intensive. The events of 26/11 have brought home the importance of the coastal security dimensions which in a larger context points to the equal importance of the oceanic as well as the littoral components of maritime security. Thus, the futuristic capabilities would need the ability to address the entire spectrum of threats starting from low-end benign functions, constabulary roles and at the higher end, the non-linear armed conflict characterised by a rapid tempo over an extended geographical continuum. Indo-Pacific is fast emerging as a military hot spot with the defence expenditure showing significant increase since 2000

---

43 For a broad overview of cost escalation and related aspects, see Keith Hartley and Todd Sandler(ed), *Handbook of Defense Economics, Vol 1,* Amsterdam: Elsevier Science B. V, 1995), Chap 11, 14 and 18. Also Keith Hartley and Todd Sandler(Ed), *Handbook of Defense Economics, Vol 2,* Amsterdam: Elsevier Science B. V, 2007, Chap 24, 29, 33 and 34.

as can be seen from Figure 7.[44]

Figure 7: Regional Military Spending- 2000-2011 (Billion USD, constant 2010 terms)

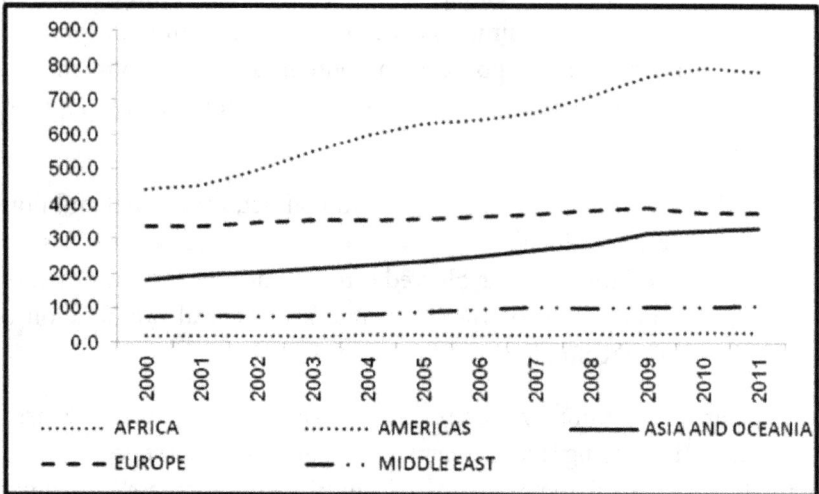

Source: SIPRI Military Expenditure (MILEX) Database.

The increased defence spending in the Americas can be attributed to the US and its involvement in prolonged military operations in Iraq (March 2003- December 2011) as well as Afghanistan since 2001 that may end in December 2014. To elaborate this point, US defence expenditure of US$ 689.6 billion in 2011 in constant 2010 $ terms, was 2.3 times that of the Chinese military spending pegged at US $ 129.3 billion and 15.4 times that of Indian defence spending of US$ 44.3 billion. The increased defence spending in Asia and Oceania that roughly equates to the geographical construct of Indo-Pacific in the absence of any military conflict assumes greater significance. At a regional level within the Indo-Pacific, the increased military spending is largely attributed to China as would be apparent from Figure 8 which raises obvious concerns about its public postulations of a peaceful rise and development.[45] The ripening strategic

---

44 SIPRI, Military Expenditure (MILEX) Database, available at http://milexdata.sipri.org/fi les/?file=SIPRI+milex+data+1988-2011, downloaded on March 10, 2013, extracted and arranged by the author.

45 ZhengBijian"China's 'Peaceful Rise' to Great-Power Status", Foreign Affairs 84 (No. 5) (September/October 2005), p. 22.

rivalries on the global scale between and US and China as well as between India and China on a regional scale have already been alluded to earlier. The recent assertiveness in the South and East China Sea disputes lend further credence to opinion by a large section of the strategic community that the Chinese pronunciations of using soft-power driven anti-hegemonistic slant may not be altogether true besides being indicative of non-conformative, agenda-setting and rule changing behaviour in the future.[46]

Figure 8: Estimated Military Spending by Top Six Select Countries in Indo-Pacific during 2000-2011(Billion USD, constant 2010 terms)[47]

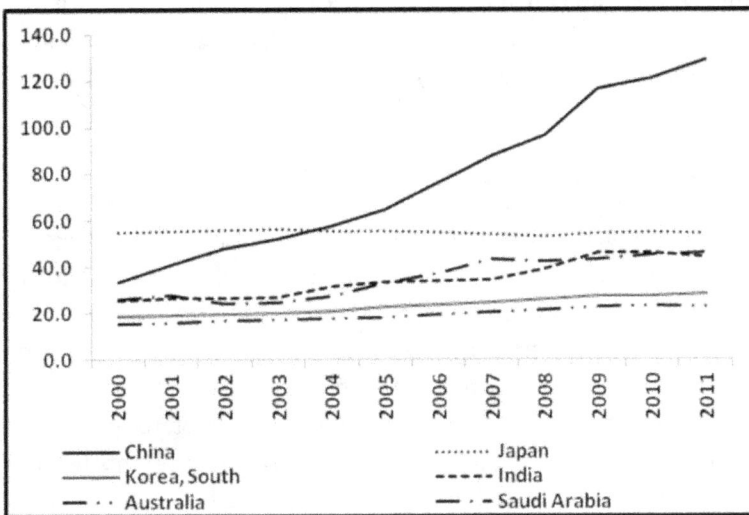

Source: SIPRI Military Expenditure (MILEX) Database.

46 For a comprehensive overview of Chinas territorial disputes seeJunwu Pan, Toward a New Framework for Peaceful Settlement of China's Territorial and Boundary Disputes, Boston: MartinusNijhoff Publishers, 2009. Also Craig A. Snyder, *Security in the South China Sea*, Corbett Paper No. 3, The Corbett Centre for Maritime Policy Studies, November 2011 and Ian James Storey, *Creeping Assertiveness: China, the Philippines and the South China Sea Dispute,* Contemporary Southeast Asia Vol. 21, No. 1 (April 1999), pp. 95-118. Also, LeszekBuszynski, *The South China Sea: Oil, Maritime Claims, and U.S.—China Strategic Rivalry*, The Washington Quarterly, 35:2 pp. 139-156., Francois-XavierBonnet, *Geopolitics of Scarborough Shoal*, Irasec's Discussion Paper, No 14, November 2012, available at http://www.irasec.com/components/com_ irasec/media/upload/DP14-ScarboroughShoal.pdf , accessed march 09, 2013. For East China Sea disputes see, M. Taylor Fravel, 'Explaining Stability in the Senkaku (Diaoyu) Islands Dispute' inGerald Curtis, RyoseiKokubun, and Wang Jisi (Eds), *Getting the Triangle Straight: Managing China-Japan-US Relations*, Washington DC: Brookings Institution, 2010, pp. 144-164.

47 SIPRI Military Expenditure Database, Op Cit, extracted and arranged by the author.

While the greater maritime orientation among the Indo-Pacific in undeniable, certain other security concerns with regional and global connotation also need due consideration. These include the fragile situation over the Iranian nuclear issue and an increasingly obdurate North Korea in recent times. The recent conflictual overtones in the Indo-Pak relations are another concern since both the nations are now considered as de facto if not de jure nuclear powers consequent to the demonstration of their capabilities in 1998. The last but not the least is the post-2014 Afghanistan scenario when the draw down of the international force is scheduled to be completed. This regional continuum extends virtually unbroken in an arc of multi-crises from North Korea in the east to Iran in the West with China and Pakistan that share close mutually beneficial security relations with these entities, serving as a filling to this sandwich, is a reality that India cannot ignore.

Present and Future Challenges

The challenges and constraints that India is likely to encounter in the Indo-Pacific can be broadly ascribed under two heads, *viz*, ideational and material. Ideational constraints arise from the absence of an integrated approach to the maritime domain. Unlike land and air dimension that are neatly divided – though not without differing interpretations and sovereign aspirations, the maritime domain is characterised by receding jurisdiction and a corresponding lessening of sovereign rights beyond the narrow stretch of territorial seas. While a gradual emergence from the era of maritime blindness that started with the Mughal era till economic liberalisation process is evident, a higher policy directive towards a comprehensive, coherent and cogent guidance still eludes India. In a similar vein, greater maritime connectivity encourages establishment of an expanded national footprint in terms of economics and influence in furtherance of national interests.

The benign, constabulary and armed roles of naval forces can be used to showcase the national technological acumen, generating political goodwill, besides demonstration of a participative or coercive pattern, as the case may be, without escalatory effects. These dimensions are neither adequately understood nor addressed at the geo-strategic level in India.[48]

---

48 C UdayBhaskar, 'The Navy as Instrument of Foreign Policy : An Indian Experience' in Hrash V Pant(Ed) , *The Rise of Indian Navy*: Internal Vulnerabilities, External Challenges, Surrey: Ashgate, 2012 , pp. 41-55.

While Indian profile, in terms of economics and military capacity has been rising, the lack of a higher policy framework continues to constrain the optimal harnessing of strategic advantages that can be obtained through the maritime medium. Such challenges are not new and have bedevilled even major powers during the course of history, especially those with continental mind-sets. This challenge would require a systemic overhaul of organisational structure, greater functional synergy and more importantly, a change in public perception. Further, in the current scenario of increased interdependence, the national posture of 'strategic autonomy' would require a radical recast towards developing 'functional partnerships' so as to leverage the true benefits of globalisation.[49] The idea of functional relationships can roughly be described as the ability to simultaneously engage in mutually contradictory cooperative and competitive engagements with other global players. Whilst this definition may sound verbose bordering on inane, a process of smart decision-making to balance the correspondence of interests with like-minded nations and assertiveness on areas of divergences would become a necessity in a complex interconnected environment.

The second major constraint in terms of material capacities arise from the sub-optimal indigenous content in critical areas. On the commercial shipping front, while India is ranked 15th in the overall global order of shipping capacity with a total of 560 ships (455 Indian and 105 foreign flagged), the foreign flagged carriers constitute a disproportionate 28.5 per cent of the national capacity.[50] Further, despite the high ranking, Indian shipping capacity forms a meagre 1.53 per cent of the global total. As far as port infrastructure and capacities is concerned, an Indian port does not find mention in the top 20 container terminals in terms of throughput capacity. To illustrate this point, 15 such ports are located in the Indo-

---

49 For the enhanced military-strategic significance of Indian maritime context whilst retaining strategic autonomy in decision making see Khilnani, Sunil. et. al., *Nonalignment 2.0: A Foreign and Strategic Policy for India In The Twenty First Century*, (India: 2012). For a contrarian perspective whilst agreeing with broad finding of aforementioned study mandating greater international collaboration see Ashley J. Tellis, *Nonalignment Redux: The Perils of Old Wine in New Skins*, Washington, D.C.:Carnegie Endowment for International Peace, 2012.

50 United Nations Conference of Trade and Development, *Review of Maritime Commerce, 2012*, extracted from Table 2.4 at p. 41.

Pacific with China leading the field with nine such terminals.[51] Further evidence of sub-optimal indigenous content in maritime commerce can be gauged from the statistics at Table 2 with close to 92 per cent of Indian maritime trade being carried in foreign bottoms.[52]

Table 2: India's Overseas Trade: 2010-11

Type of Cargo	Percentage Share handled by Indian Shipping	Percentage Share handled by Foreign Shipping
Break Bulk	3.70	96.30
Container	3.57	96.43
Dry Bulk	4.58	95.42
POL/Product and Other Liquids	15.32	84.68
Grand Total	**8.3**	**91.7**

Source: Ministry of Shipping, Government of India, Annual Report 2011-12.

As far as military capabilities are concerned, the 2011 Stockholm Peace Research Institute (SIPRI) estimates put India as the seventh largest spender on defence, climbing two places as compared to the previous year.[53] Another SIPRI press release commenting on the emerging trends in military expenditure for the period 2007-2011 states that "India was the world's largest recipient of arms, accounting for 10 per cent of global arms imports".[54]However, according to a recent analysis, the Indian Self Reliance Indicator (SRI) has been estimated to be in the region of 30 per cent.[55] The

---

51 Ibid, extracted from Table 4.2 at p. 83.

52 Ministry of Shipping, Government of India, *Annual Report 2011-12*, p. 71, available at http://shipping.nic.in/writereaddata/l892s/ar1112-97536637.pdf, accessed March 12, 2013.

53 SIPRI, *Background Paper on SIPRI Military Expenditure Data, 2011,*April 17 2012. http://www.sipri.org/research/armaments/milex/sipri-factsheet-on-military-expenditure-2011.pdf, January 02, 2013.

54 SIPRI Press Release, *Rise in international arms transfers is driven by Asian demand, says SIPRI*; March 19, 2012. http://www.sipri.org/media/pressreleases/rise-in-international-arms-transfers-is-driven-by-asian-demand-says-sipri, accessed January 14, 2013.

55 SNMisra, *Impact of Offset Policy on India's Military Industrial Capability*, Journal of Defence Studies, New Delhi: Vol 5. No 3. July 2011, p 129. As per the author of this

index has remained stagnant despite the 1993 review committee headed by Dr A P J Abdul Kalam, the then Scientific Advisor (SA), setting a goal for enhancing the indigenous content in the defence inventory from 30 per cent in 1995 to a possible 70 per cent by 2005, if the R&D share of defence budget was gradually increased to 10 per cent of the total defence budget by 2000.[56] Indian Prime Minister during his address on the occasion of DRDO award function in July 2012 had also commented that:

"The reality is that the share of indigenous content in defence procurement continues to be low. We need to take a hard look at the pipeline of our projects and focus our time and material resources on selected areas where we have demonstrated capacity to deliver projects within reasonable time and cost."[57]

The Indian Navy has also drawn critique for its low indigenous content besides cost and time overruns in its key programmes.[58] In the latest report of Standing Committee on Defence, it has been mentioned that the indigenisation levels in hull construction and propulsion machinery are of the order of 90 per cent and 60 per cent respectively. However, for the third component that is directly related to war-fighting, namely weapons and sensors, the indigenous level continues to remain at a low index of 30 per cent.[59] The Indian Navy was described as the Cinderella Service and was accorded a lower priority with corresponding smaller budgetary allocations till the mid-1980s.[60]In the 21st Century, the profile of the Indian

article, Self-reliance index was defined in the review committee report as the ratio of indigenous systems procurement cost to total system procurement cost of [for] the year.

56 Ravinder Pal Singh(Ed), *Arms Procurement Decision Making, Volume I: China, India, Israel, Japan, South Korea and Thailand*, (Oxford: Oxford University Press. 1995, p. 57.

57 *PM's address at DRDO Award Function*, July 31, 2012, New Delhi., available at http://pmindia.gov.in/speech-details.php?nodeid=1197, accessed February 20, 2013.

58 Bhaskar, C Uday, "*Indian Navy Afflicted with Common Defence Diseases: Hopelessly Low Indigenisation and Criminal Cost Overruns*" Economic Times, Aug 31, 2012, New Delhi edition, available at http://articles.economictimes.indiatimes.com/2012-08-31/news/33521387_1_defence-procurement-drdo-defence-research , accessed February 27, 2013).

59 Standing Committee on Defence, *Fifteenth Report of Standing Committee OnDefence - 2011-2012 (15thLokSabha) - Demands For Grants (2012-2013)*, New Delhi: LokSabha Secretariat, Apr 2012, p. 65.

60 Arun Prakash, *Is the future beneath the waves?,*Livefist Blog Post, December 21, 2008, available at http://livefist.blogspot.in/2008/12/admiral-arun-prakash-is-future-beneath.html accessed march 11, 2013.

Navy and along with it the budgetary share has taken an upswing but it continues to receive the lowest resources amongst the three services as can be seen at Figure 9.[61]

Figure 9: Budgetary Allocations for Indian Armed Forces and Military R&D (As Percentage Share of Total Defence Budget)

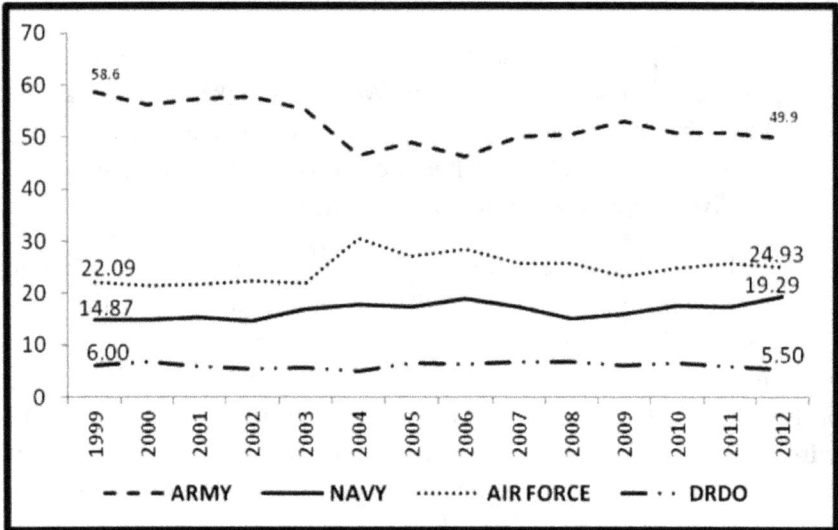

Source: Government of India, Ministry of Defence Annual Reports

On the connected issues of ship-building and naval capacity, especially the indigenous content, the Indian ship-building industry despite its potential of cross-cutting beneficial effects such as offering large employment opportunities, direct incentivisation of downstream ancillary industries besides being a tool for building strategic international linkages, continues to be marked by long gestation times and is considered as economically uncompetitive. One of the measures that merits consideration is to accord 'strategic' status to the Indian shipbuilding industry as was done by the Japanese and the Koreans in the 1970s and 1980s respectively. To match the developmental predictions, India would need a whole range of facilities for commercial and military ship building and defence industry applications. In this regard, the debate between the preferences for public and private

---

61 Extracted from relevant Annual Reports of Ministry of Defence (MoD) and arranged by the author.

sector needs a revisit for the overall national good since these sectors have their respective core competencies and attendant limitations. To offset the current limitations, a host of green field projects would be required, which by experience are best executed through the Public Private Partnership or the so called PPP route, joint ventures and foreign collaborations for infusion of high-end technology as well as bringing in the best engineering and manufacturing practices. The current procurement and production policies as an evolving mechanism have the necessary provisions for robust private and public sector participations towards the overall national aim of self-reliance. The need of the hour is a synergistic approach that leverages critical capabilities and capacities against the backdrop of military and commercial requirements. Further, the nation would have to invest in certain niche areas, even at uneconomical terms, to retain our independence in strategic decision-making and this must form the core area of indigenous efforts.

Conclusion

Human destiny has been intimately linked to the water medium as evident from the majority of the ancient and medieval civilisations being located in riverine regions. A few of these had an attached maritime construct like the Indus valley, Greek, Chinese, Roman and the Mesopotamian civilisations. The world's oldest global commons, viz, the oceans have long been serving as the determining ground in the quest for global pre-eminence. The maritime linkages have also shaped the global economy as evident by the statement from a noted analyst of marine commerce who avers that "The first is the central part which shipping has played in the global economy. At every stage in its development, sea-transport has figured prominently, and the shipping industry, with its distinctive international flavour, has played a central role."[62] A constant historical precedent of maritime commerce and sea power having been a determining scale of geo-strategic relevance is not likely to change and there needs to be a better understanding of the nuances involved and crafting an integrated framework so as to harness the maximal benefits from the maritime domain. The relevance of Indo-Pacific for India, largely an oceanic expanse, being a given imperative and the strategically cross-linked stakes demand that adequate focus is accorded to commercial and military capabilities, so that the nation is able to sustain its rising profile.

---

62 Martin Stopford, *Maritime Economics*, Third edition, New York: Routledge, 2009, p. 44.

17

Prospects for Economic Integration in Indo-Pacific Region: A Perspective from Sri Lanka

Asanga Abeyagoonasekera and Amali Wedagedara

The world is in a transition. As pointed out in the UN Human Development Report 2013, global affairs have been characterised by the levitated dichotomy between the global south and global north:

> "a resurgent South—most visibly countries such as China and India, where there is much human development progress, growth appears to remain robust and the prospects for poverty reduction are encouraging—and a North in crisis—where austerity policies and the absence of economic growth are imposing hardship on millions of unemployed people and people deprived of benefits as social compacts come under intense pressure." (Human Development Report, 2013)

This development is also reflected in the findings of a report titled *Global Trends 2030: Alternative Worlds*[1] according to which the next two decades will witness two distinctive drives in the world. Countries across the globe would be connected to China economically at an increasing phase. However, declined economic power of the US would not displace it from the global strategic sphere. Shift towards China would follow a parallel drive towards the US for 'insurance' (*ibid*, p. 97). A premonition of this trend, the 'Indo-Pacific', an emerging geo-political and geo-economic space which encompasses both Indian and Pacific Oceans, would be the

---

1 *Global Trends 2030: Alternative Worlds*, A Publication of the National Intelligence Council, December 2012. Available at http://globaltrends2030.files.wordpress. com/2012/12/global-trends-2030-november2012.pdf. Accessed on February 13.

confluence of both outreach and interests of US, China, India, Japan, Australia ... Articulated as an element of the US pivot to Asia (Clinton, 2011)[2] and the 'logical corollary' of the broadening and deepening of India's Look East policy (Saran, 2011), and the "intersecting interests of the big maritime trading and strategic powers" (Medcalf, 2012), 'Indo-Pacific' in its simplest liberal-institutionalist sense will be the guarantor of peace and stability in the times of rise and fall of great powers. As much as the roots of Asia's resurgence are situated on the rapid economic progress of the Asian giants such as China, India, South Korea and Japan a number of conflicting issues prevalent in the indo-pacific region in the form of territorial demarcations ascertain that the principal driver of the indo-pacific would be economics. What would be the forms these economic relations can assume? Would they go beyond bilateral Free Trade Agreements? Would there be new institutional set-up to accommodate them? Which countries would be the shapers of this new wave of regionalism? The present paper while answering some of these questions would attempt to bring in the perspective of a small country, Sri Lanka which is unlikely to play an active role in this regional drive.

This chapter will first attempt to identify the possibilities of Indo-Pacific through various statements made on the Indo-Pacific concept by academics, policy makers and strategic analysts. It will follow a critical analysis of the existing frameworks for integration in the Indo-Pacific area. Arguing that the integration process in Indo-Pacific is mainly driven by big power interests, the chapter examines how the process will benefit small countries like Sri Lanka. The analysis of the chapter encompasses several primary inputs in the form of focused interviews and other secondary material such as policy reports and secondary publications. Given the fact that a prospective economic integration in the Indo-Pacific region would be a reality in the near future, the small economies in South Asia have to be efficient in identifying their unique niche within the global export portfolio, undertake better investments in the education and R&D sector to enhance innovation and labour force and harness their ability to project themselves as a value destination in order to reap the benefits from

---

2   The former State Secretary Hilary Clinton while on a visit to Australia also stated that "[the Indo-Pacific] waters are [...] a key focus of Americas expanding engagement in the region, what we sometimes call our "pivot to Asia" ('US determined to remain "pacific power": Clinton', *Global Times*, November 14, 2011, Available at http://www.globaltimes. cn/content/744215.shtml.

the global and regional developments.

Indo-Pacific: Possibilities

Extension of Asia-Pacific to Indo-Pacific with an emphasis on the expanding geo-political and geo-economic significance of India has created a new upsurge in the strategic and policy discourse. Portrayed as a constructive attempt to incorporate new developments in the geo- strategic landscape of Asia, Indo-Pacific also highlights the interdependence and the sense of connectedness than existing as separate entities. Advocated by the Americans, Australians and the Indians, this new terminology insinuates several new possibilities and trajectories that the process of Indo-Pacific integration could emulate.

(a) Depicted as an element of the US' pivot to Asia, the 'Indo-Pacific' could demand new commitments from the new rising powers in Asia in terms of sharing US' burden in Asia (disseminate and strengthen liberal democracy, human rights and free trade and share defence and military expenditure) [3];

(b) Affected by the Chinese military might and the rivaling political and strategic issues with China in terms of the territorial boundaries and access to sea lanes, aspirant regional powers would want to get together to contain China;

(c) Endorsing the very meaning of the term, it would be an inclusive and plural space where everyone can act to maximise their interests and utility through constructive engagement.

Given various complexities and risks arising from the changing landscape, one might expect economics to be the driver of a possible regional integration in the Indo-Pacific region. International relations discourse has in general given less weight to the significance of economics in the great power emergence. However, the rise of China and India principally driven by their rapid economic growth, has given a new impetus to study the importance of economics. The Asian Century would mostly be the century of economics. The fact that these regional powers are embedded in each others' economies provides a strong assurance against any instability

---

3 Bisley, Nick. 2012. "The Indo-Pacific: what does it actually mean?", East Asia Forum, October 06, 2012. Available at http://www.eastasiaforum.org/2012/10/06/the-indo-pacific-what-does-it-actually-mean/.

that may arise from their competing interests in the political and strategic spheres.

What are the prospects for economic integration in the Indo-Pacific? Is there any space for a new institutional set-up? Or would it be a form of inter-regionalism with an umbrella organisation housing parallel interests and agendas?

Apart from bilateral FTAs, and other FTAs between ASEAN and other regional countries such as India, China, Korea and Japan, Indo-Pacific region has more than ten Regional Economic Cooperation (RECs) mechanisms[4]. While most of these arrangements have a regional polarisation, only Asia-Pacific Trade Agreement (APTA)[5] seems to have encompassed membership from both South Asia and East Asia. Therefore, there is still a possibility for an arrangement which would bring all these countries together.

With the objective of facilitating closer economic ties, a step towards such an inclusive arrangement was made in 2007 when Japan suggested establishing a Comprehensive Economic Partnership for East Asia (CEPEA), in order to deepen economic integration, narrow down development gaps, and achieve sustainable development. It was supposed to be a free trade agreement between the current 16 member nations of the ASEAN (ASEAN Plus Three + India, Australia, New Zealand) and attempted to achieve a more comprehensive integration than the ASEAN+3 East Asia Free Trade Area (EAFTA) proposed by China in 2001.

Debate between CEPEA and EAFTA which continued for over two years ended in 2011 when the ASEAN proposed to formulate ASEAN centered FTA: Regional Comprehensive Economic Partnership (RCEP)[6]. Negotiations for RCEP were launched in November 2012 during the 7th

---

4 RECs in the Indo-Pacific region are SAARC, BIMSTEC, SAFTA, APTA, AFTA, ASEAN, AANZFTA (ASEAN-Australia-New Zealand FTA), TPP, SCO, APEC. China-Japan-Korea FTA for which negotiations started in 2012 is still in the pipeline.

5 Previously known as Bangkok Agreement, APTA was formulated in 1975, therefore one of the oldest preferential trade agreements between the countries of developing South. Bangladesh, China, India, Sri Lanka, Nepal, Philippines, Laos and Korea are the member countries of this grouping.

6 Das, Sanchita Basu. 2012. "Asia's Regional Comprehensive Economic Partnership", East Asia Forum, August 27, 2012. Available at http://www.eastasiaforum.org/2012/08/27/asias-regional-comprehensive-economicpartnership/

East Asia Summit and they are supposed to be concluded by the end of 2015. RCEP is expected to function with a liberal membership policy allowing any of the ASEAN FTA partner to join the forum whenever they wish to. In addition, any other external economic partner can also join the forum. A successful RCEP would be the biggest trade pact of the world incorporating 45 per cent of the world population and would expedite the shift of global economic might towards Asia and "would cover a combined economic output of $20 trillion or almost one-third of the global economy"[7]. Furthermore, the multilateralization process which RCEP will bring about would untangle the 'noodle bowl' resulted by the proliferation of FTAs in the Asian region.

It would be interesting to study how RCEP process will evolve and how US would be responding to it. There are those who claim that RCEP as a Chinese initiative in order to exclude US[8]. Besides, response of the other regional trade agreements such as the Trans- Pacific Partnership (TPP) and APEC's Free Trade Area of the Asia Pacific which includes non ASEAN members would also be something to watch in the future. Another question to examine would be how much good faith involved in these initiatives. If the intention behind these initiatives at regional integration is to co-opt geo-political rivals, it could bear negative impacts on the global economy. Therefore, it is extremely important to make a comprehensive analysis of the political motives behind such processes.

Even though 'greater welfare for all' might be the ultimate objective of any form of regional arrangement, the process entails winners and losers to various degrees. Small states with much smaller economies and a little diversity would be the first and hard hit. On top of that other small countries in South Asia, with their backward approach to regional integration coupled with their protectionist trade policies, are less likely to be a part of a wider block. What would be the economic consequences of Indo-Pacific on small states in South Asia? How could they be supported and what can the new regional set-up do to mitigate their costs? By making an analysis of Sri Lanka-India economic behaviour, the paper attempts to examine the nature of impact a closer integration of the Indian market with the East Asia would have on Sri Lanka.

---

7 http://online.wsj.com/article/SB10001424127887323622904578128650479355368.h

8 http://globaleconomicgovernance2012.wordpress.com/2012/11/29/chinastrikes-back-the-rise-of-theregional-comprehensive-economic-partnership

Sri Lankan Case

Sri Lanka's is a small open economy of almost US $ 60 billion[9] in terms of the Gross Domestic Production (GDP) at market prices. When compared with other countries in South Asia, it is the fourth largest economy[10]. Like most of the other South Asian countries, Sri Lanka is also a lower middle income country with per capita GDP of US $ 2, 836. While Sri Lanka is predominantly an agrarian economy, there has been a gradual shift towards the services sector in terms of the contribution to the national economy (59.5 per cent in 2011). The industrial sector contributes 29.3 per cent while the Agriculture accounts for only 11.2 per cent.[11] In post-2009 context, the overall economy has grown at around 7 per cent annually[12], mainly driven by the strong domestic demand (Trade Policy Review: Sri Lanka 2010).

International trade is a principal mode of market expansion in Sri Lanka. In addition, it is also an instrument of acquiring a greater integration to the world economy. Hence, Sri Lanka pursues these objectives at different levels through three bilateral agreements; India, Pakistan and Iran, three regional agreements; South Asian Free Trade Area (SAFTA) Agreement, and the Asia-Pacific Trade Agreement (APTA) and BIMSTEC. India-Sri Lanka FTA, which came into being in 2000, is the very first free trade agreement to both countries. It led to a new depth in economic relations of both countries by quadrupling the volume of bi-lateral trade. In the aftermath of the agreement, India emerged as a significant export destination as well as the principal import market for Sri Lanka. Dr. Sirimal Abeyratne who carried out a systematic study on integrating Sri Lanka into the Indian supply chains states that Indo-Lanka FTA has been more important in terms of export expansion than import expansion[13].

---

9 Economics and Social Statistics of Sri Lanka, 2012. Available at http://www.cbsl.gov.lk/ pics_n_docs/10_pub/_docs/statistics/other/econ_&_ss_2012.pdf.

10 India is the largest economy accounting for GDP (current prices) US $ 1.848 trillion. Pakistan and Bangladesh follows with US $ 210.2 billion and US $ 111.9 billion GDP (current prices) respectively (World Bank Data,2011. Available at http://data.worldbank. org/region/SAS.

11 Economics and Social Statistics of Sri Lanka, 2012. Available at http://www.cbsl.gov.lk/ pics_n_docs/10_pub/_docs/statistics/other/econ_&_ss_2012.pdf.

12 Ibid.

13 Abeyratne, Sirimal. 2012. "Integrating Sri Lankan Industry into the Indian Supply

Protectionist trends among the Sri Lankan business community as well as in the political class, partly due to various non-tariff barriers, red tape prevalent in the Indian economy, have hindered proceeding to the next level of trade liberalisation between India and Sri Lanka; Comprehensive Economic Partnership Agreement which would be liberalising services and investment. In spite of Sri Lanka's Free Trade Agreement with India, Sri Lanka accounts only 5 per cent in Indian imports[14]. Recently Bangladesh has replaced Sri Lanka as the largest South Asian trade partner of India[15]. In this backdrop, how would the developments regarding Indo-Pacific integration influence Sri Lanka?

With the objective of rendering Sri Lanka an attractive destination for FDI and international trade, Sri Lankan governments have pursued a comprehensive policy framework inclusive of fiscal and monetary regulating as well as infrastructure projects. These attempts are reflected in Sri Lanka's improved statuses in various indexes. For example, according to the Index of Economic Freedom 2013, Sri Lanka is categorised as 'moderately free' and is ranked 81, well above other countries in South Asia[16]. Enabling Trade Index of the World Economic Forum which uses seven pillars[17] to determine the quality of trade policies in order to facilitate trade, ranks Sri Lanka at the 73rd in 2012[18]. Sri Lanka pursues a trade policy with the intention of maximising exports while minimising imports. However, as depicted in the following flow chart, backward position in terms of access to foreign market illustrates issues faced by

---

Chains: A Preliminary Study", Pathfinder Foundation, December 2012.

14 "SL's lack of innovation, markets limit export growth: Dr. Kelegama", Sunday Times, March 10, 2013. Available at http://www.sundaytimes.lk/analysis/31299-sls-lack-of-innovation-markets-limit-export-growth-drkelegama.html

15 Narayan, S Venkat. 2013. " Bangladesh overtakes Sri Lanka as India's largest trading partner in South Asia: Is New Delhi disillusioned with Colombo?", the Island, March 09, 2013. Available at http://island.lk/index.php?page_cat=article-details&page=article-details&code_title=74334

16 2013 Index of Economic Freedom, The Heritage Foundation. Available at http://www.heritage.org/index/country/srilanka. Accessed on March 10.

17 Domestic and foreign market access, efficiency of customs administration, efficiency of import-export procedures, transparency of border administration, availability and quality of transport infrastructure, availability and quality of transport services, availability and use of ICTs, regulatory environment and physical security

18 Enabling Trade: Valuing Growth Opportunities, 2013. World Economic Forum. Available at http://www3.weforum.org/docs/GETR/2012/GlobalEnablingTrade_Report.pdf

local exporters with respect to access to imported inputs at competitive prices, in identifying potential markets and buyers, in meeting quality requirements of the export market and access to appropriate technology and skills.

Chart 1

Enabling Trade Index 2013: Sri Lanka

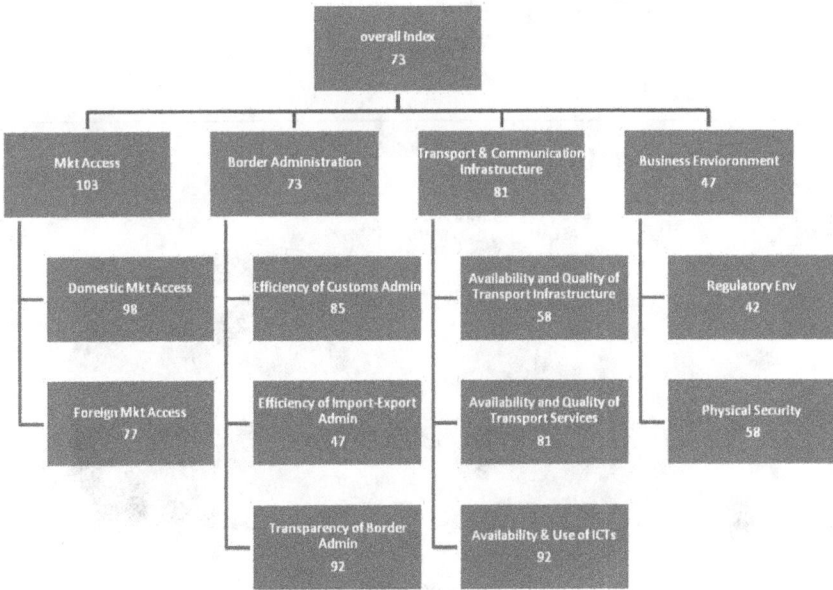

Source: World Economic Forum

Sri Lanka's stated policy of "broadening the export base, diversification of export markets, increasing domestic value additions, and creating an enabling environment for trade to support the country's envisaged growth trajectory"[19] has fallen short of meeting its goals. In addition, it also identifies gaps with regard to translating existing infrastructural facilities to actual services. For example, the index rating on 'availability and quality of transport infrastructure' is not reflected in the 'availability and quality of transport services'. Therefore, it must be noted that investments

---

19 Annual report 2011, Central Bank of Sri Lanka. Available at http://www.cbsl.gov.lk/ pics_n_docs/10_pub/_docs/efr/annual_report/AR2011/English/9_Chapter_05.pdf Accessed on March 13, 2013.

on improving infrastructure have to accompany a parallel process of enabling and empowering the population in order to overcome barriers in translating facilities available to services which people can enjoy for real.

As much as the policy infrastructure, trade profile of a country is equally important to understand the behaviour of trade in a particular country. Given its colonial roots, Sri Lanka's traditional export market continues to be the US and EU. The pie chart given bellow demonstrates the distribution of Sri Lanka's exports by region.

Figure 1

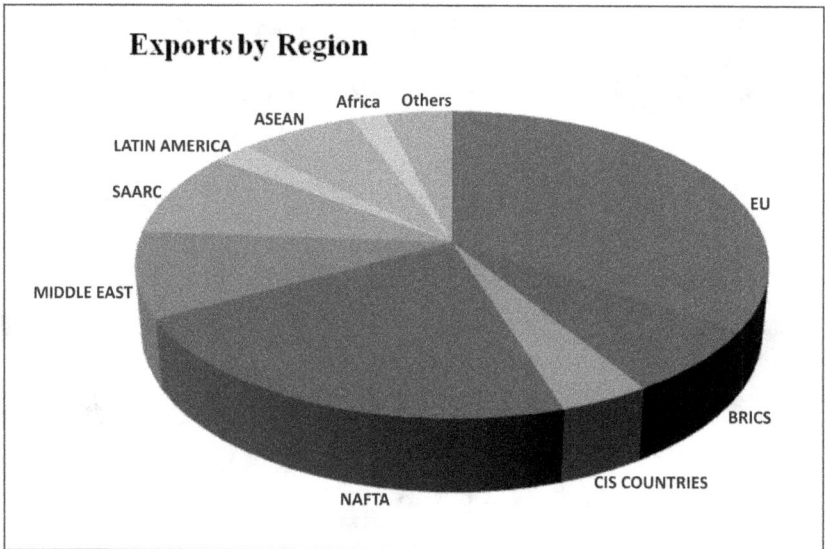

Exports by Region

Africa Others
ASEAN
LATIN AMERICA
SAARC
EU
MIDDLE EAST
BRICS
CIS COUNTRIES
NAFTA

Source: Export Development Board 2012

About 56 per cent of the exports are concentrated on EU and NAFTA while intra-regional trade accounts only 9 per cent. Other emerging markets in Latin America, ASEAN and Africa account only 2 per cent, 7 per cent and 2 per cent respectively. Owing to the negative experiences of Sri Lanka's exports to US and EU affected by the drastic impacts on the Global Financial Crisis the markets as well as political economic vulnerabilities developed from excessive dependence on the western markets as was manifested when GSP+ concessions on Sri Lanka's apparel exports to EU were lifted due to allegations on human rights violations, have generated an interest to diversify Sri Lanka's export markets. These reasons coupled with the rise of East Asia, have prompted a 'Look East policy' in the Sri Lankan economic and political discourse as well.

However, the fact that Sri Lanka doesn't have any market access mechanisms in East Asia except for APTA has emerged as an obstacle to exploiting the East Asian markets. On top of that, lack of a competitive advantage with respect to its products which are basically ready-made garments and a few manufactured goods have also affected Sri Lanka's options. Almost all Sri Lankan exports are simple products which can be copied by other competitors, therefore risk further deterioration of the market options. In addition, value of high-tech products among the exports have also had a sharp drop from US $ 102 million in 2008 to US $ 57 million in 2010[20].

Figure 2

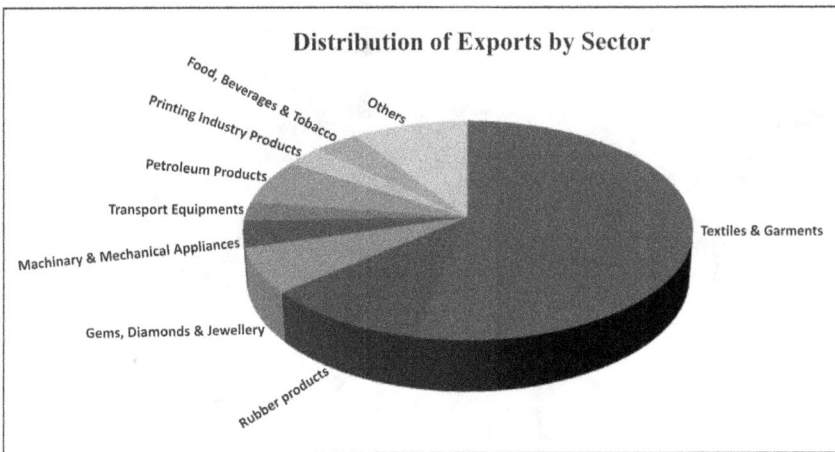

Distribution of Exports by Sector

Source: Annual Report 2011, Central Bank of Sri Lanka

Moreover, even though Sri Lanka has entered into several FTAs and RECs, Sri Lanka has failed to make a full utilisation of these arrangements. Annual Report 2011 of the Central Bank reports that bulk of Sri Lankan exports under APTA is limited to tea and coir products. Sri Lanka's bilateral FTAs with India, Pakistan and Iran narrate a similar story. Although these agreements have accelerated bilateral trade in large volumes, Sri

---

20 "SL's lack of innovation, markets limit export growth: Dr. Kelegama", Sunday Times, March 10, 2013. Available at http://www.sundaytimes.lk/analysis/31299-sls-lack-of-innovation-markets-limit-export-growth-drkelegama.html

Lanka has failed to maximise the market access opportunities and tariff concessions by transcending its primary products.

When Sri Lanka's strategic advantage apropos its exports lies in the western market, how economically sensible is it to take a shift towards the East? What is the way forward for Sri Lanka and India?

Sri Lanka's Critical Evaluation o f G e o -political Location

Proximity to the Indian subcontinent as well as its location on strategic East-West Sea Lines of Communications (SLOCS) is the biggest advantage to Sri Lankan in the Indo-Pacific region.

Map 1

Global Maritime Traffic

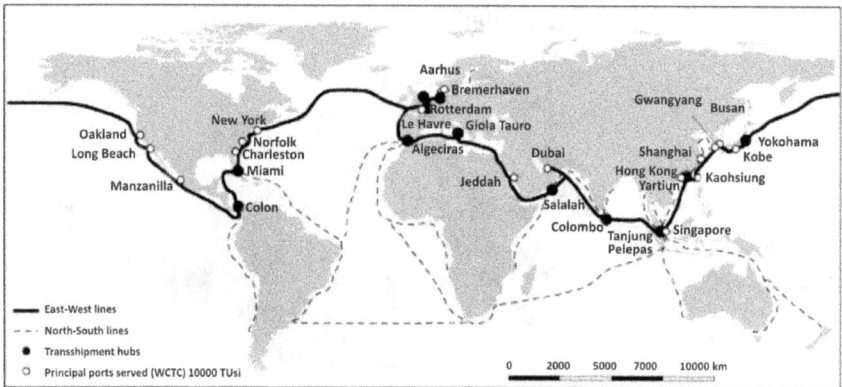

Source: Journal of Transport Geography 15 (6), November 2007, 431-442

Capitalising on Sri Lanka's physical location and its natural harbours, the country is better placed than any other nation in South Asia to pursue the agenda of being a 'trans-shipment hub'. At the moment according to the American Association for Port Authorities, Colombo port is one of the leading ports in the world and is ranked 80th in terms of the total cargo volume and the 29th in terms of container traffic in 2011[21]. Colombo port handles around 49,615 metric tons of cargo volume annually and 3,651,963 TEUs of container traffic annually. It is estimated that about 70 per cent of the transshipment cargo in the container traffic in Colombo Port belong to India. Even in the face of a possible execution of the Sethusamudram canal project, Sri Lankan ports will not be affected since the depth of the canal will not allow mega containers to pass through. Therefore, Sri Lanka ought to be mindful about this constant reality which is bound to bring greater benefits to Sri Lanka in the coming decades.

Integrate more with India

Integrating more with the Indian supply chains is the best method that Sri Lanka could integrate with the global economy[22]. The fact that India is an indispensable partner to Sri Lanka's growth is further substantiated by the degree in which Sri Lankan economy depends on India. Apart from being a destination and a point of origin to transshipments in the Colombo port, India is also a major energy source to Sri Lanka. About 35 per cent of Sri Lanka's energy requirements come from India, through Lanka IOC[23]. In addition, bulk of revenue generated in the Aviation industry comes from the weekly flights to India (42 per cent)[24]. Furthermore, Indians account for the majority of tourists visiting Sri Lanka.

These statistics reiterate the importance in untangling politics from the economic imperatives which would be vital in sustaining Sri Lanka's growth story. First initiatives towards deepening integration in the Indian market can be through further consolidating and utilization of the provisions available under the Indo-SL FTA.

---

21 World Port Rankings – 2011, American Association of Port Authorities. Available at http://aapa.files.cms

22 "Integrating industry into Indian supply chains - 'vital for growth'", *Sunday Observer*, January 20, 2013. Available at http://www.sundayobserver.lk/2013/01/20/fin36.asp Sally, Razeen. 2012. "Emerging world order and Sri Lanka's role: Lopsided foreign policy and economics", *the Island*, December 26, 2012. Available at http://www.island.lk/index.php?page_cat=article-details&page=articledetails&code_title=69065

23 "The Role of Imports in the Sri Lankan Economy", Available at http://www.bilaterals.org/spip.php?article18004.

24 Ibid.

Look at Positives and Look Outward

(a) Expanding and diversifying the export basket: A bulk of the Sri Lankan exporters is from the Small and Medium sectors who deal with innovative products and services. Improvement and expansion of these sectors are constrained by the scarcity of capital. Therefore proper policies to provide assistance to SMEs with potential such as light engineering products, plastic products, printing services, Toys and wooden furniture can revitalise the sector;

(b) Establish a nexus between the policy makers and business community: Flow of information through a close relationship between the business community and the trade officers in the missions as well as in the Department of Commerce would benefit both communities. As much as it will help the producers in finding markets, the policy makers will be informed on the export capacities, nature of export products and sensitivities of the producers.

Such close interactions between the governments, chambers and other trade related organisations would help identify gaps and limitations in our trade policy, would assist innovations in order to expand our export portfolio and tap new and emerging export markets.

Look inward

Nobel laureate economist Joseph Stiglitz has observed that:

> "To be able to grow, emerging markets must be less dependent on exports, boost domestic consumption and find their own model of sustainable economic growth, [...] To avoid repeating developed countries' mistakes, newly emerging economies should invest in education, technology, the environment and public health and find a sustainable model of economic growth"[25]

Looking inward and filling the gaps in education, technology and public health is very important in assuring that the population would not be disempowered in the face of external competition and they are competent

---

25 "Avoid mistakes of the West: Stiglitz", Available at http://www.nationmultimedia.com/business/Avoidmistakes-of-the-West-Stiglitz-30202103.html. Accessed on March 17.

enough and the economic development would be sustainable. Although Sri Lanka boasts of high ranking in the Human Development Index with respect to literacy, Sri Lankan population appears to be fallen short of relevant skills for the upcoming markets such as IT and BPO. Global Services Location Index 2011 records only an insignificant amount for 'people's skills and availability' in Sri Lanka and the country has also fallen short of relevant experiences as well as size and availability of labour force[26] which calls for more investments in R&D, increasing public expenditure on education and harnessing ICT sector of the country. IT/BPO sector brings 100 per cent value addition and has proven to be resilient even in the face of the global financial crisis.[27]

Sri Lanka is located at the 21st place and IT/BPO sector is the 5th largest export revenue earner in 2010 even after entering the market late. This sector also holds significant opportunities for future from the emerging markets such as IT sector in the Middle East.

Conclusion

Prospective economic integration in the Indo-Pacific region, be it India going to the East in the form of an ASEAN related regime or a convergence of interests in an inter-regional platform or a brand new institutional mechanism will become a reality in the future. Small economies in the region could be attentive to the new developments in the region, engage in a critical evaluation of these developments in order to take advantage of them. Integrating more with the Indian market through existing free trade arrangements, creating a unique niche for the local products, and pursuing a genuine policy to harness local potential would be highly important to ensure that these economies would not be left out in the course of global developments.

India on the other hand could pursue a more benevolent outward looking policy by focusing more towards its neighbouring countries and assisting to develop their economies. As the South Asian regional power

---

26 "Off shoring Opportunities Amid Economic Terbulence", Global Services Location Index 2011. Available at http://www.atkearney.com/documents/10192/f062cfd8-ee98-4312-ae4f-0439afc10880

27 Dr. Saman Kelegama's presentation at the 18th Annual general Meeting of National Chamber of Exporters of Sri Lanka. "SL's lack of innovation, markets limit export growth: Dr. Kelegama", Sunday Times, March 10, 2013. Available at http://www.sundaytimes.lk/analysis/31299-sls-lack-of-innovation-markets-limit-export-growth-drkelegama.html

India should focus on creating an environment conducive to resolve regional problems which obstruct the region from progressing. While it might be important to acknowledge external pressure, as the regional power it is the responsibility of India to protect the regional countries from external interferences.

Figure 3

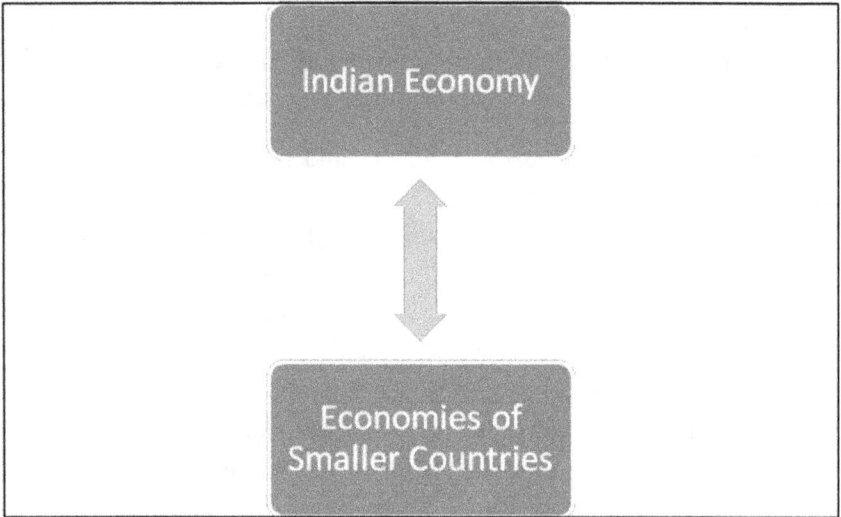

In conclusion, the Figure 3 demonstrates the degree of interdependence of the Indian economy vis-à-vis other smaller economies in the region. One may argue that India would be economically better off without its smaller neighbours; however, historical and cultural relations with India as well as other cross border spill overs (security and non security threats) inhibit India from taking off alone.

REFERENCES

Clinton, Hilary. 2011. 'America's Pacific Century', *Foreign Policy*, November 2011. Available at http://www.foreignpolicy.com/articles/2011/10/11/americas_pacific_century?page=0,0

Saran, Shyam. 2011. 'Mapping the Indo-Pacific', *The Indian Express*, October 29, 2011. Available at http://www.indianexpress.com/news/mapping-the-indopacific/867004March 02, 2013.

Medcalf, Rory. 2012. 'A Term Whose Time Has Come: The Indo-Pacific', *The Diplomat*, December 04, 2012. Available at http://thediplomat.com/flashpoints-blog/2012/12/04/a-term-whose-time-hascome-the-indo-pacific

World Trade Organisation. 2010. Trade Policy Review: Sri Lanka, November 2010. Available at http://www.wto.org/english/tratop_e/tpr_e/tp337_e.htm, March 05, 2013.

"The Rise of the South: Human Progress in a Diverse World", UN Human Development Report, 2013, UNDP. Available at http://hdr.undp.org/en/reports/global/hdr2013/download/

Index

A

African Union xvii, 134

Alfred T. Mahan 6

Andaman Sea 57, 58

Anti-access and area denial capabilities 14

Arun Prakash 145, 161

ASEAN viii, ix, xiii, xiv, xvii, 9, 10, 35, 36, 53, 54, 55, 56, 61, 62, 63, 65, 66, 69, 70, 71, 72, 73, 74, 75, 77, 78, 79, 80, 81, 82, 85, 87, 88, 89, 91, 92, 94, 95, 96, 98, 99, 100, 101, 102, 103, 104, 108, 111, 112, 113, 114, 126, 134, 151, 167, 168, 172, 177

ASEAN+3 East Asia Free Trade Area (EAFTA) 167

ASEAN centered FTA 167

ASEAN Defence Ministers Meeting Plus (ADMM Plus) 79

ASEAN Information-Sharing Portal xvii, 81

ASEAN Maritime Forum xvii, 55, 79, 80, 91

ASEAN Regional Forum xvii, 10, 55, 62, 79, 80, 81, 87, 91, 113

Asian Relations Conference vii, xi, xii, 110

Asian resurgence xi

Asia-Pacific Trade Agreement (APTA) 167

Association of South-East Asian Nations xvii, 53

Australian Institute of International Affairs xv, xvii, 37, 40, 42

Australian National University xvii, 39, 41, 42, 43, 44, 48, 67

B

Bab el Mandab 76, 130

Baladas Ghoshal 63

Bali democracy forum 114

Bandar Abbas 122

Barack Obama 63

Barry Desker 52

Bay of Bengal 10, 60, 78, 115, 145

Bruce Cumings 6, 181

C

Campbell Bay 61

Carrier Strike Groups xvii, 58

Chagos Islands 58

Chiang Mai Multilateral Initiative 91

China's Exclusive Economic Zones 86

Cocos (Keeling) Islands 40

Comprehensive Economic Partnership for East Asia (CEPEA) 167

C. Raja Mohan 9, 14, 51, 70, 82, 111

C Uday Bhaskar 158

D

Daniel Flitton 48, 50

David Scott 7, 149

Defence White Paper 2013 38

Dennis Rumley 10, 44, 45

Diaoyu-Senkaku disagreement 108

Diego Garcia 58, 124

Diogo Lopes de Sequeira 54

D. Nandakumar 60

E

East Asian economies xi

East Asia Summit ix, xvii, 6, 42, 43, 49, 50, 80, 87, 110, 168

East Asia Summit (EAS) ix, xvii, 9, 10, 42, 49, 50, 62, 80, 91, 110, 111, 112, 113

Emrys Chew 54, 72

Energy Information Administration (EIA) 146

Ernst Haushofer 6

Exclusive Economic Zone xvii, 60, 145

Expanded ASEAN Maritime Forum xvii, 79, 80, 91

F

First Gulf War 141

Flitton Daniel 48, 50

Food and Agriculture Organisation vii

Foreign Direct Investment xvii, 104, 129

fracking revolution 132

Free Trade Agreement xiv, xvii, 89, 167, 168, 169, 170, 176

G

Garnaut, John 48

Greeko-Persian wars 121

H

Habibie Centre Dewi Fortuna 101

Hambantota 59, 60

Harsh V. Pant 59

Heidelberg Institute for International Conflict Research 75

Hillary Clinton xii, 42, 52, 83, 143

Horn of Africa xvii, 75, 127, 132, 146

I

Indian Ocean Rim Association for Regional Cooperation ix, xiii, xiv, xv, xviii, 2, 3, 49, 61, 111

Indian Ocean Tuna Commission (IOTC) 77

Indo-Pacific i, iii, vii, viii, ix, xii, xiii, 1, 2, 3, 4, 5, 6, 7, 8, 9, 10, 11, 13,

14, 15, 16, 17, 19, 35, 37, 38, 39, 40, 41, 42, 43, 44, 45, 46, 47, 48, 49, 50, 51, 52, 53, 54, 55, 56, 57, 60, 62, 67, 68, 69, 70, 71, 75, 80, 82, 83, 97, 98, 99, 100, 101, 102, 103, 105, 106, 107, 108, 109, 110, 111, 112, 113, 115, 116, 117, 118, 119, 120, 121, 126, 127, 128, 129, 130, 131, 132, 133, 134, 135, 137, 138, 139, 141, 142, 143, 144, 145, 146, 147, 149, 151, 153, 155, 156, 157, 158, 163, 164, 165, 166, 167, 168, 174, 177, 179

Indo-Pacific Fisheries Council vii

Indo-Pacific Region i, iii, vii, viii, ix, xii, 1, 51, 53, 54, 56, 68, 70, 83, 97, 107, 110, 118, 121, 126, 131, 135, 144, 164

Information Fusion Centre xvii, 80, 82

International Court of Justice xvii, 35

International Liaison Officers (ILO) 80

International Maritime Bureau xviii, 75

J

Jawaharlal Nehru vii, xi, xvi, 135

Jean-Paul Rodrigue 147

John Bruni 45

John Garnaut 48

Joseph Stiglitz 176

Joshua S Goldstein 140

Julie Bishop 39, 40, 49

K

Karl Haushofer 6

Kosovo Crisis 141

L

Laccadive Sea 60

Leighton G. Luke 56

Littoral Combat Ships xviii, 65

Lombok Strait 130

Lowy Institute 38, 43, 44

M

Mahathir Mohamad 99

Malacca Strait xiii, 74

Manmohan Singh ix, 53

Masera base 124

Medcalf Rory 38, 39, 40, 41, 42, 44, 47, 48, 49, 67, 100, 105, 165

Mekong 17, 90, 91

Mekong-Ganga Cooperation 90

Michael Auslin 8, 10, 183

Michael Wesley 40, 41, 43, 44, 49, 183

Multilateral dialogue platforms: 87

  ADMM Plus 87

  ASEAN Regional Forum 87

  East Asia Summit 87

Muthiah Alagappa 55, 183

Mutual economic dependence (MED) 115

N

Najib Tun Razak 56

National Defence Policy xviii, 57

National Technical Information Service xviii, 19

Nelson Mandela 2

Nicholas Spykman 6

Non-Aligned Movement xi

O

Oil and Natural Gas Corporation xviii, 90

Operation Enduring Freedom xviii, 141

Operation Iraqi Freedom 141

Operation Unified Assistance 9

P

Panchsheel xi

Paracel islands 35

Pau Khan Khup Hangzo 77

Pax Britannica 123

Persian Gulf 54, 60, 121, 124, 127, 145

Peter Katzenstein 6

Peter Varghese 37, 47, 49

Petro Vietnam 90

P. K.Gautam 130

PLANavy 86, 93

Port Blair 61

Port of Marao 60

Priya Chacko 9, 48, 184

Q

Quadrennial Defense Review xviii, 139, 143, 144

R

Rajesh Basrur 74

Red River 54

Regional Comprehensive Economic Partnership (RCEP) xviii, 55, 88, 94, 167

Regional Cooperation Agreement on Combating Piracy and Armed Robbery against Ships in Asia (ReCAAP) 75, 81

Richard A. Bitzinger 13

Richard Riot 61

Ruchita Beri 131

S

Salman Khurshid xi

sea-based nuclear forces 14

Sea Lines of Communication xviii

Senkaku islands 35

Sethusamudram canal project 175

Seychelles xv, 60, 118, 119

Shangri-La Dialogue 56, 63, 64

Singapore Armed Forces (SAF) 65

South China Sea 10, 11, 14, 55, 56, 57, 59, 64, 65, 66, 67, 68, 69, 71, 75, 85, 86, 88, 90, 95, 96, 102, 108, 111, 130, 131, 132, 146, 157

Southern America Common Market (MERCOSUR) 134

Spratly islands 35

Srivijaya 54

Stockholm Peace Research Institute xviii, 160

Strait of Hormuz 60, 68, 76, 130, 132, 145

Straits of Malacca xviii, 10, 54, 56, 57, 59, 60, 61, 68, 71, 75, 145

Strategic Framework Agreement xviii, 64

Suez Canal 60, 130

Sumsky V. 95, 96

Sunda Straits 54

T

Taiwan Straits 10

Tetsuo Kotani 53

TNK Vietnam 90

Trans-Pacific Partnership xviii, 8, 10, 88, 91

Trans-Pacific Partnership (TPP) 88

Treaty of Amity and Cooperation xviii, 62, 100, 113

Treaty of Amity and Cooperation (TAC) 62

Trefor Moss 11, 184

V

Very Large Crude Carrier xviii, 59

W

Western Pacific 86

Z

ZhengBijian 156

Zheng He 54